The Ennobling of Democracy

The ☆ Thomas L. Pangle
Ennobling of
Democracy

THE CHALLENGE OF THE

POSTMODERN AGE

The Johns Hopkins University Press
Baltimore and London

© 1992 The Johns Hopkins University Press
All rights reserved. Published 1992
Printed in the United States of America on acid-free paper

Third printing, 1992
Johns Hopkins Paperbacks edition, 1993

The Johns Hopkins University Press
2715 North Charles Street
Baltimore, Maryland 21218-4319
The Johns Hopkins Press Ltd., London

Library of Congress Cataloging-in-Publication Data

Pangle, Thomas L.
    The ennobling of democracy : the challenge of the postmodern age / Thomas L. Pangle.
        p.   cm. — (Johns Hopkins series in constitutional thought)
    Includes bibliographical references and index.
    ISBN 0-8018-4262-X   ISBN 0-8018-4635-8 (pbk.)
    1. Democracy.   2. Civics.   3. Postmodernism.   4. Political
science—Philosophy.   I. Title.   II. Series.
JC423.P249   1991
321.8—dc20   91-20720

A catalog record for this book is available from the British Library.

Contents

Acknowledgments   vii
Introduction: The Postmodern Predicament   1

PART I
The Inadequacy of the Postmodernist Response
1 / Postmodernism and the Avant-Garde   19
2 / The Heideggerian Roots of Postmodernism   34
3 / "Weak Thinking"   48
4 / American Postmodernism   56

PART II
The Spiritual Challenges of the Post–Cold War Era
5 / The Challenge for and from Europe   71
6 / The Need to Rethink Our Rights and Our Republicanism   91

PART III
Revitalizing the Intellectual Roots of Civic Culture
7 / Reinvigorating the Legacy of Classical Republicanism   105
8 / Rethinking the Foundations of Liberalism   131

PART IV
Education: Civic and Liberal

9 / Retrieving Civic Education as the Heart of American Public
    Schooling   163
10 / Against Canons and Canonicity: Dialectic as the Heart of
    Higher Education   183

Select List of Works Cited   219
Index   225

Acknowledgments

Chapter Five grew out of my keynote address opening the Fifth Annual Conference for European Strategic Studies Institutes at the United States Mission to NATO, Brussels, September 19, 1989. Earlier versions of some portions of Chapters Six, Seven, and Eight appeared in the *Chicago-Kent Law Review* 1990–91 Symposium on Classical Philosophy and the American Constitutional Order; the American Enterprise Institute 1990–91 Symposium on the Framers of the Constitution and Fundamental Rights; and the inaugural issue of the *Public Interest Law Review* (1991). Some of the ideas in the final chapter were first presented in "Entering the Great Debate," in *Academic Questions* 2, no. 2 (Spring 1989), and in my plenary address to the Association of American Law Schools Annual Convention, New Orleans, January 7, 1989: the address was subsequently published as "Justice and Legal Education," in the *Journal of Legal Education* 39, no. 2 (June 1989). In my selective discussion of some of the Founders' thoughts on education, I am deeply indebted to my wife, Lorraine, with whom I am coauthoring a much more elaborate treatment in a book forthcoming from the University Press of Kansas: *The Learning of Liberty: The Educational Ideas of the American Founders.* I am grateful to the John M. Olin Foundation for supporting me during a summer in which I worked on this book. Finally, I would like to thank the readers for the Johns Hopkins University Press, including the editors of this series, Sotirios Barber and Jeffrey Tulis, for spirited criticisms that led to what I believe to be substantial improvements.

All translations are my own except where otherwise indicated. In the case of ancient resources, I have worked from recognized critical editions, and my citations follow universal pagination or section numberings.

Introduction / The Postmodern Predicament

This book undertakes the problematic task of offering some philosophic guidance for thoughtful citizens of American democracy. The contribution is in the nature of a prelude or protreptic. My aim here is not the elaboration of a doctrine but rather the regeneration of buried possibilities and forgotten questions. I mean to suggest an agenda for serious reflection on our fundamental situation, spurred by the awareness that we stand at a historical turning point.

It is the retreat, verging on rout or collapse, of Marxism throughout the world that most vividly marks the present moment as a hinge of history. Yet to grasp the peculiar character of this moment, we need to look beyond the dramatic and wonderful process of liberation from communist totalitarianism. We need to ask what is going to replace this totalitarianism: what guiding vision is to be the successor to Marxism? Only when we pose this question do we begin to appreciate how puzzling our situation is. Before *what*, exactly, is Marxism in retreat? *To* what are the previously enslaved nations and peoples being liberated?

The most obvious apparent answer turns out to be the source of deeper perplexities. The victory, we say, belongs to "the West," and the principled basis of the West is "democracy," together with "human rights." But is not democracy, "people's democracy," at the heart of Marxism? Was it not Marxism that brought to the fore "social, economic, and cultural" rights? Indeed, is not the philosophy of Karl Marx one of the great products of "the West"?

The principled basis of the anti-Marxist West is more precisely defined by speaking of *liberal* democracy and democratic *republicanism*, together with *individual* rights, especially individual civil and *property* rights. Yet the term *liberal* does not resonate very strongly in Western Europe. Even where "liberal" political parties exist (e.g., the Liberal parties in England and Italy, the Free Democrats in Germany), they are small or marginal. And in the United States, the term *liberal* has become steadily more controversial, and even dubious, as was evident in the presidential campaign of 1988. Anyone who raises the flag of liberalism in the West today must expect to confront hard questions. What is a liberal? What is the compelling moral justification for "liberalism"? What is "republicanism," in contrast to democracy or democratism? How do republicanism and liberalism fit together? What justifies these qualifications on democracy, on popular sovereignty? What justifies the stress, in liberalism, on the individual as such? Is "individualism" a sign of human dignity—or of fragmentation and atomization? How do liberal individualism and the free-market system with which it is intertwined harmonize with the citizenship, the civic solidarity, called for by our liberal democratic republicanism? *Do* liberalism and republicanism harmonize, or do they stand at some considerable tension with each other? Are individual rights and the competitive free market adequate to sustain the multiparty electoral, federal, and representative politics that so sharply distinguish the "Free World's" interpretation of democracy? Or is the vitality of our citizenship withering—and not by accident, but in accordance with the deepest tendencies of our "liberal democratic" way of life?

What is so troubling about our present situation, *within* the Western democracies, is the philosophic thinness of our answers to these questions. What is so disturbing is the ubiquitous mood of doubt, among our intellectuals, as to the very existence of firm foundations for inquiry into, and judgment of, our gravest political commitments. As long as we liberals could define ourselves over and against obvious political evils—first fascism and then communism—this doubt could remain lurking at a less conspicuous level. But now, as the threat from Marxist-inspired tyranny diminishes, we in the West shall have to confront more and more squarely the problematic status of our moral foundations.

Two centuries ago, when liberal republicanism was overthrowing the "Old Regime" in Europe and America, these questions concerning moral and civic foundations received a rich response. The response was elaborated in grounding treatises of political philosophy written by thinkers who characterized themselves as the bringers of the Enlightenment or the Age of

Reason. These philosophers of modernity, from Spinoza and Locke to Kant and even Hegel, spoke not simply of human rights but emphatically of "*natural* rights," issuing in moral "laws of nature and of nature's God," and accompanied by such foundational concepts as the "state of nature," the "social compact," and the "categorical imperative."

Nothing characterizes the spiritual climate of the West today so much as the pervasive disbelief in these once all-powerful philosophic pillars of modernity. Our philosophic currents are negative, skeptical, disillusioned. Indeed, one may with justification suggest that to speak of "currents" is already to mislead: the most influential trends in contemporary philosophy may be too weak and fragmentary to constitute anything so forceful as currents. Yet there is unquestionably a common ground, defined negatively. The "postmodern" has as yet nothing that is clearly its own; it is best defined, not merely by what it comes after, but by that from which it has become estranged: the modern—Modernity. But then we are in a decisive sense still defined by this Modernity. The postmodern is not "what exists after modernity"; it is rather the state of being entangled in modernity, as something from which we cannot escape but in which we can no longer put, or find, faith. What is this modernity that defines us still? What is this from which we have become alienated, in such a way that we are defined by nothing so clearly as this alienation?

At the heart of modernity is the trust or faith in scientific reason, understood as the source not only of vast powers but of authoritative guidance as to how to use those powers. The long battle that succeeded in winning intellectual predominance for modern science was simultaneously a struggle for a new culture of universal humanity to be based on scientific reason as the only solid basis for truly common bonds among all human beings as such. The struggle for science was simultaneously a struggle for a culture of universal, popular enlightenment. The new culture was to take root in a movement of liberation from age-old particularist superstitions. It was to emerge out of a revolution against illegitimate economic and political hegemonies rooted in nonrational, prescientific tribal and national and sectarian traditions. But of course the negation was to be followed or accompanied by affirmation: the new culture was to have a new content, a new goal, a new conception of the good life. Scientific morals, politics, aesthetics, philosophy, and religion were to replace the old prescientific or traditional morals, politics, aesthetics, philosophy, and religion. The very titles of some of the masterpieces of the Enlightenment reflect this great positive aspiration: *Ethics Demonstrated in Geometrical Order* (Spinoza); *An Essay con-*

cerning the True Original, Extent, and End of Civil Government (Locke);
A Philosophical Enquiry into the Origin of Our Ideas of the Sublime and Beautiful (Burke); *Religion within the Limits of Reason Alone* (Kant); *Principles of a New Science concerning the Nature of the Nations* (Vico).

Yet the cultural, moral, religious, and even the civic promises of the Enlightenment were fulfilled in a much more ambiguous and controversial fashion than the mathematical, economic, and technological promises. Modern science does not mean today what it meant for Newton. Modern scientists long ago ceased to think it essential to seek philosophic or theological foundations for their work. And on the other side, modern philosophy and religion have ceased trying to be scientific. As for "political science," our profession has pretty much abandoned the claim to provide authoritative guidance in establishing the nature of the common good and the ultimate ends of collective and personal existence. The abdication of the vocation of the political scientist as conceived by the Enlightenment is especially obvious in the subfield that passes under the stultifying rubric of "normative theory" (this is the subfield that, at its all-too-rare best, exercises a kind of museum custodian's care for the once-great texts and issues of political theory).

The great attempts by the political philosophers of the Enlightenment to provide systematic, rational, and generally acceptable foundations for public and private existence have proved to be inadequate. This is by no means to say that they have been altogether a failure. Some of the leading moral and civic notions—universal humanity and equality, government by consent, the free market, toleration and the sanctity of the private sphere—remain the bulwark of the liberal public ethos. But the original philosophic and scientific *foundations* for that ethos have eroded; and the public ethos has itself therefore become fragile and unsteady. Few educated citizens of our time dare to endorse "natural rights" or even the "rights of man." Property rights, which stood at the core of the Enlightenment conception of the rights of man, are looked upon with great skepticism by today's constitutionalists. Above all, reason itself, and the universalism implied in rationalism, is more and more viewed with distrust. At the popular level, this distrust is animated by the sharp suspicion that rationalism may be the source of "sexist," "Eurocentric," inhumanly utilitarian, and technologically driven exploitation. Behind these suspicions looms a greater source of difficulties. Modern rationalism has been hammered by succeeding generations of philosophic critics, beginning with Rousseau and culminating in Nietzsche and Heidegger—critics who advance powerful arguments contending that rationalism is incapable of providing an acceptably profound, diverse, "creative," and "historical" account of what is truly human.

Here, then, is our situation in a nutshell: we in the West find ourselves in possession of fantastically powerful technological and economic resources; these resources fuel a society that is deeply unsure of its moral purpose and foundations; as an accompaniment or consequence, this society has come to be increasingly penetrated and shaped by a new, highly problematic and skeptical (not to say nihilistic) cultural dispensation known as "postmodern-*ism.*"

This book begins from a selective encounter with a few of the most influential thinkers who epitomize or stand at the source of this new "ism." I attempt to do justice to the strengths, while delineating what I see to be the decisive weaknesses, in this still unfolding worldview. To put it bluntly, I mean to sound an alarm at what I see to be the civic irresponsibility, the spiritual deadliness, and the philosophic dogmatism of this increasingly dominant trend of thinking. I wish to help rescue the genuinely galvanizing spiritual, moral, and civic challenges of our question-ridden age from what I fear may be the banalizing and belittling effects of the new philosophic elite. What I urge is the reopening of the case for grounding in foundational reason as our only source for a firm, as well as sublime, conception of our common humanity, in its grandeur and its limitations, in its lightheartedness and its tragedy.

I seek to reopen this case partly on behalf of modernity, and, above all, on behalf of its political achievement in American constitutionalism. For I am unimpressed by the standard criticisms, as well as the all-too-common patronizing endorsements, of the great moral and political philosophies of the Enlightenment. I do not find that either the criticism or the praise reflects long meditation on the political-philosophic treatises of Spinoza, of Locke, of Montesquieu, of Hume, or of the authors of the *Federalist Papers.* Yet I am compelled immediately to add that the rediscovery of the power of the arguments underlying liberal constitutionalism carries with it a recognition of the limits or bounds of that power. The reacquisition of intimate familiarity with the grounding treatises of modern republicanism only makes the shortcomings of the Enlightenment's conception of human freedom and excellence more apparent. The study of the roots of modernity prepares one to appreciate the justification for at least the starting points of the critique of modernity launched by its truly great opponents. It is on these great thinkers, and especially on Heidegger, that our contemporary "postmodernists" are, at their best, dependent for whatever lasting force their attempted deconstructions of rationalism may have.

What I seek to stimulate, then, is not a flight back to seek shelter under the authority of our eighteenth-century intellectual forebears, but instead the gathering of our powers for a plunge into authentic confrontation with the difficulties in our philosophic origins at their deepest level. Such a confrontation requires, and indeed culminates in, a genuinely thoughtful encounter with the "other" political rationalism, the political rationalism of Socrates and the Socratic tradition.

This Socratic political rationalism has little in common with the senescent "Platonism" and "Aristotelian teleology" that peer out at us from the stilted academic portraits painted by the conventionally respectable scholarship of the past two centuries. That scholarship—decisively formed by such influential figures as the Kantian Edmund Zeller—has viewed classical philosophy through the distorting, and indeed patronizing, prism of late-modern rationalism (and then of its rebellious stepchild, modern irrationalism). To fight our way clear of modern rationalism's impositions on the texts of classical rationalism, to break out of the imprisoning blinders of the past two centuries of classical scholarship, we must find a firm foothold outside the canonical list of "acceptable" or "respectable" interpretations of Socrates, Plato, Xenophon, and Aristotle. Such a foothold is available to us in an old and all-but-forgotten philosophic tradition of what is called the Near East: authentic Socratic or classical political rationalism is a civic philosophy that flourished for the last time in the Islamic and Judaic Middle Ages in such classics as Alfarabi's *Philosophy of Plato and Aristotle* and Maimonides' *Guide of the Perplexed*.[1]

The Socratic political rationalism that these strange and wonderful medieval books open up to us is seriously at odds with modern rationalism and with the liberal republicanism founded upon modern rationalism. Yet the gulf separating the two rationalisms is not unbridgeable. Both, after all, share—even as, and indeed precisely because, they dispute—the common ground of rational argument as the way to objective and rigorous truth about the permanent human condition and the abiding human questions or

---

1. See *Alfarabi's Philosophy of Plato and Aristotle*, ed. and trans. Muhsin Mahdi (Glencoe, Ill.: Free Press, 1962), and Maimonides, *The Guide of the Perplexed*, trans. Shlomo Pines (Chicago: University of Chicago Press, 1963). Reliable English versions of other key Arabic texts may be found in Mahdi and Lerner 1972. For helpful orientation, see Leo Strauss, "How to Begin to Study Medieval Philosophy," in Pangle 1989, and "Farabi's Plato," in *Essays in Medieval Jewish and Islamic Philosophy*, ed. Arthur Hyman (New York: KTAV Publishing, 1977), 391–427.

problems that define that condition. A kind of practical compromise between Socratic and modern political rationalism is then conceivable. But such a compromise will be valid, insofar as it can be valid, only if the basic theoretical disagreements are clearly recognized, and only if the great debate is thoroughly thought (and fought) through to a conclusion. In the process, shortcomings are to be discovered on both sides, and complementary strengths as well as antagonisms or tensions brought to light. Yet in the final analysis, given the depth of the disagreements, it is necessary that one or the other of the two dialectical partners be subordinated. In the American tradition thus far, the attempted syntheses (Benjamin Franklin's is perhaps the best known and the most thoughtful) have subordinated classical republicanism to the republicanism of the Enlightenment, Socratic rationalism to modern rationalism. I suggest we seriously entertain the possibility of reversing the order. By reappropriating classical civic rationalism, we may be afforded a framework that integrates the politically most significant discoveries of modern rationalism into a conception of humanity that does justice to the whole range of the human problem and the human potential, in a way and to a degree never achieved by modern rationalism. It is with a view to provoking the reader to serious inquiry into the possible truth of this admittedly strange and surely debatable contention that the following pages have been written.

Obviously, a simple or unqualified return to classical political theory is both undesirable and impossible: impossible, because the large-scale, mass society to which classical political theory devoted its study (especially in the treatises of Xenophon) was of a fundamentally different kind from the mass society we inhabit; undesirable, because of the advances that modern republican theory has effected over ancient republican theory. For we ought not to allow the unprecedented political horrors of the twentieth century (the Marxist gulags that have blighted so much of the East, the death camps of the fascists, the ever-present shadow of nuclear holocaust) to eclipse the achievements of modernity, together with the moderate hopes we can sustain in the light of these achievements. I have in mind, not only the defeat of Marxism and fascism and the abolition of slavery, but, more positively, the achievement of dignity and political organization for free labor; the enormous improvement in basic provisions and healthcare for the mass of humanity; the growth of recognition of universal human dignity in the doctrine of human rights; and, perhaps most important of all, the protection of human rights and of self-government in constitutional mechanisms and civic practices unknown to classical republican theory. In the words of Publius (Alexander Hamilton) in the *Federalist Papers*, no. 9:

The science of politics, however, like most other sciences, has received great improvement. The efficacy of various principles is now well understood, which were either not known at all, or imperfectly known to the ancients. The regular distribution of power into distinct departments; the introduction of legislative balances and checks; the institution of courts composed of judges holding their offices during good behavior; the representation of the people in the legislature by deputies of their own election: these are wholly new discoveries, or have made their principal progress toward perfection in modern times. They are means, and powerful means, by which the excellencies of republican government may be retained and its imperfections lessened or avoided. To this catalogue of circumstances that tend to the amelioration of popular systems of civil government, I shall venture, however novel it may appear to some, to add one more, on a principle that has been made the foundation of an objection to the new Constitution; I mean the ENLARGEMENT of the ORBIT within which such systems are to revolve, either in respect to the dimensions of a single State, or to the consolidation of several smaller States into one great Confederacy. . . . The opponents of the PLAN proposed have, with great assiduity, cited and circulated the observations of Montesquieu on the necessity of a contracted territory for a republican government. But they seem not to have been apprised of the sentiments of that great man expressed in another part of his work. . . . So far are the suggestions of Montesquieu from standing in opposition to a general Union of the States that he explicitly treats of a CONFEDERATE REPUBLIC as the expedient for extending the sphere of popular government and reconciling the advantages of monarchy with those of republicanism.

But the great question that looms over even the high-water marks of modern republican theory is this. Did not theorists like Hamilton and Montesquieu depend upon, and yet inadequately account or provide for, certain absolutely crucial moral and educational foundations of civic republican culture: moral and educational foundations, the exploration of whose problematic nature was the central theme of Socratic republican theory?

It is not difficult to show that classical political philosophy is well aware of the foundation in nature—that is, in natural right—of the universal human claim to a share in dignity, or "nobility," and even inner "beauty" (*to kalon*). It suffices to recall Aristotle's most famous characterization of human nature:

By nature is the human being a political animal. That is why even when they have no need of assistance from one another they are no less directed toward living together. Not but that also the common advantage brings them together, to the extent that a share in living nobly falls to each: for it is this especially that is the goal, for all humans, both in common and individually. But they also come together for the sake of life itself, and for this hold together the political community, because perhaps there is some portion of nobility even just in living as such, if life is not too full of hardships. (*Politics* 1278b 19–27)

But Aristotle goes on to insist that the universal concern for a share in nobility or dignity points unmistakably toward human excellence or virtue. The universal concern for dignity includes a natural and universal aspiration to share, through participation in a republican community, in the rare and elevated.

It is, again, not difficult to show that classical political philosophy is aware that natural right dictates that the virtue of political justice must rest on an egalitarian pillar. Justice is equality, as both Aristotle (*Politics* 1282b14 ff., 1301b28 ff.) and Plato's Athenian Stranger (*Laws* 757) declare. But equality is not a simple thing. Equality is twofold. On the one hand, every society must provide reciprocal or corrective justice, according to which every person is to be regarded as arithmetically equal. The most obvious loci of equality in *this* sense are the marketplace and the courtroom:

In communal exchange, it is justice in this sense that is the bond. . . . The city is maintained by reciprocity according to analogy; for [citizens] seek to repay evil with evil, or they consider themselves slaves; and good with good; and if they can't, mutual exchange ceases: but they are maintained by mutual exchange. That is why they set up a public temple to the goddesses of gratitude, so that there will be reciprocity. (Aristotle *Nicomachean Ethics* 1132b32–1133a4)

But there is another and higher sense of justice as equality: "distributive justice," or "justice as fairness." Here the principle is merit, and proportional equality of the ratios between individuals and their desserts. Burden and opportunity, office and risk, and honor and disgrace ought to be distributed in proportions equal to the different contributions, efforts, proven potentials, and attainments of citizens.

The great doubt classical republican theory poses for modern republican theory is this: has modern theory, in its successful attempt to clarify and satisfy the most basic legitimate demands of political life, obscured the clear view of human excellence that is required in order to shape a public life that reflects the whole of the common good? In devoting itself to the most basic human needs, has modern republican political philosophy not eclipsed the higher dimensions of civic aspiration—and the deeply problematic reflections on our human condition to which we are led by focusing on those higher aspirations? For it is indeed the exploration of the problem of justice, or the common good, and not so much the preaching of justice, in which classical political philosophy culminates. The classics are moral philosophers, not moralists.

The questionableness of modern philosophies of natural rights—and therewith of the foundations of modern, and especially American, constitutionalism—is today very widely acknowledged. So wide, in fact, is this acknowledgment that we may reasonably suspect that the doubt of the foundations of modern republican philosophy has degenerated into a kind of formulaic dogmatism. To repeat, I do not mean to endorse the conventional criticisms of Lockean and Montesquieuian political philosophy. I am convinced that what pass today for refutations of the political philosophies of the Enlightenment are in fact bogus, because, as I have tried to demonstrate elsewhere, those refutations rest on very partial, and historically as well as philosophically naive, readings of the treatises of Locke and Montesquieu (see Pangle 1973, 1988). But on the other hand, the genuine and fundamental difficulties in the great political philosophies underlying modern constitutionalism do come to view precisely when those philosophies are tackled on their own level, and placed in dialogue once again with what they acknowledge to be their great rivals—the Bible and classical political philosophy.

When this dialogue is reenacted, one begins to see how problematic are the fashionable attempts to supplement or shore up early-modern republican theory with a recourse to German idealism. In the face of the postmodernist onslaught, the recourse to Kant's moral and political philosophy has become highly attractive. Given the moral richness and analytical rigor of Kant's philosophy, one can well understand the serious temptation to summon Kantian transfusions to the rescue of what is felt to be the rather anemic vision of humanity underlying liberal democratic political theory.

But what is amazing is how little resemblance these transfusions bear to the morally severe, metaphysically grounded, authentic thought of Kant himself. According to Kant, penetrating examination of our experience of responsible human action reveals a single, eternal, and universal principle of morality: "Act only on that maxim through which you can at the same time will that it should become a universal law." This sole "categorical imperative" is the one and only bedrock for any conception of human rights that expresses human dignity as opposed to collective Hobbesian shrewdness. To vindicate this single fundamental law, there is required a thorough critique of pure reason, showing the radical limitations of all scientific as well as metaphysical thinking. Once vindicated and analyzed, this categorical imperative emerges as much more than a merely formal or regulative principle into which anyone can fit whatever seems morally "uplifting," "sweet," or "appealing." Properly conceived, that is, in terms of the will or freedom seen as end in itself, the categorical imperative entails a small and precise set of immutably true moral virtues and a system of immutably true principles of constitutionalism. Kant elaborates the moral virtues in his *Metaphysical Principles of the Doctrine of Virtue*, which forms part 2 of his *Metaphysics of Morals*. The constitutional principles he elaborates in part 1 of the same work: *The Metaphysical Principles of the Doctrine of Right*. One sometimes gets the impression that contemporary borrowers from Kant have not heard of this treatise, in which Kant presents the substantial heart of his moral, legal, and political philosophy. Yet one cannot altogether blame our contemporary "Kantians" for trying to creep silently by this core of authentic Kantianism. *The Metaphysics of Morals* is not a treatise calculated to win Kant popularity contests, since it is here that he makes clearest his view of the extraordinary demands of a conception of human dignity and human rights that cannot possibly be reduced to the utilitarian quest for physical safety, material comfort, and the vanity of "universal recognition."

The Kantian conception of justice is grounded in the state of nature and includes the principles of natural rights (especially property rights), natural laws, the social contract, and a rather strict doctrine of sovereignty. Among the most distinctive features of the legal philosophy Kant erects on these foundations are: first, a penal philosophy that demonstrates that punishment can only be just if it is retributive (and that includes a ringing endorsement of retributive capital punishment); second, a denial, not only of the right of revolution, but of the moral legitimacy of civil disobedience; and third, a compelling moral critique of much of what we would today call the welfare state.

As for the Kantian doctrine of the virtues, its basic tone is set in the first virtues that are treated. Kant begins with a consideration of the proper moral posture toward one's self, and therefore toward one's preservation and sexuality. The first two virtues are, accordingly, the absolute avoidance of suicide, in all circumstances, and the absolute avoidance of purely sexual gratification, which Kant calls "wanton self-desecration" (*wohllüstige Selbstschändung*). The argument is a straightforward deduction from the categorical imperative, which dictates that rational humanity must always be treated, not merely as a means, but as an end in itself: "The ground of proof of the moral evil lies obviously in the fact that one gives up one's very personality (casts it aside) when one uses oneself merely as the means for the gratification of an animal drive." Kant adds that on the basis of the categorical imperative, this sexual vice must be judged worse than suicide, for "the obstinate throwing away of one's life as a burden is at least not a weak surrender to animal pleasure, but demands courage, in which there is always found respect for the humanity in one's own person" (*The Metaphysics of Morals,* pt. 1, sec. 7). Kant begins his teaching on the moral virtues in this stunning fashion because he wishes to announce from the outset the intimately demanding character of the entailments of human rights. He wishes to make unmistakably clear how far anything properly derivable from authentic human rights stands from self-indulgence, or from what we today call "sexual liberation."

Now when one turns from these authentic texts of Kant to the use made of Kant—or of his name and authority—in contemporary discussions, one cannot but gape in amazement at the disparity in tone, substance, morals, and politics. Is it really Kant, or anything genuinely Kantian, to which appeal is made? Or is it merely the case that the august name and bewitching authority of this great reasoner and moralist are being enlisted in defense of principles and policies whose laxity would set his hair on end?

Kant's philosophy is the purest, and therefore most revealing, expression of the attempt to make human rights and the will as end in itself the sustaining foundations of an elevated conception of humanity—thus radically subordinating love, the good, and happiness, and virtue or excellence conceived of as ultimately determined by these latter rather than by human rights. Kant holds that to make the good, rather than rights, the supreme principle of humanity is to condemn humanity to a conditioned, or unfree, and even animalistic existence and status. For the good, or happiness, is ultimately undefinable by reason except in negative terms (avoidance of violent death, etc.); worldly happiness is therefore determined by forces that are historical, economic, psychological, and so forth. To make happiness our standard is therefore to surrender our humanity, our freedom and rationality, to these deterministic and historical or merely subjective forces. Now is this true? That is the most important question for anyone who seriously seeks to return to Kant.

This question is not put to rest, and indeed it is in some measure obscured, by Hegel's purported improvements on Kant's moral and political philosophy. Hegel is famous for his criticism of the barren formalism of Kant's categorical imperative (*Philosophy of Right,* sec. 135). Hegel claims to have given content to the formalism by showing how the principle of the categorical imperative—the concept of the will as end in itself—can be, and is in fact, embodied in the concrete, historical institutions of a rational constitutional state administering a modern liberal ("bourgeois") society. The ethical life is then to be seen as the dutiful fulfillment of the rational tasks and patterns of behavior dictated by and instantiated in these institutions, and in the accompanying mutual recognition among citizens of their at once dutiful and emancipated rational dignity. But Hegel's stress on the need for public, legal, institutional recognition in the modern state and liberal society of what really matters only makes clearer the neglect or eclipse, in his ethical and political philosophy, of those fundamental aspects of human existence that matter so much that they can never be institutionalized in the modern state and civil society. To see this vividly, one has only to consider what Hegel says, or does not say, in his *Philosophy of Right* about happiness, love, God, heroism, sainthood, friendship, philosophy, and what Hegel admits is "virtue in the strict sense of the word"; while bearing in mind the status of these subjects in the chief political works of Plato and Aristotle (see esp. *Philosophy of Right,* secs. 19–20, 93, 123, 150, 158, 163, 242).

The philosophically most profound work in our century that has attempted to plumb the depths of what it would mean to recur to Kant for an enlargement and enrichment of the moral and political principles of modern constitutionalism ends with these guiding words:

> The old foundations of law and of the state are more problematic than they were before. . . . Thus *Kant's problem is absolutely our problem.* It is certainly not simply "the same" but *it repeats itself . . .* the *conditionality* of humanity and above all of history, which is the starting point for all transcendence, must be subjected to an *interrogation* that is philosophic, i.e., *unconditioned.* But the question will never really be unconditioned except if, *in the knowledge applied to historical passion, the question uncovers the question of the good.* It is not our task here to examine more closely the *answer* to this question—and also the Christian answer of Augustine. That the decisive question remains *true,* even if it does *not* find an answer, the example of *Socrates* can teach to whomever asks as did he.
>
> (Krüger 1931, 236; emphasis in the original)

Serious recourse to Kant and Hegel eventually requires a reconsideration of the Socratic alternative and of the great debates between Socratism and revealed religion.

Thus far I have indicated this book's point of departure and its goal. Let me now briefly outline the path my argument takes. My critique of postmodernism in Part I is followed, in Part II, by a tentative exploration of the spiritual and civic future of Europe. Through that speculation I try to make plausible some slender, but real, possibilities for a European cultural renascence, rooted in the highest potentialities suggested by past (precommunist) and present (anticommunist) movements toward a dynamic European community of peoples and nations. These possibilities and potentialities are juxtaposed against the contemporary American scene in order to suggest the stimulus the American spirit might conceivably receive from such a European reawakening, or from our meditation on such a possibility. Insofar as Milan Kundera may have been right in asserting that "the postwar annexation of Central Europe by Russian civilization caused Western culture to lose its center of gravity," and if "we cannot dismiss the possibility that the end of Central Europe marked the beginning of the end for Europe as a whole" (Kundera 1980, 230), then we cannot dismiss the possibility that the liberation of Central Europe might help Western culture regain its center of gravity.

Part III outlines some of the first steps in the reconsideration of moral and civic fundamentals that would be required to rise to the European challenge whose nature and possibility I have sketched. These chapters constitute the theoretical heart of the book, in which I try to introduce the reader to what I believe to be the authentic, if forgotten, battlelines of the fruitful debate between modern constitutionalism and ancient political rationalism.

In the fourth and final part, I try to suggest the basic principles that ought to guide a genuinely liberating liberal education, an education that would prepare young people both for participating in an awakened republican political life and for carrying on the sort of responsible, critical inquiry into our grounding principles whose first steps I have sketched in the preceding chapters. These concluding chapters continue, if only tacitly, my dialogue with postmodernism. The most impressive philosophic voice of contemporary postmodernism, Jean-François Lyotard, has stressed that postmodernism proceeds on the assumption that the university as it has been known in the West is finished: the university, viewed in the postmodernist optic, has lost all ground for any credible unifying and guiding claim or purpose it might once have had, and the time has come to devise other loci of nontechnical education (Lyotard 1979, esp. 82–85; 1986, 165–66). As will be obvious, I do not deny that the contemporary university—and, indeed, our entire educational system—is in spiritual crisis, and that as a result the university and the educational system are undergoing accelerating decline. But I believe that regenerative reform, based on return to the original, genuine, and now forgotten or buried Platonic conception of "liberal education" (*paideia eleutheria*), may still be possible in some places—however slender the possibility. I do not attempt to make, and in any case am not competent to elaborate, specific suggestions for the reorganization of educational institutions. My theme is rather the spirit of our institutions, and above all the educational goals or objects of aspiration that we ought to hold in our mind's eye as we give serious thought to the challenge of forming and liberating the souls of the young. Even, or precisely if, Lyotard is right—if it is true that we are compelled to begin to construct new, less "official" sites for true education—sustained reflection on the goal of authentic liberal education is all the more essential.

PART I

The Inadequacy of the Postmodernist Response

1 / Postmodernism and the Avant-Garde

What Is Postmodernism?

Like so many other doctrines bearing the suffix *-ism,* the concept of post-modernism is nebulous, diverse, and even contradictory in its meanings or in the meanings given to it. The term *postmodernism* has rather different connotations in literature, in architecture and the fine arts, in political theory, and in history, as, for that matter, do the terms *modernism* and *the modern.* Yet there is a familiar, and not unrevealing, shared set of stylistic motifs. This surface has been aptly depicted by Susan Shell:

It is everywhere around us, winking at us from rock videos and commercials, from the eclectic facades of the newest buildings, from the artful exercises in edible minimalism served up at the choicest restaurants. The assault is a matter of style as much as substance, or rather, of the eclipse of the difference between style and substance. . . . [It has] been brewing for quite some time, as readers of Nietzsche well know. What is new about the current assault is its evident good cheer. . . . Today's nihilism is no *angst* and all play. *Spiel macht frei.* The French *geste,* in the sense of move or gesture, sets the tone. The important thing is the difference between gesture and posture (or imposture). To gesture is not to take a stand, but to reveal, without necessarily meaning to. Statements (which claim to be true or false) take a back seat to the knowing (or not so knowing) wink. The dizzying horror of the abyss is replaced by the virtuosity of performance—a kind of perpetual mid-air tap dance, in which the ground isn't needed—not, as in the land of 'toons, because its absence isn't noticed, but because the ground itself is no longer sought. It may seem odd to address the plight of the academic humanities by way of recent developments in largely popular style. But in fact the sources of that style are largely academic: the artful playing off of contradictory images (at least contradictory in terms of their conventional historical meaning) that typifies so much of that style—from Philip Johnson to Madonna—is a direct appropriation, via British bottling of Gallic (and Germanic) wine that has already begun to fizzle out abroad. What is perhaps more remarkable to us as Americans is the success of what has until recently been a mainly European event in storming the bastions of the American Academy, bastions that were until recently not only unreceptive but openly hostile to it.   (Shell 1989)

To begin to find our way to the philosophic heart of the matter, we may observe that in a debate with his fellow postmodernist Jean-François Lyotard, the leading American postmodernist, Richard Rorty, defers to his friendly antagonist by declaring that "it is from France that the most original contemporary philosophic thought comes to us" (Rorty 1985a, 578). What then is French postmodernism? Lyotard himself, in an ironically elementary exposition of postmodernism called *Le Postmoderne expliqué aux enfants* (1986), suggests we begin to orient ourselves by way of reflection on the changes in the nature and the self-understanding of avant-garde art (including literature).

But in order to follow Lyotard's "explanation for children," we need to begin from another writing of Lyotard's, in which his starting point is made more visible: his "Philosophy and Painting in the Age of Their Experimentation: Contribution to an Idea of Postmodernity" (1989b).[1]

The Reaction against Hegel

In this latter essay we learn that, like so much that is truly interesting in modern French thought, Lyotard's postmodernism is best defined over and against Alexandre Kojève's Hegelian rationalism, viewed as perhaps the fullest and purest expression of modernity. For Kojève, Hegel's is *the* final teaching (once slightly emended and supplemented by Kojève). Hegel's teaching explains the present era as the completion of history, which can now be seen to have been a rational, if contradictory (dialectical), process

---

1. Lyotard's account of the meaning of the avant-garde, modern and postmodern, is by no means customary, and from any conventional point of view his categorizations and interpretations of twentieth-century artists will often appear strange, not to say perverse. Lyotard is unique in the degree to which he insists that the postmodern cannot be separated (though it must be distinguished) from the modern: in Lyotard's view, the postmodern is present in the modern from the very beginning, and gradually makes its presence more and more evident. Lyotard's view certainly does not typify the orthodox opinions of artists, critics, and art historians, and I have not chosen to focus on him as "representative." On the contrary: I have chosen to focus on Lyotard because of his bracing originality, the breadth of his historical and philosophic self-consciousness, and the uniquely illuminating character of his intransigent attempt to locate the deepest (that is to say, the religious) impulse of the avant-garde.

through which the articulate essence of the human condition has been completely disclosed, formed or re-formed, and satisfied. All coherent aspirations have in principle been realized, all fundamental contradictions resolved, in the emerging universal and homogenous world society of free and equal men and women made secure and comfortable by a technology that has in principle overcome nature (as standing in opposition to reason). No transcendence of the given world appears required or credible anymore, except to those who have yet to join fully in the emerging rational society.

Lyotard quotes from a 1936 essay Kojéve wrote for Vasily Kandinsky, in which Kojève sketched an account of abstract art on his Hegelian basis (Kojève 1970a). According to the paradox-loving Kojève, all figurative and so-called representational painting prior to the twentieth century stands revealed now as "abstract art." For in every case a partial, because less than perfectly rational, perspective was assumed, in accordance with the historical "subjectivity" of the artist. Only now, or more precisely beginning with a famous untitled Kandinsky watercolor of 1910, has a truly "objective," nonfragmentary, and "concrete" sort of painting become possible.[2] What appears to the old-fashioned eye as twentieth-century "abstract" painting is in fact the first type of painting that does not abstract anything out of nature. Rather, this formally abstract art expresses the "concrete totality," the nothing-in-particular, that is the vision of the self-conscious mind at play in its awareness of its complete comprehension of, and therefore integration into, the whole of being at the end of the historical process that has remade being into rational existence.[3]

To see the full bearing of Kojève's letter, we must draw on Kojève's other

2. The famous Kandinsky watercolor is reproduced in Kandinsky 1985 (p. 101). Although the painting continues to be identified as executed in 1910, it has recently been argued that the work's date was misremembered by Kandinsky and his widow, and that in fact it dates from 1913 and is not the first abstract painting: see Long 1980, 157 n. 17.

3. This is not the place to enter into the question of the relation between Kojève's interpretation of what Kandinsky was doing or trying to do in founding abstract art and Kandinsky's self-interpretation. Kandinsky's most authoritative statement, *Über das Geistige in der Kunst* (On the Spiritual/Intellectual in Art, [1912]), certainly seems to suggest that he was influenced by the symbolist movement, theosophic mysticism, and Nietzsche more than by anything interpretable in terms of Hegel; but the artist's self-understanding at the time remains ambiguous, and was in any case incomplete or in a state of development (he did not yet know, of course, of Kojève's mature Hegel interpretation). It would appear that the later Kandinsky was much closer to Kojève; see the crucial formulation quoted in Hess 1956, 87: "With the passage of time, one becomes decisively conscious of the fact that . . . the abstract painter encounters his 'inspirations,' not from arbitrary pieces of nature, but from nature as a totality, from its manifold manifestations, that he sums up in himself and brings out in the work. This synthesizing basis seeks for itself the most fitting form of expression, and that is the 'nonrepresentational.'" The discussions in Long 1980 and in Weiss 1979 are helpful, but these writers do not seem aware of the connection between Kandinsky and Kojève.

works in order to bring out the crucial religious and political implications. Kojève is saying that Kandinsky's misnamed abstract expression is, or may be, the first thoroughly and unqualifiedly *atheistic* art. He is saying that this is the first art form that need be neither openly nor surreptitiously an expression of longing for the beyond, or for the absent that would "complete" existence and that can be intimated only through some sort of aspiration or inspiration. By the same token, Kojève means that this is the first art form that expresses no fundamental moral or political criticism of the given world: the first art form upset by the social world only to the extent that certain parts of the social world have not yet "caught up" to what is already evident, and evidently right, in the social world. Twentieth-century avant-garde art finds its spiritual satisfaction in the given work, as not pointing or looking beyond itself, as the expression of the satisfied rational self-consciousness at play in a world in which it is in principle totally at home. This play, to be sure, is no longer "human": it knows no serious anguish, longing, moral struggle, overcoming, or possibility of tragedy. For "History," as "Negation," or as "human action," history as dynamic contradiction between conflicting "causes" or conceptions of justice, is finished. The rational and just society has been realized, at least in principle. The only important "struggle" left is the struggle to apply and consolidate the rational truth articulated in Hegel's *Philosophy of Right*.[4]

Art thus becomes a kind of rational infantilism—the highest activity, one might say, of spiritual life when there is nothing left of importance to accomplish. The perfect literary manifestation is Raymond Queneau's *Cent mille milliards de poèmes*.[5]

It is against this staggering claim of Kojève-Hegel, and its reflection in the work of surrealist artists like Queneau, that Lyotard rebels, in the name of a return from Hegelianism to the aesthetics of Kant, as supplemented by

4. See, esp., Kojève 1962, 434–37. With a view to what will follow, it is relevant to note that Kojève's atheism was not incompatible with a certain playful tolerance of mysticism, so long as the mystic remained totally silent or spoke only in logical contradictions. This side of Kojève appears in his correspondence with his reluctant disciple Georges Bataille (Kojève 1970b) and was explicitly developed in Bataille's "self-conscious atheistic mysticism" and "negativity without a task": see Bataille 1955, 21–44, and his letter to Kojève published in 1961, 169–72. The critique of Bataille's 1955 *Deucalion* essay, and its inability to escape the Kojèvian matrix, was one starting point for Jacques Derrida's introduction of Heideggerian thought to France: see Derrida 1967, 369–407.
5. Queneau, 1961: this little book of poetry, still readily available at children's bookstores, involves the reader's participation in artistic "creativity" at every step, by compelling one to decide how each poem is to read; and the reading/creating can help consume free time at the end of history, since one can calculate that the reading/creating of the book consumes more than one hundred million centuries. For Kojève-Hegel set to music as it were, consult the surrealistic novels of Queneau, especially *Le Dimanche de la vie* (1947).

the French *philosophe* Diderot. According to Lyotard, the postmodern must be understood as emerging out of and against the modern avant-garde. But both the postmodern and the modern avant-garde must be properly understood (i.e., in Kantian rather than Hegelian terms). What then is the avant-garde, modern and then postmodern, when it is conceived in Kantian terms?

The Adaptation of Kantian Aesthetics

At the heart of the modernist avant-garde (including literature) is, Lyotard argues, an attempt to recover the experience that Kant calls the "sublime" (*das Erhabene*) in *The Critique of Judgment*. This experience of the sublime is to be conceived in contrast to the experience of the beautiful (*das Schöne*).

The experience of the beautiful is the experience of a particular sensuous object or representation that corresponds to no general conception in our minds, but whose sensual perfection evokes pleasure in and of itself, without reference to other interests. This pleasure is accepted as valid by a consensus of "taste." (Simple example: the pleasure we all take in seeing or exhibiting a flower or a still life.)

The experience of the sublime, in contrast, is the experience of a general and even vague conception of the awesomely limitless or infinite that may be evoked but cannot adequately be represented by particular sensuous objects or images. (Simple example: the sublime is evoked by the sight of the stormy sea.) In regard to the sublime we find a more unsteady consensus of "taste."

Now, the *modern* avant-garde, says Lyotard in his "explanation for children," is "consecrated" to the attempts to express in art this experience of the sublime: "Art is modern that consecrates its 'little bit of technique,' as Diderot puts it, to presenting that which is unpresentable" (Lyotard 1986, 27–28). But can we gain a somewhat more specific notion of just what this "unpresentable" is, and of how the unpresentable is to be presented in art? Lyotard gives, by way of Kant, only one or two tantalizing examples:

Kant himself indicates the direction to follow, in naming the *nonform*, the *absence of form*, as a possible index of the unpresentable. He also says of the *abstraction* the imagination experiences as it searches for a presentation of the infinite (another unpresentable) that this abstraction itself is like a presentation of the infinite, its *negative presentation*. He cites the "Thou shalt not make any graven image, etc." (Exodus 2:4) as the most sublime passage in the Bible.

At the risk of making exoteric what Lyotard prefers to leave in esoteric ambiguity: the modern avant-garde, in rebellion against atheistic modern rationalism, seeks a *deus absconditus*.

So, if this is the heart of the modern avant-garde, how then does the *post*modern avant-garde come to sight, for Lyotard, revealing the impulse of postmodernism? How does the postmodern take over where the modernist rebellion against rationalism leaves off? Modernism, we may say, culminates in an avant-garde that reveals the inadequacy of what is given, of what *appears* "real," by expressing the "sublime" disproportion between the little that *can* be presented in art and the grandeur of what is conceivable or sensed but remains unpresentable except in evocative absence. Yet this experience splits into two possibilities: "The accent can be put on the weakness of the faculty of presentation, on the nostalgia for presence which the human subject experiences"; *or* "the accent can be placed rather on the power of the faculty of conceiving, in its 'inhumanity' so to speak" (Lyotard 1986, 30). "Here then," concludes Lyotard, "is the difference":

The *modern* aesthetic is an aesthetic of the sublime, but nostalgic; it permits the adducing of the unpresentable only as an absent content, while permitting the form to continue to offer to the reader or viewer matter for consolation and pleasure, thanks to its recognizable consistency. But these sentiments do not constitute the truly sublime sentiment, which is an intrinsic combination of pleasure and pain, to wit, the pleasure in reason exceeding all presentation, and the sorrow that the imagination or the senses cannot conceive.

The *post*modern would be that which in the modern adduces the unpresentable in the presentation itself; that which refuses the consolation of good forms, of a consensus of taste that permits a common experience of nostalgia for the impossible; that which inquires into new presentations, not to enjoy them, but to experience better that which is unpresentable. A postmodern artist or writer is in the situation of a philosopher: the text he writes, the work he accomplishes are not in principle governed by rules already established. . . . These rules and these categories are that for which the work or the text searches . . . From this it follows that the work and the text would have the properties of the Event [*l'événement*], inasmuch as they arrive too late for their author. . . . It seems to me that the essay (Montaigne) is postmodern, and the fragment (the Athenaeum) modern.

(Lyotard 1986, 32–33)

Lyotard elaborates in a discussion of works by the artist Barnett Newmann:

The inexpressible does not reside in an over there, in another words [*sic*], or another time, but in this: in that (something) happens. In the determination of pictorial art, the indeterminate, the "it happens," is the paint, the picture. The paint, the picture as occurrence or event, is not expressible, and it is to this that it has to witness.[6]

6. Lyotard 1989c, 197. Lyotard focuses on Newmann's painting *Vir Heroicus Sublimis*. First shown in 1951, it is now in the Metropolitan Museum of Modern Art in New York. A color reproduction may be found on p. 395 of *The Encyclopedia of American Art* (New York: Dutton, 1981). Lyotard also draws on Newmann 1948.

Yet what has been said thus far does not account for the "privation" that characterizes the emerging postmodern avant-garde. In Lyotard's words, "an Event, an occurrence—what Martin Heidegger calls *ein Ereignis*—is infinitely simple, but this simplicity can only be approached through a state of privation." To understand these words, we must follow Lyotard and Newmann back behind Kantian aesthetics to Edmund Burke's *Philosophical Enquiry into the Origin of our Ideas of the Sublime and Beautiful* (1757). Kant draws from Burke, but, according to Lyotard, because Kant rejects Burke's thesis as psychological reductivism, "he strips Burke's aesthetic of what I consider to be its major stake—to show that the sublime is kindled by the threat of nothing further happening" (Lyotard 1989c, 204). What does Lyotard mean by this "threat of nothing further happening?"

Lyotard appeals to Burke's understanding of the sublime as an experience rooted in our fear, and ultimately in our greatest fear, the fear of violent death or of nothingness. The sublime is a mixture of pain and pleasure: the first moment of the sublime is terror, followed immediately by the relief of terror through distancing. More specifically: in sublime art, the threat of the termination of life, of the termination of the occurrences that make life alive, is first evoked, and the soul is "astonished" with fear—"dumb, immobilized, as good as dead." But then "art, by distancing this menace, procures a pleasure of relief," which Burke christens "delight." "Thanks to art, the soul is returned to the agitated zone between life and death, and this agitation is its health and its life. For Burke, the sublime was no longer a matter of elevation (the category by which Aristotle defined tragedy), but a matter of intensification" (Lyotard 1989c, 205).

This "intensification," this essentially artificial attempt to rediscover and resuscitate the life that is alive (filled with fear of annihilation and glimpsing a promise of redemption through art), in the midst of an era that threatens us with lifelessness, is for Lyotard the clue to the deepest meaning of the emergence of the postmodern avant-garde.

Lyotard is making no claims about "influences": "Manet, Cézanne, Braque, and Picasso probably did not read Kant or Burke. It is more a matter of an irresistible deviation in the destination of art" (Lyotard 1989c, 206). The postmodern aesthetic experience is of "ontological dislocation": the threat of meaninglessness, emptiness, nothingness, is evoked and countered—but by less and less. For every convention, rule, or category inherited from traditional art must be subjected to questioning and experimentation in order to wrest the "occurrence" of the work of art free from the meaninglessness inherent in the routinizing world of modernity—a world that claims to sum up the whole past and that in so doing seems all too susceptible to becoming the grim cage of completed Hegelian rationalism, the end of all possibility of either transcendence or "intensification" of existence. And of course this postmodern avant-garde art becomes more and more alien to "ordinary life"—the life lived in everyday monotony with a deadening lack of intensity. As Lyotard scornfully comments, "the social community no longer recognizes itself in art objects, but ignores them, rejects them as incomprehensible, and only later allows the intellectual avant-garde to preserve them in museums as the traces of offensives that bear witness to the power, and the privation, of the spirit" (Lyotard 1989c, 206). Unfortunately, as Lyotard has to admit, this is hardly the end of the matter. For the postmodernist consciousness *does* have profound political and social effects. Lyotard does his best to minimize or explain these away, but he cannot ignore them.

The Political Implications of the Sublime

The avant-garde search for the sublime, Lyotard concedes, "seems only to aggravate the identity crisis that communities went through during the long 'depression' that lasted from the thirties until the end of 'reconstruction' in the mid fifties." The "question" posed by the avant-garde consciousness was "translated" (and thereby "betrayed") as a waiting for some fabulous subject or identity: "Is the pure people coming? Is the Führer coming?" Lyotard has to admit that the "aesthetics of the sublime" was "thus neutralized and converted into a politics of myth" (Lyotard 1989c, 208–9). But he refuses to accept that what he calls postmodernism has any responsibility for, or remains subject to, these fascist and Stalinist consequences. To see the issues Lyotard is here skirting, we need to turn to his more political discussion of the sublime, presented near the end of what he calls "my book of philosophy," *Le Différend* (Lyotard 1983, 236–46).

Here Lyotard notes that according to Kant, there is an essential continuity, from the experience of the sublime in art, to "enthusiasm," "an extreme mode of the sublime" that is produced above all by *political* "events." For Kant, the leading example of such an event is the French Revolution. As Lyotard puts it, paraphrasing Kant, "enthusiasm as 'event of our time' . . . is the most contradictory of aesthetics, the aesthetic of the most extreme sublime." In "enthusiastic" reaction to political "events," the onlooker experiences the awareness that what is happening points beyond itself to universal and even infinite meaning. Now Lyotard stresses that Kant knows and warns that this all-too-natural movement from the sublime in aesthetics, to political enthusiasm, is dangerous and even sick. As Lyotard paraphrases Kant, "historico-political enthusiasm is then close to dementia, it is a pathological attack, and as such it has in itself no ethical validity." Nevertheless, "the enthusiastic pathos does retain, in its episodic unleashing, an aesthetic validity, it is an energetic *sign*." "The infinity of the idea draws to itself all the other capacities, that is to say, all the other faculties, and produces an *Affekt* [emotional state] of 'a vigorous sort,' characteristic of the sublime."

Lyotard wonders whether Kant has dealt adequately with the political danger he perceives in the aesthetics of the sublime. A fair question; but in Kant, there is at least a clear and unambiguous principle by which political enthusiasm, rooted in the aesthetics of the sublime, can and must be judged, dominated, and regulated. This principle is the categorical imperative and its entailments, the "natural rights of man." For Lyotard, this guiding core of Kantian political aesthetics has become utterly incredible as well as dangerous. Lyotard sees Jacobin terror as the not-so-surprising outcome of the Declaration of the Rights of Man and Citizen of 1789. He goes so far as to argue for an important resemblance between Hitlerism and the imperialistic French Republic's crusade for the Rights of Man (Lyotard 1986, 83–94). But what then, for Lyotard, replaces the limit on political enthusiasm provided by the now-discredited Kantian moral law and the universal rights of man? Not much. Nothing except a vague and nostalgic evocation of what Lyotard admits is a bankrupt Marxist notion of world proletarian revolution: "Marxism has not finished, but what keeps it going?" asks Lyotard in 1983. He answers in these elliptical terms:

Wrong expresses itself by sentiment, suffering. . . . Capitalism pretends to universality. The wrong that capitalism inflicts on speech would then be a universal wrong. But if the wrong is not universal, the silent sentiment that signals a diversity [*un différend*] remains to be heard. . . . It is thus that Marxism has not finished, as sentiment of the diversity. (Lyotard 1983, 245–46)

Or, as Lyotard puts it in *Le Postmoderne expliqué aux enfants,* his book written to win the young over to postmodernism:

It must be made clear that it is not for us to *furnish a reality,* but rather to invent allusions to the conceivable that cannot be presented. And one cannot expect from this attempt the least reconciliation between the "language games." . . . Our response is war against everything, bearing witness to the unpresentable, activating the differences, saving the honor of the name. (Lyotard 1986, 33–34)

Given the purely "sentimental"—if still wildly activist— validity that Lyotard continues to attach to Marxism, it is not surprising to find that the political consequence of his aesthetics that does worry him, and for which he admits he might bear some responsibility, is the fact that "there is a kind of collusion between capital and the avant-garde." On the one hand:

The forces of skepticism and even of destruction that capitalism has brought into play, and that Marx never ceased analyzing and identifying, in some way encourage among artists a mistrust of established rules and a willingness to experiment with means of expression, with styles, with ever-new materials. There is something of the sublime in the capitalist economy.

But in addition, there is in the capitalist art market a "confusion between innovation and *Ereignis* [event]" owing to the deceptive principle that "a work of art is avant-garde in direct proportion to the extent that it is stripped of meaning." After all, as Lyotard is honest enough to ask, "Is it not then like an event?" Yet Lyotard refuses to entertain the thought that the postmodernist consciousness in fact encourages what he knows to be the most dangerous political proclivities, and the most corrupting market forces, of the past fifty years: "the enigma," the mystery in the "occurrence, the *Ereignis*" is "not dissolved for all this" (Lyotard 1989c, 209–11).

Postmodernism is the rebellion against the rationalism it sees as culminating in the Hegelian "transcendental illusion." Postmodernism is the rebellion against all magnificent "meta-narratives," as Lyotard calls them, that pretend to explain in worldly and universal terms, and that thereby diminish and constrict, the "intensity" of existence in its diversity and openness to the magical or the divine. Every claim or attempt to explain the whole of existence both distorts existence and, what is worse, tends toward a "totalitarian" claim to be able to judge and order existence morally and politically.

Yet in passing Lyotard draws our attention to the fact that the "sublime" has an altogether different interpretation in late Greco-Roman philosophy. He refers us to Longinus's *On the Sublime*, the original treatise on the topic and in a sense the fountainhead of all discussion of the sublime. Lyotard remarks that Longinus's treatise, following Aristotle, defines sublimity in terms of "elevation." When we turn to the text of Longinus, we find that the sublime (*to hypsos*) is there defined not merely in terms of "the elevated" (the literal meaning of *to hypsos*). Longinus goes on to insist that the *apparently* elevated quickly withers unless it arouses, in and with elevation, sustained critical wonder and rational thought. The sublime in *this* sense Longinus finds epitomized in an author who is today held to be the least sublime of the classics: Xenophon.

For this is what is in its very being truly great: that to which belongs continued theoretical speculation, and which is so provoking to thought that rebellion against its power is impossible, but the memory is strong and hard to escape. . . . The first characteristic of the sublime is its superiority in the penetrating force of its effect on the activities of intelligence, as we have defined it in our studies of Xenophon; and the second characteristic is passion in its intensity and being-possessed.[7]

This intriguing suggestion of a possible alternative rationalist "aesthetics" is brushed aside by Lyotard, because his unquestioned historicism convinces him that classical rationalism is but the first step on the way to the life-destroying finality that we find epitomized in the "Hegelian" end of history.

The New Pagan Moralism

Doubtless there is a powerful, if obscure, religious impulse at the heart of Lyotard's postmodernism. But we must not be seduced into interpreting his postmodern antirationalism as a simple return to disguised traditional religiosity. The error of such an interpretation becomes clear if we attend to the judgment Lyotard passes on monotheism—that is, on Judaism (for Lyotard does not have much patience with Christianity).

Lyotard delivers his clearest postmodernist verdict on monotheism by way of "Figure Foreclosed," a critical commentary on Freud's *Moses and Monotheism* (Lyotard 1989a, 69–110). Freud diagnoses Judaism as an extraordinarily powerful obsessional neurosis. Lyotard insists that Freud has not gone far enough: he advances "the hypothesis that the characteristic features of Judaic religion, and of the West to the extent that it is a product of that religion, are not to be sought in obsessional neurosis but in psychosis" (1989a, 102). Drawing, perversely, on his teacher Emmanuel Lévinas's *Four Talmudic Readings*, Lyotard discerns what he regards as the following unmistakable signs of "Jewish psychosis." First, "detachment from reality" as evidenced in the "foreclosure, and the renunciation of compromise, myth and figure, the exclusion of female or filial mediation, a face-to-face encounter with a faceless other." Second, "predominance of the text": "psychoanalysis teaches us that the predominance of the ear bears witness to the fact that the ego has come under the sway of the id, and has taken the side of

7. Longinus *On the Sublime* 8.1. It is worth adding that Longinus selects the following as an example of the truly sublime in the Bible: "And God said, 'Let there be light.' And there was light" (ibid. 9.9). The importance of Xenophon as a standard for classical "aesthetics" is confirmed by the rank assigned him by the greatest classical philosopher of aesthetics in the modern age, Shaftesbury (1964, 1:167, 2:309). While contrasting him with the more "sublime" Plato, Shaftesbury nonetheless characterizes Xenophon as "the most elevating and exalting of all uninspired and merely human authors."

the inside against the outside. The advance in intellectuality is not an advance in truth." Third, "overestimation of the father." Fourth, "disavowal": "self-depreciation is a recognizable trait. Freud identifies it and analyzes it in depth in his study of melancholia, and he establishes the connection between this symptom, narcissism, and psychosis" (1989a, 95–99).

But Freud, according to Lyotard, managed to repress the degree to which his own being, as scientist or psychoanalyst, was implicated in the diagnosis of Judaism: Freudian science, like so much of Western science, "is a product of that peculiarly Jewish predominance of the father" (1989a, 106). Lyotard can therefore summarize the postmodernist program in these unsavory words: "We are appealing against a (counter)revolution that is Jewish in origin, and that has become a civilization of unmediated discourse and power. And we are calling for an unknown revolution" (1989a, 85).[8]

Lyotard rejects monotheism in the name of *paganism*, a word that figures prominently in the title of more than one of his books. What does he mean by *paganism*? Certainly not Platonic philosophy, which Lyotard stresses was antipaganism par excellence. Lyotard's "paganism," he explains, can be adequately understood only when we recognize it as the mirror image of the Platonic critique of the pagan gods in book 2 of *The Republic*. Lyotard certainly regards Platonism as the canonical litmus test of piety—and hence of impiety. "By pagan, I mean impious, at the least. . . . This is exactly what horrified Plato in paganism, which is for him the worst sort of impiety"(Lyotard 1977a, 10, 50). The Platonic text to which Lyotard refers is the first explicit text of "theology" that has come down to us. In that text, Plato's Socrates insists that a god worthy of worship must be a being who causes only good and not evil, who does not change shape, and who does not lie. Accordingly, Lyotard proclaims, "the gods would be the causes of evil as well as good, they metamorphose (and therefore lie)." He proceeds to substitute, playfully, a new canonicity for the Platonic canonicity: "The canonical phrase for these types of disourse is: I tell you, they [the gods] are as weak as you and me" (Lyotard 1983, 41).

This does not mean, however, that Lyotard appeals to the practices or beliefs of classical republicanism against the thought of the classical philoso-

---

8. Lyotard 1983, 159ff., takes his critique of Judaism, and Lévinas, somewhat further by raising—and answering only in ambiguous and contradictory remarks—such questions as: "The order received by Abraham to sacrifice his son: is it more intelligible than a memorandum administering the round-up, the convoy, the concentration, the slow death and the quick death? . . . How does one know that Abraham is not a paranoid subject to homicidal (infanticidal) urges?" For even less wholesome analogies between Judaism and Nazism, which I prefer not to repeat, see the context.

phers. For Lyotard's paganism is an extreme form of feminism. He excoriates the "sexism" of the classical republic, with its citizen armies and devotion to rationalism as expressed in deliberative assemblies, in which he sees the germ of Socratic, "phallocratic" rationalism:

The philosopher is as such a secret accomplice of the phallocrat. For philosophy is not just one discipline among others. It is the quest for a constituent order that gives sense to the world, to society, to discourse; it is the mental illness of the West. . . . the language of philosophy, this metalanguage, is *from the beginning* the language of masculinity in the Western sense, and, in particular, in the Greek sense.

Where, in fact, did it get constituted? In those communities of free men, speaking the Greek language, carrying arms, honoring the same gods, and submitting to equality under law, which formed in the breast of the feudal Greek society the kernel of the *politeia*. . . . And this remains true for the revolutionary assemblies in the modern world: the American, French, and Bolshevik revolutions. . . . One can establish historically the congruence between the constitution of this institution that is politics, a masculine order, and the institution of the discourse constituting philosophy.

Lyotard's postmodernist paganism is antirational and antiphilosophic feminism; women do not philosophize, at least not like men, since reasoning does not suit them, according to Lyotard. Lyotard means this as a compliment. Woman as "the little girl" will lead us all out of the trap of deliberative rationality, which has issued in the mental illnesses of Socratic philosophy, psychotic Jewish monotheism, and the American, French, and Bolshevik revolutions. "It is *ceasing to philosophize* that is required"; "the antonym of the adult male questioner is the *little girl*"; "women are discovering something that could bring about the greatest revolution in the West"—"another sexual space, a topology of erotic powers, comparable to that which Freud designated in the infant under the name (rather hypocritical) of *polymorphous perversity*" (Lyotard 1977b, 213–14, 224, 227–30).

Lyotard attempts to adumbrate further his "paganism" through intimations such as these:

Pagans always call their gods "the strongest"; because they know they have the advantage when it comes to deceit: the gods are in fact not less, but more, slippery [*passible*] than men: not any more just, but more inhuman. They enjoy the advantage of a limitless proteanism, to which they owe, perhaps, their immortality. Still and all, they have to be seduced, and one can get the upper hand, for a moment . . .

A pagan god is, for example, an effective narrator. You hear a story recounted to you, it makes you laugh, cry, reflect, it makes you do something, undertake some action, suspend a decision, or yourself tell a story.   (Lyotard 1977a, 45–46)

To comprehend what Lyotard means by *paganism,* one must bring into view the intimate link between this new religiosity and Lyotard's extreme moralism. Lyotard remarks on more than one occasion that the injunctions "Let us be pagan" and "Let us be just" belong together. Justice is the supreme, and the sole pure, virtue for Lyotard. But this means that he has a peculiar notion of justice in its fullness. According to Lyotard, if justice is to have its full force, it must manifest itself as a compelling prescription, whose force is not blunted by, or subordinated to, any attempt to deduce the imperative from some naturalistic need or ontological proposition: this was the classic mistake of Plato, continued by Marx.

> Ordinarily, when the problem of justice is raised, it is from a problematic of the Platonic type. It will be said that the distribution of all that circulates in a given society is just if it conforms to something defined in Plato as justice itself. . . . In such a case, then, the question of justice refers back to an initial discourse that is descriptive, or denotative, or theoretical. . . . The same is true of Marxism to the extent that it acknowledges the indispensable role of theory. . . . this type of operation . . . is also that of liberalism (the latter has a general idea of what is just because it has also a certain representation of man, of humanism in general, and of individualism).
>
> (Lyotard and Thébaud 1985, 19–21)

Lévinas's Judaism avoids this mistake and correctly grasps this essential aspect of justice:

> This is what, for me, makes the thought of a Lévinas so important: it shows that the relation with the other, what he calls "the Other" of "the absolute Other," is such that the request that is made of me by the other, by the simple fact that he speaks to me, is a request that can never be justified. The model here is the relation of God to the Jewish people, with God's initial statement to Moses: "Let them obey me!"
>
> (Lyotard and Thébaud 1985, 22; cf. 52–53)

Lyotard, we may say, seeks a conception of compelling moral authority that wells up in such a way as to be free of the taint of any permanent hierarchical relations whatsoever—among human beings, or even between human beings and the divine source, which is then the only source left for such authority. This fantastic notion is the essence of what Lyotard means by *paganism*. It is a name for the situation in which one passes severe judgment "in matters of justice, that is, of politics and ethics, and all without criteria. That's what I mean by paganism" (Lyotard and Thébaud 1985, 16).

Postmodernism as epitomized by Lyotard may be said to be a confirmation of Nietzsche's prediction about the arising world:

> On the basis of many conversations, questioning, listening carefully, this is what I have found at the bottom of the decline of European theism: it seems to me, that the religious instinct is indeed in the process of growing powerfully—but precisely the theistic satisfaction it refuses with deep distrust.
>
> (*Beyond Good and Evil*, No. 53)

To understand the roots of postmodernism, we must indeed turn back to Nietzsche, as mediated and completed/contradicted by Martin Heidegger in his searching and sympathetic critique. In the words of Gianni Vattimo, Lyotard's Italian counterpart:

Only by putting ourselves in relation to the Nietzschean problematic of the eternal return and the Heideggerian problematic of the surmounting of metaphysics do the scattered and not always coherent theorizings of the postmodern acquire philosophic rigor and dignity; and only when they are related to the postmodern reflections on the new conditions of existence in the late-industrial world do the philosophical intuitions of Nietzsche and Heidegger define themselves in a definite manner as irreducible to the simple *Kulturkritik* that characterized all of philosophy and culture in the early twentieth century. To take the Heideggerian critique of humanism or the Nietzschean announcement of complete nihilism as "positive" moments for a philosophic reconstruction, and not merely as symptoms and denunciations of decadence, . . . is possible only if one has the courage—not only the imprudence, we hope—to listen attentively to the discourses, about art, about literary criticism, about sociology, on postmodernity and its peculiar traits.   (Vattimo 1987, 9)

2 / The Heideggerian Roots of Postmodernism

According to Nietzsche and Heidegger, the late nineteenth century ushered in a historical period that for the first time permits us a clear view of the fully evolved meaning of the commitment to science and rationalism that came increasingly to dominate Western civilization in the preceding centuries. Western civilization must now be recognized as the culmination of a tradition whose history reveals the unfolding "nihilistic" consequences of the attempt to ground life in reason. What does this mean? In what sense is "nihilism" the essential outcome of rationalism?

One may begin to summarize (while never forgetting that every summary is a crude simplification) by saying that Nietzsche and Heidegger observe that our rationalist, scientific culture in its maturity conceives of itself, and of all human existence, through certain fundamental categories, modes of analysis, and criteria of evaluation. What exists is to be comprehended in terms of what is *permanent*, underlying and governing all change; *universal* (or cosmopolitan), supervening over cultural differences and "ethnic stereotypes"; *objective*, transcending subjective "prejudices"; *utilitarian*, but without any clear ultimate purposes beyond the negative overcoming of various forms of suffering; conducing to *peace*, through *harmony*, achieved by resolving all discord by descending to a plane of indubitable agreement; *necessitated* and therefore *predictable* (in principle)—rather than mysteriously occurring and consequently a source of looming uncertainty and hope; objectively *conscious*, or capable of becoming an *object* of scientific consciousness; and *monotheistic*, in the sense that the only legitimate religious awareness is of a single, transcendent or transhistorical godhead whose dispensations are not in fundamental conflict with rationalism.

Truth, both truth in general and the truth about or nature of any existing thing, is held to be what is intelligible in these and other kindred categories. Whatever does not initially appear to fit these categories is to be analyzed into elements and principles that do fit such categories. All other apparent facets of existence are treated as mythic or illusory—as relics of tradition or as products of naiveté, pretense, mere imagination, and ignorance.

But the experience of history, informed by a genuine and profound meditation on the deepest experiences of our souls, teaches us that what is most precious and gripping in human existence cannot be adequately grasped or comprehended through such categories. The attempt to identify the truth, or what exists, with what can be made comprehensible in the terms indicated leads to a mutilation of truth and of human existence. The genuinely venerable in human life—that around which all else in human existence orbits—consists of virtues, gods, things of beauty, communal obligations, and model individuals and ways of life that are the radically diverse manifestations of an elusive, because utterly temporal or historical, Being. This Being is the manifold, fluid infinity of creativity, disclosing itself through the unfolding, strife-ridden drama of a wholly unpredictable history. It is Being in its mutable manifestations that allows merely existing entities to take on meaning and hence emerge from a blurred chaos or cacophony into definition and relation. Being is not eternal: it depends on history and hence humanity, and as humanity becomes extinct, Being will subside.

To say that Being discloses itself only in time or history is to say that that which gives architectonic meaning, and thus order, by evoking reverence and love always comes to sight and exists within the bounds of a cultural "horizon." It is to say that the deeply or irresistibly moving can be adequately grasped only by experiences rooted in one or another contingent, unique sacred tradition. A people's or an individual's aspirations find expression in works of art, heroes, and sacred objects of worship that are never "common," in the sense of being fully expressible or communicable from one cultural horizon or historical epoch to another. Yet at the same time, precisely because the diverse horizons are essentially in conflict, they are continually changing and being changed by one another. Indeed, the most compelling sources of obligation, and objects of aspiration, come to be most vividly defined in the course of spiritual struggles and wars among competing, alien peoples and cultures and ages—which are doomed to misunderstand one another. In the actual course of struggle, each of the warring nations or peoples becomes more self-conscious in its claim to distinction. Each seeks to exert a stronger claim to allegiance and devotion on the part of individuals, even while gaining a fuller intimation of the contestability and diversity of the values that emanate from the mysterious fountainhead of Being or Time or History. Every profound attempt at understanding anything human is always perspectival, because committed or engaged, and hence imbedded in a particular culture locked in struggle with other competing cultures with opposed interpretive perspectives. To be seized by Being is to be compelled to judge: it is to be compelled to take a passionate moral stand, that is neither whimsical nor predetermined nor fully explicable, and from that stand to issue judgments upon all of existence—judgments that in some sense define all of existence.

Truly to possess or be possessed by what Nietzsche calls "values" (*Werte*), as opposed to mere preferences, is an experience that partakes more of rupture, loving discovery, and unexpected inspiration than of deliberation, reductive analysis, and "common sense." Such "decision" (*Entscheidung*) in response to the historical "event" (*Ereignis*), as Heidegger calls it, can never escape severe challenge and hence controversy. To define oneself, and one's people or culture, is to rank oneself and one's people or culture over (or under) *and against* others. At the heart of a serious or dedicated existence are not peace, harmony, and leveling, but instead conflict among antagonistic claimants to supreme allegiance and to the prerogatives and responsibilities of rule. In the words of Heidegger in his great work *Nietzsche*:

A fundamental experience derived from the history of the establishment of values is the knowledge that the establishment of even the highest values does not take place at a stroke: that the eternal Truth never shines forth in the heavens overnight, and that no people in history has its truth fall in its lap. Those who establish the highest values, the creators, the new philosophers, must according to Nietzsche be experimenters; they must make their way and break a trail in the knowledge that they do not have *the* Truth. From such knowledge it in no way follows that they may view their concepts as betting chips in some game, where they can just exchange their concepts for some others; what follows is precisely the opposite: the severe rigor and the binding character of thinking must experience in the things themselves a grounding such as philosophy hitherto has not known. For only thus is there created the possibility of a grounded position erecting itself against the others and the strife becoming an actual strife and thus the actual source of truth.

The grounding of goals is a "grounding" in the sense of an awakening and liberation of those powers that lend to the established goal its thoroughly commanding and mastering strength of binding obligation. Only thus can historical existence take on a primordial flourishing in the region opened up and marked out by the goal. . . . it is essential to the creative establishment of goals and its preparation that it comes into action and existence, as a historical phenomenon, only in the unity of the fully historical existence of human beings in the form of particular peoples. This does not mean isolation from other peoples any more than domination over others. The establishment of goals is in itself confrontation, the opening up of battle. *But true battle is that in which those who battle mutually surpass themselves and the fight for this surpassing unfolds within* [emphasis in original]. This kind of meditation on the historical event of nihilism and the conditions of its overcoming from the ground up—the meditation on the necessary metaphysical grounding, the thinking through of the way and the means for awakening and making ready these conditions—Nietzsche sometimes terms "the great politics."

(Heidegger 1961, 1:37, 184–85)

The attempt or claim by reason, once it assumes sovereign authority, to look upon life with transhistorical detachment, neutrality, and objectivity results inevitably in either dishonesty or easygoing shallowness. Reason, in seeking or demanding fixed and universal standards, necessarily corrodes the diverse faiths and decisions supporting the endlessly competing standards of justice and moral judgment. The contemporary rationalist movement toward equalization of values, or equalization of the objects of value; the stress on tolerance; the easygoing "agreement to disagree"; and the liberal "open society" are all symptomatic, according to Heidegger, of the dissolution of standards and the loss of dedication in life. Rational self-consciousness is, no doubt, an essential *tool* for the clarification and articulation of a people's highest "values"; but hypertrophic reason, at least in the Western experience, endangers and banalizes "values" by its relentless tendency to reduce to a lower, "common" level what is *distinguished*, and hence truly evocative of sacrificial love and devotion. What Nietzsche calls "values" can never be done justice by reason, for "values" in the fullest sense are always rooted in elusive historical wellsprings (called "subjective" or "subconscious" by the scientific mind) that are spiritually richer, psychologically more powerful, and morally more compelling, than narrowly rationalistic consciousness and its apparently timeless and universal modes of comprehension and evaluation. Nietzsche's formula for the nihilistic outcome of the history of rationalism is "God is dead!" By this he means primarily the self-destruction of the monotheistic Christian God through the full development of the spiritual forces that monotheism, after allying itself with Platonism, unleashed. But more generally he means the loss of the possibility of apprehending, let alone believing in, all the essentially diverse and contested high ideals or objects of devotion and dedication mankind has known.

To the extent that human beings try, through rationalism, to overcome their contingent particularity and strife-torn moral diversity, to the extent that they try to orient their lives by hopes for peace and certainty or agreement rooted in permanence and universality, they are seeking to flee the fundamental experience that is *the* clue to reality or Being. The entire Western tradition can be seen as dominated or haunted by such a search for an escape from life or existence or Being. At the same time, this vast and distorting effort has been itself an expression of life or existence or Being. This paradox is in fact another crucial clue to the radically paradoxical character of the ultimate source of things. What has truly lent power to the West's historical creative attempts to escape from history and from creativity has been the underlying experience of life, from which life, rebounding in horror, sought escape. The lacerating awareness of history, exposed mortality, and strife-torn diversity is what powered the semiconscious drive to the reshaping, and hence covering over, of existence.

But this means that hidden within the contemporary nihilism is a source of liberation from the nihilism. Science, and its ever more pervasive technological imperative to control, regiment, and predict, threatens to pave over and obscure, perhaps forever, the creative awareness that has hitherto underlain all human existence; but science is itself a creative expression of existence or Being and, in addition, on account of its peculiar historical evolution within the Western tradition, science as we now know it is intimately linked with historical awareness as well as intellectual probity (i.e., rigorous, and ruthlessly honest, self-examination). Science contains within itself some of the seeds of its own overcoming.

Science can begin to reflect on its technological preoccupation with the "how," and its obscure incapacity to express the truly important—the "what" and above all the "why" (see the opening pages of Heidegger's *Introduction to Metaphysics*); science can begin to wonder at the infinite perfectibility or progressiveness of science, with the implications for the infinite mysteriousness of the "nature" science studies; science can become penetrated by an uneasy consciousness of the degree to which its "knowledge" is contingent upon the scientist—that is, on the human-merely-human, and hence necessarily historically bound, perspective; science can become seized by an awe or dread at the power for evil and good that its technology amasses. What is more, the very emptiness of technological culture, the very nakedness or "destructive" character of the modern art that exhausts itself in negative rebellion against scientistic culture, clears a space that can bring home to many the vacancy, the absence of meaning, in contemporary existence. The cataclysmic threat posed by scientific or rationalist culture in its maturity is then accompanied by, and indeed helps provoke, precisely because of its cataclysmic scope, an unprecedented awakeness to that basic human condition and experience whose obscurity is so massively threatened.

Today, there opens for the first time the prospect of self-conscious—that is, no longer escapist—acceptance and tempering of the human drive to reshape or recreate meaningful existence. For the first time, this drive may find expression with a newly acquired sense of limitations or paradox. There opens the prospect of self-conscious creativity, or the self-aware reshaping of an irretrievably historical existence. Our historical epoch or situation calls us, in a way no previous epoch called men, to embrace the human fate with resoluteness: if Nietzsche is right, to create new values, or, if Heidegger is right, to await the welling up of new gods, in a spirit of gratitude and reverence for the past against which we rebel, and with a grave sense of responsibility—as well as hope—for the future of our collective and individual creations or "projects" or "offspring."

Our initial response to this call must be a resolute opposition to the unchecked or unquestioned rationalism that optimistically promises "progress" toward a life made "happy," or freed of suffering, by the power of utilitarian technology. The tempting, and therefore blinding, mirage of painless, peaceful, prosperous creature-comfort as the true goal of all mankind's strivings is the natural outcome of rationalism's success in bringing to the fore what is common to all humanity, what is the same or similar in all historical cultures—what seems, to the rational or scientific perspective, to underlie the merely "apparent" or "superficial" diversity of historical experience. What are most obviously and massively common are, in the first place, the body and its needs, and the psyche understood as reducible to, or a mere servant or extension of, the pleasures and anxieties rooted in the body. Rationalist society therefore naturally tends to stress material welfare, while ignoring the spirit or soul. Almost equally obvious and universal, or sought after by all men in all cultures, is the gratification of vanity, the petty dependence on the approval and admiration of one's fellows and neighbors. Once given legitimacy in a rationalist and egalitarian mass democracy, this dependence grows like a cancer, issuing in the ever-more-absolute sway of conformist "public opinion" and "public relations" over the spiritually dwarfed and morally cowed and atomized individual. On the political level, democratic universalism and communalism tends relentlessly toward the bureaucratization of civic existence under the soft, numbing tyranny of what Max Weber calls "procedural rationality." The attempts, epitomized for Heidegger by Ernst Cassirer, to revive or keep alive neo-Kantian universalistic ethics and aesthetics represent a naive and self-deluding moral veneer for the overwhelming historical movement toward narrow individualism, passivity, and spiritual barrenness.

Heidegger insists that the time for attempts at resuscitation of Kantian or post-Kantian rational universalism is past. What is needed instead is a philosophically sophisticated rebellion against rationalism, a general subversion of the hegemony of rationalist self-consciousness and metaphysics in the name of a still-vague postrationalist future. This requires in the first place a painstaking, critical study of the history of Western thought, "deconstruction" of the authority of the texts and authors of the rationalist tradition, and uprooting of their claims, or attempts, to provide rational foundations for life. By examining these bewitchingly constructed foundations and foundational texts, by probing to the bottom these purported grounds, we can become first conscious of, and then liberated from, the charm of philosophic and metaphysical claims to foundational knowledge of such supposed entities as "the objective mind," "nature and nature's God," "natural right or law," "the categorical imperative," "the health of the soul," "the end or purpose or fulfillment of human nature," "Divine Law," "the historical dialectic," and so forth. By tracing out the way in which the great texts have been, not so much deceptively, as *self*-deceptively constructed and construed, by bringing to light their unconscious or semiconscious rootedness in particular historical situations, and in an overarching philosophic and linguistic tradition made up (unsystematically) of these historical situations, we can begin to uncover the limits of rational consciousness within the great texts that have shaped our discourse and consciousness.

At the same time, there is needed a wary nurturing of some of the fragile elements or remains, within Western culture, and even within the great rationalist philosophic texts, of the sub- and suprarational, the particularistic and rooted, the transcending (but not transcendental) historical leaps of creativity. Yet our renewed openness to the divine must never lose sight of the "nihilistic" dangers that lurk in monotheism, otherworldly religiosity, and rationalist, especially scholastic, "theology." And on the other hand, the rebellion against rationalism must avoid a relapse into "worldview formation" (*Weltanschauungs-Bildung*), "myth," and the "philosophy of feeling" (*Gefühlsphilosophie*), which "today more than ever before, from all regions of spiritual life, threaten philosophy" (Heidegger 1975, 467). The revival of piety must be a "piety of *thinking*." The renewed openness to the divine must involve a search for ways out of the horizon of the life-denying, monotheistic and rationalist, West. What this quest calls for, among other things, is a sympathetic listening to, an attentive study of, Eastern or non-Western or pre-Western ("pre-Socratic") experiences of, and philosophic reflections on, existence.

From Nazism to the Threshold of Postmodernism

The preceding summary does not adequately capture the chilling character of Heidegger's thought. It is necessary to add that his embrace of Nazism has left a grisly shadow over everything that he ever said or wrote. Heidegger himself sometimes "explained" what he rather ambiguously called his "error" of "commitment" as a result of misunderstanding, political naiveté, deception and self-deception. But, while he seems not to have endorsed the extremes of Nazi anti-Semitism, and while he delivered some public criticisms of so-called "Nazi philosophy" (the first course he offered after resigning as Nazi rector of the University of Freiburg in the summer term of 1934 was pointedly entitled "Logic"), he nonetheless maintained his membership in the party from 1933 until 1945, repeatedly expressing his admiration for Hitler and for the "ideals" of the "movement." Never at any time after the war did he condemn the Holocaust or repudiate his fellow Nazis. He stubbornly refused to pass ethical judgment on this or any other movement or action: as he put it in the course of a 1968 interview, "Who today can permit himself, and in the name of what authority, to impose an ethic on the world?"[1] This statement implies more than that Heidegger found it inauthentic, and hence impossible, to discover a foundation for moral judgment beneath or above or outside of whatever occurs as the decisive "event" in history. For Heidegger made it clear that his attraction to the Nazis—more specifically to their opposition to rationalism, or to universal moral standards, and their appeals to "resoluteness," "decision," "permanent revolution," "roots," "community" or "wholeness," "values," and passionate environmentalism linked to "purity"—was intimately tied to his conviction that the most urgent immediate task of contemporary life was, and is, the critical confrontation with the deracinating, atomizing effects of scientific technology and capitalism. In his *Introduction to Metaphysics*, the 1953 published version of lectures he delivered as a somewhat suspect Nazi professor under Nazi surveillance in 1935, he said: "What is today however being put about as the philosophy of National Socialism, but has not the slightest thing to do with the inner truth and greatness of this movement (namely,

---

1. *L'Express*, December 2–8, 1968, 55–56.

with the encounter between planetary technology and modern man), fishes in these murky waters of 'values' and 'totalities'" (Heidegger 1953, 152).

In a famous and amazingly frank interview with the German magazine *Der Spiegel*, an interview that Heidegger carefully vetted, and that he insisted be published only posthumously (it appeared on May 31, 1976, a few days after his death), Heidegger explained these words from the *Introduction to Metaphysics* as follows:

> Since then, in the past thirty years, it has become clearer that the planetary movement of modern technology is a power whose history-determining greatness can hardly be overestimated. It is for me today a decisive question, how in general a political system—and which one—can be adapted to the technological age. To this question I know no answer. I am not convinced that democracy is the answer.
>
> . . . I would indeed characterize the political strivings of the Western world, and thereby democracy, and the political expression of the Christian worldview, and also constitutionalism, as halfway measures, because I see in them no actual confrontation with the technological world, since behind them I always see standing, from my perspective, the assumption that technology in its essence is something that humanity has in hand. In my opinion this is not possible. Technology in its essence is something that humanity on its own cannot control.
>
> . . . Everything works. That is precisely what is uncanny: that it works and that the working drives on ever further to a broader functioning, and that the technology more and more rips and uproots humanity from the earth.
>
> . . . Insofar as I at least can get my bearings by our human experience and history, I know this: that everything essential and great can arise only on the condition that man has a home and is rooted in a tradition. But contemporary literature, for example, is far-reaching in its destructiveness.
>
> . . . Yet it seems to me that you all take technology as too absolute. I see the position of humanity in the world of global technology not as an inextricable and inescapable fate; rather I see the task of thinking precisely here, that within its limits it helps humanity in general finally to achieve an adequate relationship to the essence of technology. National Socialism certainly moved in that direction; but those people were far too limited in their thinking to achieve a really explicit relationship to what is going on today and has been going on now for three hundred years.[2]

Heidegger did claim to have learned something from his "mistaken" attempt to shape or guide or exploit Nazism. He seems to have admitted that, in focusing on the spiritually deadening and decadent outcome of nihilism in the contemporary world, he had underestimated the blindly brutal and ferocious possibilities also immanent in this nihilism. He linked up this lesson with his steadily intensifying dissatisfaction with his first great philosophic attempt (*Being and Time*); among other things, he had in that work, he felt,

2. *Der Spiegel* 30, no. 23 (May 31, 1976):193–219; quotations from 206, 209, 214.

failed to appreciate sufficiently the drive to mastery and domination implicit in Western rationalism. The evolution of the West, as Heidegger sees it, has been animated by an attempt to make what exists conform to what can be grasped, hence mastered, controlled, or willed by human beings; and even Heidegger's own first approach remained too "humanistic" in this sense.

It was through his long wrestling with Nietzsche above all that Heidegger tried to clear the path of his thinking. In the preface to the *Nietzsche* volumes published in 1961, Heidegger wrote that the publication "consists of *Lectures* that were delivered in the years 1936 to 1940 . . . to which are joined *essays*. They originate in the years 1940 to 1946. . . . Considered as a whole, the publication may allow a view of the path of thinking that I followed from 1930 until the *Letter on Humanism* (1947)."

In Nietzsche, Heidegger found the thinker who had come closest to overcoming Western rationalism or metaphysics and who, by virtue of this magnificent failure, made most explicit the hidden, fundamental thrust and gravest limitation of rationalism. As we have already seen, the agreement between Heidegger and Nietzsche is deep and broad. It is by no means easy to discern where Nietzsche ends and Heidegger begins, in Heidegger's exposition. Put another way: it is possible to wonder whether some of the criticisms Heidegger claims to bring against Nietzsche are not, in fact, self-criticisms taken from Nietzsche himself. Yet Heidegger is aware of this question or difficulty, and he insists that in the final analysis Nietzsche fails to do justice to his most pregnant philosophic inspiration. I must limit myself here to brief suggestion of a few illuminating aspects of Heidegger's criticisms that are most pertinent to revealing the path toward, and hence the nature of, postmodernism.

Heidegger was arrested by an early Nietzschean formulation to the effect that Nietzsche's own thought can be understood as "inverted Platonism" (Heidegger 1961, 1:180). But inverted Platonism remains a kind of Platonism—a "rotated" Platonism. (Heidegger stresses that neither he nor Nietzsche means by "Platonism" the thought of Plato himself, as it is available in a dialogue like the *Phaedrus*: "Plato is too great for Platonism.") Insofar as Nietzsche fails to "twist free" of his struggle against Platonism, he remains defined dialectically by that against which he struggles. "Platonism" denigrates the merely "apparent" world of the body or the sensuous in the name of the "true" world of the supersensuous, apprehended by the intellect; Platonism erects eternal ideas or ideals over the changing, historical world of human willing and making; Platonism looks to nature as the standard to which an imitative art must conform. Now insofar as Nietzsche's thought remains inverted Platonism, it does not sufficiently escape the still-Platonic gravitational pull of the tendency to conceive of itself as an elevation of "lie" over "truth"; "appearance" over "reality"; the sensuous, or a physiological psychology, over the supersensuous; will and creation over eternal idea; art over nature. Heidegger does not mean that Nietzsche simply stands Platonism on its head, or inverts it in a simple way; Nietzsche struggles to "twist free," and in some measure therefore liberates himself from Platonism. But not entirely; the struggle continues; the trap cannot be evaded and the escape is not yet complete.

Commenting on a remark of Nietzsche's that "there are fateful words that appear to express knowledge, and, in truth, *hinder* knowledge; among them belongs the word 'appearance' [*Schein*]," Heidegger says: "Nietzsche does not become master of the fate that lies in this word, i.e., in the matter" (Heidegger 1961, 1:247–48). The clear sign, for Heidegger, is Nietzsche's substitution of *appearance* for *reality*, or his dismissal of the very notion of "Being" and his insistence that "only Becoming is." The world as it appears to us is the only world, and it is a world of mutable Becoming, not fixed Being. But then Becoming, and only becoming, is. So Becoming is somehow Being. Aware of this, Nietzsche is impelled to give an account of this fluid Becoming in terms of his doctrines of the Will to Power and the Eternal Return of the Same. But is this not an arrant relapse into metaphysics and even cosmology? In order to escape such a relapse, Nietzsche presents these doctrines in an unprecedented way: they are at once *the* truth and Nietzsche's creation, his "tempting attempt," the product of his personal "perspectivity"—which he self-consciously "interprets" as "will to power"—in the service of his "values" (which he has also "created").

But is this an escape from metaphysics, or, rather, the starkest confession as to what all metaphysics, even the subtlest, has always been—the insistence on the part of a thinker that the world must conform to his willed conception? Besides, do not the two aspects of this perspectivalism undermine each other? Insofar as the Eternal Return of the Same is Being, is it not the most stultifying cosmic expression of the machine monotony of technology that is the "essence" of things as revealed by rationalism? On the other hand, insofar as perspectival "creativity" is at the bottom of all understanding, insofar as created values are the foundation of all thought and action, does not the arbitrariness and willfulness essential to the creative act undermine any belief in the validity, the binding and obligatory truth, of that which is created? For Nietzsche, Heidegger says, "Reality, Being [*Sein*], is Appearance [*Schein*], in the sense of perspectival letting-come-to-sight." To exist is to appear, to be somehow intelligible, and hence to appear within some frame-work; but to exist is at the same time to be "creative" or tò transform precisely the framework of existence. For humans, this means, above all, first to obey and then to rebel against and transform, or "transvalue," some moral principle or "value." Heidegger therefore summarizes Nietzsche's basic metaphysical thought as follows:

> If the real (the living) is to *be* real, it must on the one side establish itself in a defined horizon, thus remaining in the appearance of truth. But if, however, this reality is to *remain* real, it must, on the other side, at the same time transfigure itself beyond itself, in the coming to sight of what is created in art, i.e., it must go against the truth. While truth and art both similarly belong from the very beginning to the essence of reality, they must confront and oppose one another.
>
> (Heidegger 1961, 1:250)

"But now," Heidegger adds, "because for Nietzsche appearance as perspecti-val also has the character of the unreal, of illusion, of deception," Nietzsche must "decisively" affirm what he does in *Will to Power*, no. 853:

> There is only *one* world, and it is false, cruel, contradictory, seductive, without meaning—A world thus constituted is the real world. *We have need of lies*, in order to win a victory over this Reality, this "Truth"—i.e., in order to *live*. —That lies are necessary in order to live is itself part of the terrifying and questionable character of existence.

Heidegger continues:

> Art and truth are both necessary for reality; as the equally-necessary they stand in discord. This relationship first becomes horrifying, however, when we recognize in thought that creativity, i.e., the metaphysical activity as art, acquires yet another necessity in that moment when the situation of the greatest event [*die Tatsache des grössten Ereignisses*] is known—the death of the moral God. At this time, now, for Nietzsche, existence [*Dasein*] can be endured/overcome only by creativity. The conducting of reality up to the power of its law, and its highest possibilities, is what alone guarantees Being [*Sein*]. But creativity is, as art, the will to appearance; it stands in discord with truth.
>
> (Heidegger 1961, 1:251)

As Heidegger said in his *Introduction to Metaphysics*, on the same page (152) as the passage praising the Nazis previously quoted:

> The subtitle of his planned masterpiece, *The Will to Power*, reads: "Attempt at a Revaluation of all Values." The third book is entitled: "Attempt at a New Establish-ment of Values." The entanglement in the thicket of conceptions of values, his failure to understand the questionable origin of these conceptions, is *the* reason why Nietzsche did not attain to the true center of philosophy.

After all, Nietzsche did not, in fact, succeed in "creating new values"; he left that task to his "supermen"; but his "supermen" remain a fiction.

Nietzsche's thought is the fullest or most self-conscious manifestation of the truth that so long as man conceives of existence as attaining order and meaning through conformity to man and his "humanistic values," man will languish in the trammels of nihilism. Somehow man must come to terms with the fact that the meaning or meanings that Being "sends" in and through history, while they (and therefore Being itself) cannot exist without man and man's effort, are yet rooted in some source larger than man and his grasp: a source that is obscured by monotheism.

This last thought attains a bit more concreteness in Heidegger's critique of Nietzsche's philosophy of art. Heidegger praises Nietzsche for having grasped the experience of art, in the fullest sense (the poetic source of meaning-giving visions for whole peoples and epochs), as a/the decisive clue to Being. Heidegger applauds Nietzsche's attack on the democratic notion of the audience, or the "reception," as the key to artistic experience. But Heidegger disagrees with Nietzsche's insistence that art, in its highest form, must be seen above all from the perspective of the *artist* (as "creator"). The deeper and truer perspective is attained by way of the *work of art* itself, which, as Event, has a life or existence that always grows, in history, decisively beyond the limits of its creator and, a fortiori, its audience.

The critique of Nietzsche, the reaction to the Nazi experience, and the autocritique of his own great early effort seem to have led Heidegger toward a more humble, quietistic, even mystic position. The most popular, but not for that reason necessarily crude, formulation of Heidegger's late position is found in the *Der Spiegel* interview previously cited:

To put it briefly, perhaps a bit ponderously, but after long thought: philosophy will not be able to effect any direct transformation of the present state of the world. This is true not only of philosophy but of any simply human reflection and striving. Only another god can save us [*Nur noch ein Gott kann uns retten*]. The only possibility that remains for us is, in thinking and in poetry, to prepare a readiness for the shining forth of the god or for the absence of the god in the debacle [*im Untergang*]: so that we go down looking toward this absent God.

. . . We can't *think* him into presence here, we may at most awaken the readiness for the expectation.

. . . The readying of readiness must be the "first aid." The world cannot be through man, but it also cannot be without man, as what and how it is. This stands together with my view that that which I name with a very traditional, ambiguous, and now worn-out word "Being" [*das Sein*], needs humanity for its revelation, truth, and taking-on of form. The essence of technology I see as lying in what I name the "framework" [*Gestell*]—an often ridiculed and perhaps clumsy expression. The sway of the framework means: humanity is framed in place, assigned tasks, and commanded by a power that is revealed in the essence of technology and that man himself does not control. To bring us to this insight: thought seeks no more than this. Philosophy is at an end.

... Through another kind of thinking, a mediated effectiveness is possible, but nothing direct, in the sense that thinking will transform the world condition in a causal way.   (p. 209)

Despite or because of the fact that in the same interview Heidegger insisted, as we have seen, that "it is for me today a decisive question, how in general a political system—and which one—can be adapted to the technological age," in his later work he retreated from any direct or overt attempt to influence or inspire political action. In the 1960s, he spoke with favor about the negating or ground-clearing activity of the New Left and its rebellion (spearheaded intellectually by his old student Herbert Marcuse) against scientism, liberalism, and the bourgeoisie. But for the most part he stressed the need for meditative waiting and personal spiritual preparation for renewed cultural possibilities, whose advent lay in an as-yet-unseen religious future. He turned his attention to the nurturing of a more thoughtful and philosophically informed poetry and art, to a dialogic encounter with Eastern religion, to quasi-mystical possibilities within Western religion and thought, to the analysis of the dangers and possibilities of technology, and, above all, to an ever-more-searching critique of the history of Western philosophy. Heidegger never ceased indicating his loathing for every kind of mere conservatism, his anguish at the contemporary "world-night," his fear of an increasingly mechanized, comfortable future, and his radical hopes and longings for a shattering new age of either transfiguration or debacle (*Untergang*).

3 / "Weak Thinking"

The postmodernist movement attempts to appropriate many of Heidegger's basic conceptions of thought, language, and existence while transforming these conceptions so as to substitute for Heidegger's anguish and longing a stance that would bespeak a greater gentleness; an ironically self-conscious superficiality; the promotion of humane, but destabilizing, anarchic impulses; and an endless movement to, and then through, discrete "micrologies" or "language games" that include "narrations" of experiences as "events." What is aimed at is what Lyotard has christened "*la sveltesse*" (Lyotard 1984): the exhilaration of a discordant diversity or "difference" metamorphic enough to prevent the rootedness that engenders serious conflict but simultaneously strong and purposeful enough to "contaminate" and subvert the hegemony of rationalist, technologically regimented existence.

The key disagreement among the postmodernists appears in their conflicting estimations of how far a just, or nonexploitative, authentic version of a postmodernist culture stands from liberal bourgeois society as we now know it. In Lyotard, there is still a piercing sense of the ugliness of contemporary "capitalist" existence. Yet Lyotard's moral indignation blinds him to political philosophy. His tirades against the hegemonic character of rationalism in general, and of Socratism in particular, as presented in Plato's dialogues, provide him with the perfect excuse for indulging apparently redemptive moral or even religious feelings without having to expose those feelings, and the opinions they generate and are generated out of, to the sustained acid test of Socratic questioning. Lyotard thus avoids the initially painful process of Socratic self-purgation and cuts himself off from the serene, consuming pleasure of Socratic self-knowledge and self-liberation.

In *Just Gaming*, Lyotard does find himself, or allow himself to be, exposed to some revealing dialectical challenges that reward close scrutiny. This is the case despite the fact that in the midst of the dialogue, Lyotard defines "dialectics" as a kind of reasoning that "has nothing to do with Plato's reason" (Lyotard and Thébaud 1985, 27). For Lyotard cannot, in fact, altogether fend off the X-ray power of dialectics. When his persistent interlocutor (Jean-Loup Thébaud) tries to sum up and then concretize Lyotard's teaching on "paganism," the following remarkable exchanges ensue:

Thébaud: In other words, you dissociate the true from the just so that the just not be subject to the critique that you have leveled at the true. This is the first operation in order to maintain, or to recast, justice.
Lyotard: Right. . . .
Thébaud: What do we do with a thesis like "it is unjust; I rebel"? How is one to say this if one does not know what is just and what is unjust? If the determination of the just is the object of a perpetual sophistic debate? . . .
Lyotard: . . . We are dealing with two systems of prescriptions that encroach upon each other and that are incompatible. That leads to war.
Thébaud: You are saying, two systems of prescriptions. There is [German Chancellor Helmut] Schmidt's set of prescriptions and then there is the Red Army Faction's system of prescriptions?
Lyotard: That is right.
Thébaud: And you are saying that, at this point, one is just and the other unjust?
Lyotard: No. I am saying that they are incompatible. I am not judging.
Thébaud: . . . But if you do not have any criteria to say that a given thing is just or unjust?
Lyotard: It goes to show to what extent it is difficult to decide. For example, is it just that there be an American computer in Heidelberg that, among other things, is used to program the bombing of Hanoi? In the final analysis, someone like Schleyer thinks so. In the final analysis, the "Baader-Meinhof" group thinks not. Who is right? It is up to everyone to decide!
Thébaud: And you think it is unjust that there be an American computer in Heidelberg?
Lyotard: Yes, absolutely. . . . I feel committed in this respect. . . . If you asked me why I am on that side, I think that I would answer that I do not have an answer to the question "why?" and that this is of the order of transcendence. . . . I am indeed playing the game of the just.
Thébaud: How can you say that it is a language game like the others when it has the distinctive feature of including a transcendence, a finality . . . ?
Lyotard: I do not know; you are making me talk beyond what I am capable of articulating. . . . It is not known who obligates; there is nothing to be said about it. . . . I hesitate between two positions, while still hoping that my hesitation is vain

and that these are not two positions. To put it quickly, between a pagan position, in the sense of the Sophists, and a position that is, let us say, Kantian.

(Lyotard and Thébaud 1985, 24, 69, 71, 73)

It would do Lyotard an injustice not to remark that he stands apart from all other postmodernists in the degree to which he does still feel and express some strong moral passion for justice and liberation. What is more, Lyotard still stands—and to some extent is aware that he stands—on the threshold of the possibility of Socratic self-discovery. He still seriously wrestles with the Socratic challenge, above all, of Plato's *Gorgias*. He cannot leave behind a doubt or uncertainty about the collapse of the fundamental distinction between rhetoric and dialectic. Lyotard is aware that the "Platonic discourse that inaugurates science is not scientific, precisely to the extent that it attempts to legitimate science." Without recourse to the sort of argumentation found in the dialogues, Plato's scientific knowledge "would be in the position of presupposing its own validity and stooping to what it condemns: begging the question, proceeding on prejudice." But Lyotard cannot discern how Plato can be thought to have succeeded in his most fundamental enterprise, because Lyotard is unable to see or distinguish clearly the truly dialectical aspects from what he calls the "narrative" or "poetic" aspects of the Platonic dialogues. This failure is understandable, given Plato's exquisitely artful blending of the two strands of "narrative" and "dialectic"—at the cost, admittedly, of a superficial obscuring of the latter. But Lyotard's reading of the dialogues remains a failure—a failure to follow meticulously the guidance Plato offers in the *Phaedrus* as well as the *Gorgias* to the interpretation of his written words (Lyotard 1983, 38–48; 1979, 50–51; Lyotard and Thébaud 1985, 3–6).

Above all, Lyotard has failed to see the extent to which what he correctly calls the "legitimation of science," in Plato, stands or falls with a relentless dialectical cross-examination of our opinions as to the just. Lyotard has failed to see that *political* philosophy (in the Socratic, not the Enlightenment, sense) is the first and fundamental philosophy. This failure is traceable finally to the fact that Lyotard, like his mentor Heidegger, appears to have no experience of such Socratic political philosophizing. A painstaking attention to the surface of the *Gorgias* might have helped Lyotard to begin to find his way to this Socratic heart of things.

In the writings of the sweeter-tempered Gianni Vattimo, the central figure in "*il pensiero debole*" ("weak thinking"), one sees the more recent and placid reaches of the stream flowing from Heidegger/Nietzsche to postmodernism. Postmodernism in this sense, we may observe, might well have satisfied the ironic Hegelian Alexandre Kojève.

Where Lyotard, in a deflected echo of Heidegger, evokes feminist pagan gods of a future, "impious" religiosity, Vattimo seems to know piety only in the form of what he calls the *"pietas"* of patronizing respect for the great old, and senescent, works of European culture. This *"pietas"* consists in the fact that our awareness that those works are manifestations of Being tempers the "historicist relativism" that arises from our certainty that they constitute "the history of errors" (Vattimo 1987, 183–84).

Where Lyotard still looks to the "intensification of life" through art, Vattimo accepts the "death, or better put the decline [*tramonto*], of art":

Like many other Hegelian concepts, that of the death of art has also revealed itself to be prophetic in respect to the developments effectively verified in advanced industrial society. . . . Is it not perhaps true that the universalization of the domain of information can be interpreted as a perverted realization of the triumph of the absolute spirit? . . . and yet it is not a perversion in any exclusively degenerative sense, but rather contains, as is the case often with perversions, cognitive and practical consequences that we ought to explore, and that probably delineate the shape of the future.
(Vattimo 1987, 59)

Mass culture formed by the mass media, the mechanization of reproduction, kitsch, the self-negation of high art in Samuel Beckett's work and Theodor Adorno's aesthetics, the replacement of "meaningful" art by the simply decorative and playful, all point to the truth of art in our time. That truth can and should initiate us into a new conception of art, seen not as dying but as in "decline." But the "great tradition" has been revealed by Heidegger to be rooted in falsehood, and even in destructive and self-destructive falsehood. So then "decline" is a merely relative notion, useful as a kind of orientation. In the decline we discover a new, if "weak," meaning of the aesthetic—and, through the aesthetic, of Being itself:

The situation in which we are living, of the death or, better put, the decline of art, can be read philosophically as an aspect of this more general happening which is the *Verwindung* [recuperation] from metaphysics, of this Event, which concerns Being itself. And how so? To clarify this, it is necessary to show how, though perhaps in a sense that has not hitherto been noted in the literature on Heidegger, the experience that we are having now of the decline of art is describable as the Heideggerian notion of the work of art as "the setting to work of truth."   (Vattimo 1987, 68–69)

One sees better what Vattimo is getting at if one turns back to his earlier work, *Le avventure della differenza* (Vattimo 1980, esp. introduction and chs. 3, 5, 6, and 7). There Vattimo tells the story of an original enchantment, and then progressive disenchantment, with the Nietzschean idea of the "superman" and the "dreams" of a "unity" somehow to be found or created in a future human existence. Vattimo focuses in particular on the changing meaning of a capital term in postmodernist thought: "the difference." In Heidegger, "the difference" refers to the "ontological difference"—that is, the distinction between "Being" and "beings." This difference may be characterized as the ever-changing historical interplay between entities, finding their meaning, and hence definition, within diverse, changing historical "horizons," and the Being or the To-Be-ness that is, not the "ground" in any metaphysical sense, but the elusive "Presence" or "Coming to Presence" of these changing historical horizons, and hence of all the entities in their meaningful context. Now in recent French Heideggerian thought, beginning especially with Jacques Derrida in the late 1960s, there is a tendency to view the Heideggerian conception of Being, in contrast to beings, as a sort of relapse into a nostalgia for "The Source"—for something metaphysical, if not theistic. Vattimo tries to rescue Heidegger from this charge by arguing that Heidegger's texts allow for a much "weaker" notion of Being, a notion that would not simply denigrate the "era of decline" in which we live, but that would instead justify an "ontology of decline."

If we take seriously the identification of Being with Time, then Heideggerianism can and should be freed from Heidegger's own longings for a "strong" time, a time of "strength." "Strength," will, commitment, resolute purposiveness: all these are tied, arguably, to the "force and violence" of metaphysics, and are to that extent less in tune with Being than is the historical dispensation into which we are entering. Being has indeed come to presence, in past ages, through metaphysical visions; but we now can see how imperfect and self-enshrouding or self-forgetting were these "violent" and willful or humanistic presences of / impositions on Being. We see all around us the grim rigidification of existence that is the technological "hangover" of these metaphysical impositions. This "seeing" that *we* have is Being's becoming present for us, in this time. Our time is in a sense privileged, by this "end-of-history" insight—but we lose that privilege the minute we forget that our time, too, is somehow enshrouded, in ways we cannot see. Some of the shrouds that limit our vision will be seen, insofar as they are ever seen, only in a later age, that, looking back, will see what we do not see—while losing sight of much that we do see. But we cannot live in, or even for, that later age. We cannot say what light may illuminate and what darkness will enshroud existence in the next age or in the many future ages. Here and now, for us, in this age, we must give up any pretension to see more than we can or to be more than we are. We see negatively the vicious residue of rationalism, monotheism, and metaphysics; and, positively—what do we see? Very little. Our "eyes" are weak; "nobility" or "beauty" (to kalon) as well as pietas are historical relics for us, and he who claims otherwise speaks inauthentically. But in their weakness, our eyes perhaps see what strong eyes miss. Weak eyes see the weakness of Being. For our time, to be is to "oscillate" in fluid indeterminacy, and this need not appear as "growing old," but in fact can be seen as "maturation."

But what precisely and concretely does this mean for civic life?

The "weak thinkers" refuse the invitation Heidegger extends to join him in his vague longings and waitings for cataclysmic cultural revolution, but they accept Heidegger's overthrow of pre-Heideggerian philosophy, religion, and art. Can Heidegger's critique be so easily accepted, while rejecting the momentum of that critique? The "weak thinkers" remain morally committed to a vaguely anarchistic democratism, simultaneously warning us of the exclusivistic tendencies of moral dogmatism, of the danger that standards can lead to oppressive hierarchies, of the ease with which devotion to causes, even beautiful causes, can obfuscate the elemental fellowship of human beings as human beings. Such warnings are always necessary. They are particularly apt when directed to the late Enlightenment—to the totalitarian temptations rooted in left-wing Hegelianism and in Marx, and to the scientism and neo-Darwinism that have marked and marred so much of American philosophy. These warnings remain timely, it seems to me, as applied to Jürgen Habermas's so-called "emancipatory" theory of "communicative action." With its dangerously vague philosophic abstraction, its politically naive indifference to constitutionalism and legalism, and its remarkable self-righteousness, Habermas's alternative to and attack on postmodernism constitute one of the strongest arguments I have encountered for a certain superiority of postmodernism. But the cause of rationalism does not stand or fall with this particular champion. Once Habermas and what he represents is, as I believe ought to be the case, set aside, one may seriously ask whether the warnings of the "weak thinkers" are not more properly directed against modern antirationalism than against the older forms of rationalism. Was it traditional rationalism and traditional metaphysics (I include everything from Plato to natural law, to Montesquieuian constitutionalism) that lent the crucial veneer of "depth" and respectability to the Nazis? Was it not precisely the leaders of the attack on Plato, natural law, and traditional metaphysics—thinkers of the stature of Carl Schmitt and Martin Heidegger—who inspired and enflamed the student youth and the academic establishment in their devilishness?

But the more immediate danger lies in another direction. The postmodernists—from Vattimo and Lyotard on the continent to Paul De Man and Richard Rorty in America—openly boast of the "weakness" of their thinking. Even when they still speak of a "tragic" weakness, they admit that "tragedy" is on their terms a dubious or "weakened" notion. In the words of Vattimo's collaborator Alessandro dal Lago, "from the fact that there is no promise of 'outcome,' nor promise of decision, beyond the attempt to take to its extreme consequences the possibilities implied in the weakness, the tragic aspect of weak thinking can be attenuated. The tragic, for one who is habituated to it, can thus lose its lacerating qualities" (Dal Lago 1985, 89).

In celebrating their incapacity and disinclination to seek grounds for life's most necessary moral and political choices, do the postmodernists not license escape from those choices, or from responsibility for thinking them through? In stressing the "oscillation" of all thought, do they not inadvertently cultivate a climate of moral vacillation? Is the unintended consequence not a tendency to flatter whatever now exists, and to serve whatever academic, cultural, and political powers there be? To quote one of the leading "weak thinkers," Franco Crespi, "the absence of an absolute anthropological foundation (humanism, substantive rationality, etc.) puts into crisis the critical capacity of social theory, which finds itself deprived of references to ideals that call it to oppose itself to what exists" (Crespi 1988, 244).

In their educational program, the postmodernists boldly dedicate themselves to the "subversion" of what they term the "authority" of traditional texts, whether legal, literary, philosophic, or religious. This subversion begins from the dogmatic denial of the very possibility of cross-cultural or transhistorical dialogue, and culminates in the explicit rejection of any traditional conception of humanity. As Vattimo has insisted, it is now simply impossible for the sophisticated postmodernist even to recognize the challenge of the "radical otherness" of another age or culture:

As the condition of the radical otherness of another culture is revealed as an ideal that has perhaps never been realized, and that certainly is impossible for us to realize, it follows that in the process of assimilation-contamination, even the texts belonging to our own tradition, the "classics" in the literal sense of the word, by which we have always before measured our humanity, progressively lose their cogency as models and thus become part of the vast construction site of residual rubble.

(Vattimo 1987, 169)

The effect of this posture toward education, I submit, is hardly the cultivation in students of passionate concern for deciphering what can be learned from the text or from the work of art. What is most likely to be fostered instead is indeed a *pensiero debole*, a weak thinking, characterized by a superficial sense of satisfaction that masks a fundamental emptiness of the spirit. This vacuum is not only deadening to the citizenship and humane spirituality of the young; out of or into this deadening vacuum have swept, and may sweep again, longings and irrationalisms of shattering and frightening proportions.

Responding to the challenge to provide some more specific indication of his political goal, Lyotard has declared that postmodernism is an "orientation" that "corresponds to the evolution of social interactions, where the temporary contract is in practice supplanting permanent institutions in professional, emotional, sexual, cultural, familial, and international matters, as well as in political affairs." To be sure, this "evolution is certainly ambiguous." The "temporary contract is favored by the system" because it contributes in all sorts of ways "to better operativity." The information revolution "could become the 'dream' instrument for controlling and regulating the market system, extended to scholarship itself, and ruled exclusively by the principle of performativity." But if we think of our lives as "just gaming," as consisting in the playing of heterogeneous "language games," and if we insist on avoiding "consensus" in the "rules of the games," and, above all, if we all learn how to use sophisticated computers and gain access to data banks, we can somehow hope or believe that all this will lead to emancipation. The solution, Lyotard continues, is really

in principle, quite simple: give the public free access to the memory and data banks. Language games will then be games of perfect information at any given moment. But they will also be non-zero-sum games, and by virtue of that fact discussions will never risk fixating in a position of minimax equilibrium because they have exhausted their stakes. For the stakes will be in that case constituted by knowledge (or information, if you will), and the reserves of knowledge, which are language's reserves of possible utterances, are inexhaustible. This sketches the outline of a politics in which the desire for justice and the desire for the unknown will be equally respected.

(Lyotard 1979, 107–8)

These words, which conclude Lyotard's book on "the postmodern condition," appear to be seriously intended, although I cannot help but suspect that they represent another example of ironic "postmodernism for the children"—that is, another "game." Unfortunately, this really is just about the most concrete reflection on the postmodernist civic alternative that one will find in the works of Lyotard or Vattimo.

4 / American Postmodernism

The postmodernist rush to escape the depths (in every sense) of Heidegger while preserving something of his philosophic and literary pyrotechnics is a bit like a bottle of strong spirits on a cold winter's night: it promises pleasant dreams; but where and in what condition will we wake up? In the case of Paul De Man, a major source of postmodernism in America, postmodernism turns out to have been a covert, hence all the more troubling, attempt to replace or supersede a youthful journalistic involvement in fascism and anti-Semitism.[1] But in general my unease is caused less by what American postmodernists have endorsed or done than by what may prove to be the real, if insufficiently recognized, consequences and entailments of their thought.

Postmodernism at its least dangerous is the incoherent, if humanly understandable, attempt to preserve some of the attractive consequences of humanistic Enlightenment rationalism while putting a knife into the heart of

1. See De Man 1988. De Man's friend and fellow postmodernist Geoffrey Hartman has mounted a defense that seems to me doubly damning (Hartman 1988). De Man's "development" is elegantly summarized by Shell 1989: in his early days, De Man "identified his success as a literary theorist with the Teutonic destiny of the Flemish people over and against the universalizing, 'Judaizing' spirit of France. What De Man later came (apparently) to renounce was not his early insistence on the privileged status of literature and literary criticism over other modes of thought, but only its attachment to a theory of racial superiority. His own 'denazification' did not take the form of a positive assertion of liberal values, of the truth, say, of the universal declaration of the rights of man, but of a more radical questioning of language itself." The starting point for his postwar reflections is seen with some clarity in De Man 1953, esp. p. 1018. There De Man makes the following radically un-Socratic pronouncement: "The negation of absolute knowledge implies the negation of any knowable good." He adds that "moral value is entirely relative."

that rationalism. Richard Rorty, endorsing the view that "the preservation of the values of the Enlightenment is our best hope," nevertheless insists that it is his task to "cut the links which connect those values with the image of the Mirror of Nature [Rorty's pejorative term for rational grounds such as were insisted on by the Enlightenment]" (Rorty 1979, 335–36). Rorty concludes a more recent book by assuring his readers that he does not mean to say "that the attempt to think in terms of abstractions like 'child of God,' or 'humanity,' or 'rational being' has done no good. It has done an enormous amount of good, as have notions like 'truth for its own sake' and 'art for art's sake.' Such notions have kept the way open for political and cultural change" (Rorty 1989, 195–98).

The problem comes when this "handy bit of rhetoric" is taken seriously, as "a fit subject for 'conceptual analysis'"—"in short, when we start asking about the 'nature' of truth, or art, or humanity." So just how should these "handy bits of rhetoric" be used, in Rortyan postmodernese? What do they mean, in Rortyan liberalism? "The right way to take the slogan 'We have obligations to human beings simply as such' is as a means of reminding ourselves to keep trying to expand our sense of 'us' as far as we can." But this turns out to be not very far: "If one reads the slogan in the right way, one will give 'we' as concrete and historically specific a sense as possible: It will mean something like 'we twentieth century liberals.'" On the other hand, "if one reads it the wrong way," Rorty warns, one will come up with a notion of "us" that is not exclusive enough. One may be led to adopt a notion of "us" that opens the door to nonliberals, or to exponents of pre-twentieth-century cultures (Socrates, Jesus, Moses, Isaiah, Zarathustra, Gandhi, etc.). Rorty focuses on the danger of including just one such problematic case, that of the sort of democratic theory represented by the Founders of the United States: "If one reads the slogan the wrong way, one will think of our 'common humanity' or 'natural human rights' as a 'philosophical foundation' for democratic politics." This "makes one think of democratic politics as subject to the jurisdiction of a philosophical tribunal—as if philosophers had, or at least should do their best to attain, knowledge of something less dubious than the value of the democratic freedoms and relative social equality which some rich and lucky societies have, quite recently, come to enjoy" (Rorty 1989, 195–98).

So impervious is Rortyan liberalism to outside criticism that Rorty goes so far as to declare some pages earlier in this same book (46) that those who endorse the relativistic liberalism of the "rich and lucky" societies holding sway today are "civilized," while those who do not endorse the Rortyan relativistic liberalism are "barbarians." Rorty adopts as his own Joseph Schumpeter's famous remark that "to realize the relative validity of one's convictions and yet stand for them unflinchingly, is what distinguishes a civilized man from a barbarian."

In thus issuing judgments on what distinguishes the "civilized man" from the "barbarian," Rorty is, of course, no longer speaking as a coherent relativist, or even as a coherent Rortyan, but only as a morally confused human being entangled in flagrant self-contradiction. This sort of self-contradiction is the hallmark of relativists, who are, after all, human beings and therefore cannot escape human nature or the permanent human condition. To apply to Rorty the words Leo Strauss wrote in refuting Isaiah Berlin's attempt to defend the exact same proposition from Schumpeter, Rorty

cannot escape the necessity to which every thinking being is subject: to take a final stand, an absolute stand in accordance with what he regards as the nature of man or as the nature of the human condition or as the decisive truth, and hence to assert the absolute validity of his fundamental conviction. This does not mean, of course, that his fundamental conviction is sound. One reason why I doubt that it is sound is that if his authority were right, every resolute liberal hack or thug would be a civilized man, while Plato and Kant would be barbarians.   (Pangle 1989, 17)

As Rorty goes on to admit in this passage under discussion, "we" relativistic liberals, who constitute the "civilized," cherish our freedoms "on the *public* side of our lives," while "on the private side of our lives," there are certain rather different claims that are "*equally* [Rorty's emphasis] hard to doubt": "our love or *hatred* [my emphasis] for a particular person, the need to carry out some idiosyncratic project." This striking reminder of the nature of Rorty's peculiarly apolitical or uncivic liberalism brings to the fore a question: prior to the elaboration and examination of the loves, hatreds, and private projects of Rortyan relativists, can one be so simply confident that they alone have exclusive title to be called "the civilized"?

But we see just how exclusive Rorty's conceptions of community and obligation are when we ask what happens when very sophisticated and intelligent nonliberals, such as Nietzsche and Heidegger, or Calvin and Thomas Aquinas, or Rousseau, or Aristotle, or Marx, or Gandhi, insist that the public sphere of a sound society must reflect and embody "some idiosyncratic project" representing a broader, richer notion of the "we" than is known to Rorty's tepid community. Rorty's reponse is most revealing. "The best one can do with the sort of challenges offered by Nietzsche and Heidegger" is "ask these men to *privatize* their projects, their attempts at sublimity—to view them as irrelevant to politics." And what if they wish to argue with such a request (as they do, of course, or they would not be Nietzsche and Heidegger, but cozy conformists to Rortyan "we"-ness)? "In my view, there is nothing to back up such a request, nor need there be," Rorty responds. In fact, we are under no obligations to the "barbarians" who stand outside our consensus—and, on the other side, we can demand of them no sense of obligation to us: "We are under no obligations other than the 'we-intentions' of the communities with which we identify" (Rorty 1989, 45–47). The circle of human obligation for Rorty turns out to be very restricted in scope.

Lyotard is rather more aware than is Rorty himself of what is at stake and what is afoot in Rortyism. At a crucial point in his debate with Rorty, Lyotard gives this response:

> Richard Rorty is afraid that I lack confidence in liberal democracy. I am pleased that he is afraid. I would like to infect him with my fear, or my loss of confidence. I see something in the example that he gives with regard to *us*. He says: "We don't hope to have the last word, we just hope that in the twenty-first century, they will say of Richard Rorty, 'He is one of us,' just as we now say of Jean-Jacques Rousseau, 'He is one of us.'" Now I when I examine this example, I see that in fact the model of democracy for Richard Rorty is Jean-Jacques Rousseau. For him, Rousseau is *the* democrat. If I go to the end point of my thinking, I will say that we must, in fact, make democracy controversial again: not democracy in the usual sense of the word, democracy in the sense where it is opposed to despotism, but democracy precisely in the sense in which it is *not* opposed to despotism. I remind you that in Kant's elaboration of the political problem, a very sharp distinction is drawn between the *forms of power* and the *forms of government*. Now democracy is a form of government, just like monarchy. But of the forms of power there are just two: the republic and the despotism. And Kant adds this, to which not enough attention is paid: it is evident, he says, that democracy is necessarily despotic. I won't say more, but I ask of Richard Rorty that he revise his excessive confidence in democracy, even liberal.
> (Lyotard and Rorty 1985, 582–83)

Our "conversational" fellow American Rorty is no doubt politically more attractive than his less easygoing, more "tragic" French fellows (the terms come from Lyotard, in his rather patronizing debate with Rorty). Recoiling from the antidemocratic and antiliberal implications of Heidegger and Lyotard, Rorty has sought shelter in a marriage of Heidegger and John Dewey, brokered by Wittgenstein.

This astounding match is made conceivable only on the basis of Rorty's simplified reinterpretation of Heidegger. In Rorty's hands, Heidegger's texts are boiled down to the point where Heidegger's own passionate central concerns—with transhuman Being, hence with gods, and hence with transfiguring artistic elevation—evaporate. What is left is what Rorty calls "a

Schwarzwald redneck," whose severest political challenge to liberalism can be dismissed literally without argument: "On the general question of the relation between Heidegger's thought and his Nazism, I am not persuaded that there is much to be said except that one of the century's most original thinkers happened to be a pretty nasty character." But Rorty cannot resist this remarkable addendum: "If one holds the view of the self as centerless . . . one will be prepared to find the relation between the intellectual and the moral virtues, and the relation between a writer's books and other parts of his life, contingent" (Rorty 1989, 111).

How contingent is contingent? Is there really no correlation between liberal intellectualism and the moral and civic virtues that support and are required for liberal republicanism? Is there no correlation between a writer's repeatedly preaching against cruelty—as Rorty does—and his practices? Does the "centerless" liberal self celebrated by Rorty have not even a center that resists bad faith? Does the distinction good faith / bad faith then become another traditional "handy bit of rhetoric"? The answers to these questions become more pressing when we learn that Rorty in fact rejects Heidegger's own self-interpretation in favor of a rather crude Nietzschean interpretation of Heidegger's thought and motivation. For it turns out that at the bottom of Rorty's thought there is, after all, a foundational answer to the most fundamental question. Rorty raises that question in his own terms by asking why we play any "language game"—and, in particular, why we play any particular moral or philosophic or political "language game." "The only available answer" seems to Rorty to be "the one Nietzsche gave: It increases our power" (Rorty 1989, 115). Rorty's deepest thought is a somewhat muffled, but for that reason all the more sinister, endorsement of a singularly unsublimated form of the Will to Power doctrine. Rorty is honest enough to admit that "the sort of pragmatism" advocated in his book *Contingency, Irony, and Solidarity* is a form of thought Heidegger "took to be the most degraded version of the nihilism in which metaphysics culminates" (ibid., 116).

Heidegger indeed made it clear that he saw in American pragmatism the ultimate apotheosis of scientism—that is, of naive faith in the progressively benevolent character of technological thinking and of the reorganization of human existence through the controlling and predictive capacities of technology. This Heideggerian assault is not far from the mark in the case of Dewey, who is, of course, famous for celebrating "the technique of social and moral engineering," and who articulated the leitmotif of his political thought as: "approximation to use of scientific method in investigation and of the engineering mind in the invention and projection of far-reaching social plans is demanded."[2] Dewey's laudable preoccupation with citizenship education (a concern that tends to diminish in the relatively apolitical Rorty) was conceived rather strictly in terms of scientific thinking:

The future of democracy is allied with the spread of the scientific attitude. It is the sole guarantee against wholesale misleading by propaganda. More important still, it is the only assurance of the possibility of a public opinion intelligent enough to meet present social problems. (Dewey 1939, 148–49)

In his sole thematic treatment of German philosophy, Dewey insisted that the lesson to be drawn from the Nazi outcome of German philosophy is that the American way of life is threatened by a German "heritage" that seeks to confine the scientific canons of communication to "a compartment that is external to social life"; the German "heritage shows itself, with harm to democracy, *whenever and wherever* we fail to use science as a means of rendering communication more intelligent in *all* matters requiring social decision" (1942, 46–47; my emphasis). Amazingly enough, Dewey finds the antidote to German thinking in German practice: Dewey turns out (in 1942!) to be a strong admirer of applied German scientism:

Germany is a monument to what can be done by means of conscious method and organization. An experimental philosophy of life in order to succeed must not set less store upon methodic and organized intelligence, but more. We must learn from Germany what methodic and organized work means. (Dewey 1942, 142)

"That such an experimental philosophy of life means a dangerous experiment goes without saying," Dewey adds. But "the question of the past, of precedents, of origins, is quite subordinate to prevision, to guidance and control" (ibid., 140–41). It is this worship of scientific "guidance and control" that undergirds Deweyan progressivism, or his self-confident assertion that we stand in a historical position from which we may judge the inferiority of the past.

As Harvey Mansfield, Jr., stressed in his *New Republic* debate with Rorty, this scientism, which is the linchpin of Dewey's own authentic thought, is, to say the least, kept in the background in Rorty's presentation.[3]

2. Dewey 1948, 173 (see also 26, 36–38, 43, 125); and see Dewey 1935, 70–73 (see also 87); cf. Dewey 1939, 101–2; Dewey 1946, x.
3. Mansfield 1988 responding to Rorty 1988. See also Nichols 1990, 531: "In Richard Rorty's recent restoration of pragmatism to higher philosophical respectability, Dewey's faith in scientific methods and confidence in the mutual support of democracy and science seems to evanesce." My understanding of Dewey's political theory is deeply indebted to Nichols's rich and penetrating discussion.

But from time to time it leers out from the shadows. In a footnote, Rorty characterizes Dewey's "peculiar achievement" as that of having "remained sufficiently Hegelian not to think of natural science as having an inside track on the essences of things, while becoming sufficiently naturalistic to think of human beings in Darwinian terms" (Rorty 1979, 362). Rorty does not ever really explain how a "Darwinian" social and political thought can counterbalance (rather than intensify) the explicitly antihumanistic, antidemocratic thinking of Nietzsche and Heidegger. More generally, Rorty avoids facing and thinking through the political and moral dangers inherent in a modern scientific conception of human beings. If one might have hoped Rorty would learn something politically useful from Heidegger, it is this.

Rorty attempts to sidestep the issue by veiling Deweyism's scientistic core. Dewey "was at his best when he emphasized the similarities between philosophy and poetry, rather than when he emphasized those between philosophy and engineering" (Rorty 1982, 56). But the hole this leaves in Deweyism is gaping. Dewey's moral and political philosophy was pretty thin in its original version: if, or insofar as, one guts Deweyism of its distinctive core, the dedication to scientism, and to scientistic citizenship education, what of controversial substance is left—beyond vague, albeit warm, appeals to consensus and avoidance of violence? Dewey ceaselessly inveighed against irrationalism, in philosophy (especially German), religion, and politics. In his debate with Lyotard, Rorty explains his Deweyan "discipleship" this way: "We pragmatists," "given our uncritical conception of rationality, are not inclined to the diagnosis irrationalism; since for us, 'rational' means simply 'persuasive' and 'irrational' 'evoking force'" (Rorty 1985a, 578).

Rorty perhaps shows his hand most fully in a critique he has written of Habermas and Lyotard, where he declares that his political program or goal is a revival of Deweyan "social engineering," conceived as "the substitute for traditional religion." In order to fulfill this ambition, postmodernism must, Rorty argues, return to the philosophic orientation of Sir Francis Bacon, whose leading insight, according to Rorty, is "Knowledge is power." "This," Rorty says, summing up his own position, "seems to me to embody Lyotard's postmodernist 'incredulity towards metanarratives' while dispensing with the assumption that the intellectual has a mission to be avant-garde, to escape the rules and practices and institutions which have been transmitted to him in favor of something that will make possible 'authentic criticism.'" According to Rorty, Lyotard's severe doubts about the regimenting forces of the contemporary scientistic consensus represents "one of the Left's silliest ideas" and "necessarily devalues consensus and communication." This notion, Rorty declares in exasperation, makes the left-wing version of postmodernism "wildly irrelevant to the attempt at communicative consensus which is the vital force which drives bourgeois culture" (Rorty 1985b, 173–74).

But I certainly do not wish to leave the impression that I believe that the Heideggerian or Lyotardian attack on the application of scientific thinking to social and political issues ought to carry the day. On the contrary, what I find most defective in Rorty's philosophy of science is his failure adequately to defend the possibility of a truly rational and humane political science against these attacks. A proper defense of political science or rationalism requires, of course, a clear and sympathetic understanding of the best arguments of the deepest critics. On this basis, and only on this basis, one can begin to see one's way toward a thorough revamping of today's "social science" with a view to meeting the criticisms of it. In this regard, Rorty could have learned something more, it seems to me, from the late John Dewey's reflections on the possible symbiotic relation between scientific method—conceived of as a moral method, and by no means as a "value-free" or "relativistic" one—and responsible democratic citizenship. For Dewey is not always so simplistically scientistic as his critics (and defenders such as Rorty) seem to assume.

From the confrontation with fascism and communism, Dewey became acutely aware that "a more adequate science of human nature might conceivably only multiply the agencies by which some human beings manipulate other human beings for their own advantage." Writing in 1939, he apologized for his previous focus on English thought to the neglect of the wisdom of the American Founders, and especially Jefferson: "In the past I have concerned myself unduly," he admitted, "with the English writers who have attempted to state the ideals of self-governing communities." "If I now prefer to refer to Jefferson," he went on to say, "the chief reason is that Jefferson's formulation is moral through and through." Dewey found "the heart of Jefferson's faith" in "his words 'Nothing is unchangeable but the inherent and inalienable rights of man.'" Dewey applauded the fact that in this observation, it is "the *ends* of democracy, the rights of *man*—not of men in the plural—which are unchangeable." Although "the words in which [Jefferson] stated the moral basis of free institutions have gone out of vogue, . . . his fundamental beliefs remain unchanged if we forget all special asssociations with the word *Nature* and speak instead of ideals and aims . . . backed by something deep and indestructible in the needs and demands of humankind" (Dewey 1939, 155–57; see also 131ff.).

Nor did Dewey's debt to Jeffersonian rationalism stop at the notion of permanent foundational rights. He was also inspired by Jefferson's classical republican preoccupation with "general political organization on the basis of small units." Jefferson's reflections, when directed critically against modern scientific organization, helped Dewey to discern "one of the most serious of present problems regarding democracy": "the way in which individuals at present find themselves in the grip of immense forces whose workings and consequences they have no power of affecting." With Jefferson's help, Dewey clarified the difference between mere "association" and "community": "electrons, atoms, and molecules are in association with one another." "Associations are conditions for the existence of a community, but a community adds the function of communication in which emotions and ideas are shared as well as joint undertakings engaged in." Such community has requirements that are gravely threatened in modern large-scale democracy: "Vital and thorough attachments are bred only in the intimacy of an intercourse which is of necessity restricted in range. . . . Democracy must begin at home, and its home is the neighborly community." In this light Dewey was led to some of his most sober reflections on the fundamental problem facing modern democracy. Civic education, or "apprenticeship in the practical processes of self-government, which Jefferson had in mind," is critical. But there is more to it than this: civic education "involves development of local agencies of communication and cooperation, creating stable loyal attachments, to militate against the centrifugal forces of present culture" (Dewey 1939, 159–61).

Equally important, and equally eclipsed in Rorty's "Deweyism," is Dewey's insistence on the link between republican civic virtue and the intellectual virtues of the authentic scientist or philosopher. This Deweyan thought is elegantly captured by James Nichols:

The hope for fruitful harmony between science and democracy is given plausibility by the observable character of a genuine "morale" to be found among free scientific inquirers: "fairmindedness, intellectual integrity, the will to subordinate personal preferences to ascertained facts and to share with others what is found" [Dewey 1939, 148]. Democracy needs to be infused with this moral scientific spirit. A certain kinship between democracy and science, consisting in such shared traits as experimental innovativeness, openness, and devotion to progress, and eminently displayed in such persons as Jefferson, makes their cooperative harmony a reasonable hope as well as an indispensable goal. (Nichols 1990, 384)

Since neither Rorty nor any of the other most famous "postmodernists" have written very much about political and legal theory per se, one must also turn to those distinguished political and legal theorists who have begun to elaborate the civic implications of postmodernist thought more systematically. Among these, it seems to me that Sanford Levinson, McCormick Professor of Law at the University of Texas, stands out. His treatise on the subject, *Constitutional Faith,* is uniquely revealing by virtue of its lucidity, comprehensiveness, and constitutional competence—and the boldness with which it limns for us the future constitutionalism entailed by (especially Rortyan) postmodernist political theory.[4]

What Levinson calls "the core" of his treatise is a wrestling with the question of what could possibly bond Americans together "in a coherent political community" after "the triumph of a distinctly (post)modernist sense" (Levinson 1988, 6–7). The United States, Levinson stresses, is unique in the degree to which its nationhood, culture, and private as well as public morality are constituted by, or wholly dependent upon, shared attachment to a distinctive set of constitutional principles, understood as "timeless moral norms" derived from "reason or the nature of things" (60). If appeal was made to God by the Founders, it was to the God discoverable in, and limited by, reason and nature (59–65, 88). But "these ideas have barely, if at all, survived" (61). According to Levinson, we have been taught by Nietzsche to see that like all other moral bonds, attachment to the Constitution is—and always was—a matter of faith rather than, or even as opposed to, reason: we no longer can believe "in the persuasive force of detached reason" (52). "Whatever the process by which understandings of concepts like 'the Constitution' emerge, it is doubtful that logical argumentation plays a crucial role" (36–37). Faith, not reason, rules human existence. If the United States or any other nation is to endure, the question is not whether it ought to have a religious basis, but only what kind of "civil religion" is possible and necessary (73). Accordingly, jurisprudence and law must be conceived on the analogy to religion and religious fervor, or the lack thereof. Law professors may best be understood as "legal theologians" or even "prophets" (27, 63); the law school may best be conceived on the model of a "divinity school" or "a secular department of religion" (179); the Constitution itself is to be seen as a "sacred text," and "the United States Supreme Court as the principal keeper of the religious flame" (16).

Yet "the sacred" must be radically reconceived in light of the depths opened up by "(post)modernist" insight. Religiousness and faith can no

4. Levinson 1988. Page references in the following paragraphs are to this text. I have made use here of my review of Levinson's *Constitutional Faith* in the *Social Science Quarterly* 70 (1989): 782–83.

longer be understood in any traditional sense, at least by men of "intellectual honesty" or "sincerity." All faiths that we have known or experienced heretofore, including especially the American "constitutional faith," were naive or deluded inasmuch as they were devoted to some notion of "truth"—some idea of "fixed moral principles." Our recognition of this fact, our coming to "(post)modernist" self-consciousness about our constitutional faith, is the death knell of constitutionalism: "The 'death of constitutionalism' may be the central event of our time, just as the death of God was that of the past century (and for much the same reason)" (52, 172).

But the death of the old constitutional faith liberates us for a new kind of constitutional faith, a radically new religiousness that does not "define religion as necessarily including affirmations of supernatural beings" (55). The new, godless or agnostic, civil religiousness consists in a rationally ungrounded "commitment" to a *future* law and "Constitution" rather than past law and "constitutional*ism*." In this new dispensation, "what is evoked in the classroom, including my own classroom, are political visions rather than political truths, and the future will, in some ways, be constructed out of the visions that most persuade" (172). This constitutional faith commits "only to a process of becoming and to taking responsibility for constructing the political vision toward which I strive" (193; cf. 130). The new keynotes are "interpretation as deconstruction," "civil religion" as "political vision," and—above all—"Event." For in the new, postmodernist religiousness, "Event" is Revelation, but a revelation now conceived of as emerging out of Being in History or Time—as shimmering before us in a future merely inspired, rather than controlled and limited, by any past revelation (130). We are to look upon "alleged" constitutional interpretation, just as we look upon all "alleged" textual interpretation, as a self-conscious activity involving the destruction of old and creation of new meanings; and even this degree of concern for fidelity to, or limitation by, legal texts "must be balanced by fidelity to the model of action bequeathed by the Founders" (134). That model is one of "blatant and conscious illegality," of revolutionary, antilegal usurpation of the existing Articles of Confederation (131). "History is shaped as much by deciding what it means to bear witness to the event as by any alleged explication of the text" (134).

Levinson does not shrink from adumbrating the vistas this new, deconstructive prophetic thinking opens up for the country in more detail. "There is nothing that is unsayable in the language of the Constitution," he observes (191). As examples, he approvingly quotes Justice Frank Murphy's endorsement of the possibility that amendment or, indeed, just simple "creative" interpretation of the Constitution might legitimate "the abolition of private property without compensation," and "the establishment of a proletarian dictatorship with political rights to be denied to persons who were not proletarian and/or party members" (136). In almost the same breath, Levinson applauds the Court's "subsequent vindication of the Nazi-sympathiser Baumgartner" as having in no way violated his naturalization oath because of his fidelity to *Mein Kampf*. Here Levinson stresses that his discussion is not "merely academic," and in proof he offers the "vision" of a South African revolution that would bring to our shores a wave of Afrikaner immigrants whose admission to citizenship would introduce a powerful racist or proto-fascist faction into the community (148–49). Levinson leaves us in no doubt that he, for his part, at least at this historical moment, and under the influence of the present moral "conventions," would deplore and vigorously oppose such a revolutionary "event" in the polity. But his "sincerity" compels him to bring to our attention the authority of Richard Rorty, who teaches the "rather gloomy" truth that the abandonment of the idea of "truth" necessarily entails abandonment of the "belief in a single true self—to whom fidelity is then presumably owed": the "hope" for such a selfhood or trustworthy center of moral gravity in any human being is "chimerical." On the authority of Rorty, we must learn to accept that the "truth" of the "self," like all other "truths," changes as the self is seized by fundamental "events," with their attendant changes in our "conventions" (176). Nor can or ought we appeal from the "chimerical true self" to trust in the stability of American decency: this would fail to face the explosive power of the "event," or of History, especially in our present state of cultural disintegration: "Social life as we know it is being challenged and may even be dissolving into an ever-greater Heraclitean flux" (73). "The fact that the public rhetoric of American political culture remains organized, in substantial ways, as a faith community centered on the Constitution may mislead us." This "once-strong, indeed culturally dominant, mode of thought can collapse almost literally overnight" (52). "Hegel's comment is all too relevant: 'How blind they are who may hope that institutions, constitutions, laws . . . from which the spirit has flown, can subsist any longer!' (6). "Rorty quotes Sartre's remark that the establishment of fascism would establish 'fascism as the truth of man, and so much the worse for us'" (176).

What we are living through today, according to Levinson, is the culmination of a process that began with the American Revolution: a process through which the idea of "popular sovereignty as a motif emphasizing the energy and moral authority of will (and willful desire) rather than the

constraints of a common moral order to which the will was bound to submit" has "become the view emphasized today at most major law schools."
"Law is stripped of any moral anchoring," and "political institutions thus
become the forum for the triumph of the will" (64–65).

Levinson goes well beyond Rorty. But he must, in order to think through
and bring out the full civic and legal consequences of Rorty's own truncated
political meditation. To see the authenticity, and at the same time the relative
thoughtlessness, of the Rortyan roots of "post-Constitutionalism," we have
only to watch Lyotard's exposure of Rorty in their debate. In order to grasp
the full significance of this, one must be aware that in a critical appreciation
of Lyotard published the same year, Rorty had assumed that Lyotard and
his followers, like Rorty himself, "are willing to drop the opposition between
'true consensus' and 'false consensus,' or between 'validity' and 'power'"
(Rorty 1985b, 162).

> *Lyotard:* A theme dear to Richard Rorty is that one can obtain a consensus by
> persuasion. I will make here two remarks. First, to persuade is not to convince.
> Persuasion is a rhetorical operation, and the Greeks knew that that operation uses
> trickery, mental violence. Accordingly, I pose the question, can our duty to be free
> be an object of persuasion? Do not make the mistake of supposing that this is a
> simple problem. . . . as you listened to the talk of Richard Rorty, you heard the
> expression "to attain a free consensus." How does one know a consensus is free?
> How can any consensus be free if it is obtained by persuasion? I believe that the whole
> question of imperialism, including soft imperialism—what I call the conversational
> imperialism of Rorty—is contained in this point.
>
> *Rorty:* From the point of view of the pragmatist, and also, I think, of the Wittgen-
> steinian, and also, I think, of anyone who renounces what we call nowadays "the
> metaphysics of presence" you cannot make any distinction between persuading and
> convincing that does not go back to the difference between physical violence in the
> simple and ordinary sense of the word and the absence of physical violence. . . . you
> cannot maintain the Greek distinction between rhetoric and logic. As a consequence,
> the only distinctions accessible to you are those between the presence and the absence
> of the secret police, journalists, television, etc. . . . and these symptoms suffice for
> the needs of political reflection.   (Lyotard and Rorty 1985, 582, 584)

Fortunately for all of us, the debate between Lyotard and Rorty does not
begin to exhaust the possibilities of a European–North American dialogue.

PART II

The Spiritual Challenges of the Post–Cold War Era

5 / The Challenge for and from Europe

Europe has once again become a cynosure, from which emanate hopes and promises of a world-historical dimension. Is this a temporary or a lasting reassertion of primacy? Are we startled witnesses to the unexpected eruption of a Vesuvius that has somehow mustered its dying forces for one final, glorious episode? Or is Europe recovering its native spiritual vigor after a protracted illness that assumed, deceptively, the symptoms of old age?

The Cold War that held Europe in its icy grip for half a century has come to an end. The Western liberal democracies, rooted in eighteenth-century philosophical conceptions of individual rights and representative government, and grounded in the free-market economy created and legitimated by the political philosophy of the Enlightenment, first defeated fascism (with the help of communism), and are now finally witnessing the collapse of communism, centered in the Soviet Union and China and rooted in the Marxist philosophy of the nineteenth century. We are entering the rather desperate throes of an endgame, which in politics is not like the endgame in professional chess. The losing side does not quietly concede. On the contrary, it often lashes out in ferocious and irrational lunges, attempting to redeem its fate through fantastic gambles. When great empires decline and fall, they have a tendency to go down finally in flames that engulf the world. As is brought out with particular vividness in the diaries of Kurt Riezler (personal secretary to Theobold von Bethmann-Hollweg, the chancellor of Germany), World War I was caused more by the weaknesses than by the strengths of the German and Austro-Hungarian empires.[1] I do not therefore mean for one moment to suggest that we are entering a period of enhanced security. I suspect we are, rather, entering a time of danger unprecedented in its character and degree. We and our children are about to begin to endure the curse of living in truly interesting times.

But these unprecedented dangers—the dissolution of the framework that has structured global political existence for the past half-century—also open up new vistas. If ours is a time of danger and uncertainty, it is also, naturally and necessarily, a time of hope and of awakening to dramatic new challenges. Thus far, what has emerged is not so much the birth of new dreams as the resurrection of old, forbidden longings and ideals: what Marju Lauristin, a leader of the Estonian Popular Front, calls "the ideals that our people have carried in their hearts for fifty years."[2] If we are called to new thinking and new questions, we soon find that the new meditations involve the rediscovery of forgotten old thoughts and questions, whose inherent, long-repressed power springs forth as the great artificial weight of the past half century begins to lift. Such is the question I now raise and pursue: What is a good European?

We are not accustomed to ask, to think about, this question. For the past half century, Europe, in the sense meant by this question, has not existed. When the "good European" Stefan Zweig committed suicide in Brazil in 1942, he left a note saying: "My spiritual homeland, Europe, has destroyed itself. I salute all my friends! May it be granted them to see the dawn after the long night!"[3] That dawn may at last be breaking. Europe in our lifetimes has been sundered between and subordinated to the Soviet Union and the United States. Every country and individual was obliged either to take sides or suffer the contempt that awaits those who try to remain neutral in the greatest moral, spiritual, and political conflict of their age. But now a new possibility is emerging—or an old, dormant, all-but-forgotten possibility is reviving: the possibility that Europe, and the Europeans, may become not merely an economic, but a political, a cultural, a moral unity. The possibility reemerges that a unified Europe could once again be inspired and uplifted by the goal articulated in such different and sometimes conflicting ways by

1. *Kurt Riezler: Tagebücher, Aufsätze, Dokumente*, ed. Karl Dietrich Erdmann (Göttingen: Vandenbroeck & Ruprecht, 1972). See the discussions in Stern 1975, 77–118, and Thompson 1975, ch. 3.
2. Quoted in the *New York Times*, August 24, 1989, 8.
3. A facsimile of the handwritten note is printed in the "Publisher's Postscript" to *The World of Yesterday: An Autobiography by Stefan Zweig* (Lincoln: University of Nebraska Press, 1964), 437–40.

Kant, by Hegel, by Heine, and, above all, by Nietzsche. The possibility reemerges that Europe may again aspire to constitute a planetary spiritual aristocracy: a moral and intellectual leadership of the world altogether different from the shortsighted, antagonistic drives for political and economic empire of the narrowly nationalistic late nineteenth century.

America's Decline and Decoupling from Europe

To grasp the potential power of this aspiration, we must give due weight to a rather controversial premise underlying my question about what it might mean to be "a good European." The United States is on the verge of triumph over her great antagonist, Russia. But this victorious America, I submit, runs grave risks of spiritual decline, risks that victory may well intensify.

To begin with, the victory is, of course, a tribute to the greatness of American liberal democracy, and not merely a sign of the decadence of Marxism. The victory testifies to the resolve, patience, steadfastness, and prudence—despite all the lapses and mistakes—of the American electorate and its Cold War leadership over many years. These virtues of foreign policy were impressively reaffirmed in the defeat of Saddam Hussein. Nor is it only foreign policy that offers testimony to the continuing strength of the moral fiber of the United States. The civil rights movement has eradicated or greatly diminished longstanding civic vices, through the practice of admirable civic virtues—virtues of fraternity, humanity, fairness, obedience to the law, courage, and compassion. As a result of the nation's rededication to these civic virtues, substantial new opportunities have been opened up, in education, employment, health, political participation, and hence dignity for large sectors of the population, including notably American women. At a somewhat less noble or heroic level, Americans can take justifiable pride in their economy, whose resilience bespeaks hard work, discipline, commitment to education, and respect for talent and initiative. But these and other justifiable sources of pride are shadowed by a pervasive malaise that grips the vitals of the nation. Deeply implicated in this malaise is a growing detachment of American culture from the European tradition that has since the beginning been the matrix of the American soul.

The moral and political vitality of the United States is rooted ultimately in two great European sources. The first is religion, originally Protestantism, but eventually also Roman Catholicism and Judaism, each of which found a haven under the American principles of toleration. The second is the specific conception of human nature elaborated by Locke and Montesquieu and adopted in the *Federalist Papers*. Only from this conception of human nature can we derive the fixed, universal, and permanent moral principles—human rights, religious toleration, and checked and balanced representative government—that lie at the heart of the U.S. Constitution. It is from these two European wellsprings—one of revelation, one of philosophic reason—that Americans have drawn their sense of higher purpose, their objects of dedication, their capacity for self-control, endurance, and self-overcoming, their bonds of fraternity, and the highest foci of their intellectual reflection and artistic expression.

Now the melancholy fact is that these twin fountainheads run drier and drier among the opinion leaders, teachers, and scholars or men and women of letters in America today—and the obvious consequences are increasingly, and inevitably, spread among the great mass of the citizens, beginning with the young.

The religious traditions on which the American polity was founded are very imperfectly remembered; and insofar as strong remnants do remain lively in the public mind, these are regarded with suspicion or contempt in most American universities, journals of opinion, and circles of intellectual sophistication. Mainstream Catholic as well as Protestant theology is awash in profoundly antibiblical, radically atheistic, and even polytheistic modes of thinking derived from truncated, vulgarized, and poorly digested studies of Heidegger, Nietzsche, and Marx.

When one turns from the religious to the rationalist or philosophic foundations of the American polity, one again is struck by an impression of desuetude. As I noted in the Introduction, it is rare indeed to find the American intellectual, professor, journalist, or scholar who believes in natural rights, in the "transcendent law of nature and of nature's God," as these were understood by Lincoln and the Founders of the United States, and enunciated in the *Federalist Papers* and Declaration of Independence. The idea that nature should or could provide the fixed standard for human existence, the notion that American life and institutions represent the embodiment of timeless, transhistorical and transcultural principles of right, is regarded as naive even by most American high school students. Historical or cultural relativism, in more or less sophisticated versions, reigns almost unquestioned in the American consciousness.

As a result, the American commitment to human rights has become more and more blurred and ambiguous. Undermined at home by demands for reverse discrimination and assaulted in the United Nations and abroad by Third World tyrants' self-serving perversions of the meaning of human rights, the original American understanding of a small granite core of inalienable rights inhering equally in every individual, and entailing specific civil rights, threatens to become obscured. In the international arena, the clearcut and objective natural and civil rights of individuals, for which both the French and American Revolutions were fought, are increasingly submerged in the amorphous and sticky jelly of so-called economic, social, and cultural rights. At home, simplistic and often demagogic demands for equality of results or conditions steadily replace the self-respecting demand for equality of opportunity, making it ever more easy to justify, ever more difficult to protect against, the assault on the dignity of the individual and the individual's claim to be judged strictly on his or her personal merits. Group and historical rights have a place in the shaping of political institutions, guaranteeing genuine representation of all the constituents of a diverse population; but today claims made in the name of group and historical rights too often lack mooring in the concept of individual natural rights, dedication to which has bound Americans together in a moral enterprise "conceived in liberty, and dedicated to the proposition that all men are created equal."

The watchwords of the more advanced intellectual life of the United States today are *empowerment* and *deconstruction,* terms signaling the fact that among academic elites, the pervasive relativism is neither open-minded and tolerant nor easygoing and dispassionate. What is characteristic of the most "advanced" intellectual life in America today is not simply a loss of belief in, or even a loss of sympathetic comprehension of, the faith and philosophy of the American republican founding. What is most characteristic of "politically correct thinking" is a morally indignant reaction against the lifeblood—not merely the literary, artistic and historical, but, most ominously, the philosophic and constitutional foundations—of the nation. So-called "critical legal theory" joins forces with the more radical branches of feminism, and with those who condemn the American experience as one long bout of racism, to strip the moral legitimacy from what is labeled the essentially male chauvinist, racist, plutocratic, exploitative, and ideological character of American constitutionalism and common law. On the other side, among the more libertarian and positivistic elements in the Benthamite "law and economics" movement, the idea that courts and judges, citizens and statesmen, should be bound or even guided and inspired by the original intentions and principled reflections of the Founders is more and more treated as a a species of backward and benighted naiveté.

This rejection of the American political and constitutional heritage is in some measure the continuation or application of a more profound rejection, growing throughout the academy, of the entire European heritage of Western philosophy, theology, literature, and constitutionalism. The study of the great texts of the past is more and more perverted by a so-called "deconstructive" enterprise that lionizes the deliberate "subverting" of rational discourse by arrogant and often philistine critics who treat the works of the past as a pathologist treats the corpses of the carriers of a plague. The great books are condemned as the priestlike "canon" through which "Eurocentric," white, male, privileged elites supposedly wield their cultural and psychological imperialism over the souls of non-Europeans.

The most authoritative and telling testimony to today's dominant elite opinion at the level of higher education is the American Council of Learned Societies Report "Speaking for the Humanities." This report, published with fanfare in the *Chronicle of Higher Education* in January 1989, and endorsed by the Modern Language Association, was written by the directors of eight "Humanities Centers" at prestigious universities joined by twenty other leading humanities scholars. It was the humanities establishment's definitive and highly defensive response to what it called "attacks" on the current state of education in the humanities.

These "attacks," by the secretary of education, the chairman of the National Endowment for the Humanities, and a few eloquent leading scholars, "clearly respond," the report admitted, "to a widespread and understandable popular disenchantment with the work of universities." "The crisis," the report further admitted, "is authentic." The crisis, as the report sees it, is rooted in this question: "What is to be the relationship between works traditionally taught as great—the vast majority of them by Western white males—and writing reflecting the experience and aspirations of other groups, either within Western societies or from other societies?" But the report does not mean that this is or ought to be a truly *open* question.[4] The answer is clear, dogmatic, authoritarian, and self-righteous. One can no longer seriously entertain the possibility that the great works and thoughts of our heritage may continue to supply the decisive guidance for our lives:

One cannot proceed, in the humanities, by looking to past curricula, past conceptions of value and meaning, to provide the models that will allow us to meet the current crisis with which the humanities are now most profoundly concerned. Part of our responsibility is, in fact, to learn to understand those models and the reasons for their failure.

4. John Searle, a distinguished logician and professor of philosophy, has recently observed of this report how difficult it is "to convey the smugness of its tone, the feebleness of its argument, or the weakness of its constant appeals to authority" (Searle 1990, 40).

From within the seclusion of their academic establishments, America's new educational elite have launched what is tantamount to a cultural revolution that aims to replace "Eurocentrism" with a dramatically new focus—supposedly on the cultures of Asia, Africa, and Latin America. There would be no cause for alarm if what we were talking about were the initiation of a genuine, critical dialogue between some of the great thinkers and ideas of the Western heritage and their counterparts in the North African, or Chinese, or Hindu, traditions. On the contrary, such a development—students learning classical Arabic, Chinese, or Sanscrit in order to engage firsthand the challenge of Ibn Khaldun or Algazel or Mencius or the Rig Veda—would be a cause for rejoicing, not least because it might be a powerful stimulus to the revitalization of serious thought and argument over the competing philosophies and religious visions of the Western heritage, with its rootedness in universal human rights, or natural right, and universalistic monotheism.

In fact, however, the new fashion is antithetical to a serious and sympathetic preoccupation with the issues that preoccupy both the Eastern and the Western classics. The new fashion is born from theories of recent Western European and American intellectuals and critics who invoke, all too often on superficial acquaintance, the authority of Freud (filtered through Lacan), Marx, and Heidegger. The fashion consists in treating the arguments and creations of philosophers, theologians, and poets as ideological cover, as unconscious defenses for deeply imbedded institutions of hegemony and domination. Speaking of the leading goals of humanities education, the Learned Societies' report says that such education ought "particularly to expose and analyze those values that lie hidden beneath the surfaces of language and art." Unspecified "developments in modern thought," the report proclaims, "have made us alert to what is left out when 'the best that has been thought and written' is selected or when discussion focuses on 'man.' We have learned to ask whether universalist claims do not in fact promote as a norm the concerns of a particular group." It does not take the report long to deliver its authoritative answer to this question "we have learned to ask." "Fundamental questions about standpoint, cultural difference, aesthetic, moral, and political values," the report declares, "belie universalist claims." "Traditional claims to disinterest reflect unacknowledged ideologies."

The approach to texts regarded in this way is hardly one of respectful attentiveness, as the prelude to critical appreciation and dialogue. Instead, it becomes the purported moral duty of the "liberators" to unmask and

"deconstruct" all "privileging of discourse." The report rejects with sophisticated scorn even those claims explicitly made by past authors to provide
reasoned arguments for their political commitments: it has been "demonstrated" the report confidently declares, by "the most powerful modern
philosophies and theories," that "claims of disinterest, objectivity, and universality are not to be trusted." Naturally then, although the report makes
a passing bow to the idea that the humanities "are to act as witnesses for
the American belief in a profound connection between an alert mind and
the exercise of civic virtue," no civic virtues are ever specified, no reference
is made to any important document in the American civic tradition or its
direct antecedents, not a word is said about human rights, and the very
possibility of any significant human universality or universal humanity is
ringingly denied. "What most matters in modern thought," the report as-
sures us, "challenges claims to universality." The report is well aware that
the "ideal of objectivity and disinterest is at the root of modern Western
thought"; but it insists that only the naive and deluded still "mistakenly
believe that ideal also to be at the heart of the principles that underlie modern
democracy—the belief that members of a society can act against their own
self-interest, recognizing a larger social good." While "we may wish to argue
that a commitment to democracy is *not* ideological but a recognition of a
universal truth, disinterestedly achieved," the report dismisses this wish as
an old-fashioned fond hope: "we ought to be—and we are," the professors
declare, "able to defend our ideological commitments without recourse to
such arguments. A firm recognition of our own interests, and of the fact that
in teaching democratic principles we are being ideological strengthens rather
than weakens our position. . . . We should not equate truth with our own
political ideology."

Everything becomes "political," and the "political" is unabashed "defense" of "our own interests," articulated through "ideology," which is
openly conceived of as being in sharp contrast to truth, objectivity, or the
capacity of members of a society to "act against their own self-interest,
recognizing a larger social good." Politics as defense of warring interests
replaces politics as civic virtue, and political thought, understood as "ideology," is assumed to be incapable of authentic rational justification or arbitra-
tion. The "political" becomes, almost by definition, the covert and semiconscious—and hence all the more irrational—endless Nietzschean struggle for
power: no middle ground exists between the defense of existing hegemony
and the "empowerment" of the hitherto powerless (who will set up their
own new hegemonies). The ubiquitous "political" becomes a pure contest

of Nietzschean wills or power structures, in which the notion of a common ground of reasoned and imaginative or sympathetic dialogue is dismissed as superficial and deceptive, necessarily exploitative, a clear sign of bad faith, where it is not a sign of culpable simplemindedness.

And on the other hand, when the actual contents of the "liberation from Eurocentrism" are specified, there stand revealed the amazing spiritual vacuity, absence of real erudition, and narrowly reactive political character of the new orientation. The age-old poetic, theological, civic, and moral voices of the Great Books, sifted and tested through the centuries, and brimming with critical controversy and argument, tend to be replaced, not with any of the equally great and difficult classics of Islam or Buddhism or Confucianism or Hinduism, but instead with revolutionary tracts and autobiographies written by various recent Third World ideologues whose highest intellectual standards are set by the writings of Franz Fanon. Through these new required works, students are to be taught to admire souls corroded by hatred—of non-European traditionalism and religion even more than of European colonialism—and are to take as their new models men and women whose minds are enserfed to the self-hating intellectual frameworks concocted by European leftists of the postwar period.

Contemporary commentators who discuss European-American relations ignore or turn away from this most momentous and dynamic fundamental aspect of the evolution in those relations: American education is today in the throes of an awesome cultural deracination, not only from its own, but from the entire Western —that is, predominantly European—cultural legacy. At the very least, we have to recognize that this decoupling at the higher or deeper levels of culture is racing in competition with the economic coupling or integration that (we are earnestly promised) will intensify steadily as a result of the "new Europe."

The effects of the cultural and intellectual changes I have been sketching are, of course, not the sole source of the deepening malaise of American life, but they surely contribute to it. One does not need to look far for symptoms of the debility to which I refer: the political apathy and disenchantment of Americans, borne out by steadily decreasing voting and steadily increasing disrespect for elected representatives; the powerful disinclination on the part of those representatives to shoulder the responsibilities, to run the risks, of truly governing the nation and facing the harsh choices such governing requires; the erosion of organized labor and of the solidarity and political awareness of the working class; the disintegration of the family and the dissolution of relations between the sexes, manifested in rampant sexual promiscuity, staggering rates of divorce, child abuse, child abandonment (especially by divorced fathers), single parent and parentless households, and households in which marriage has been unknown for generations; the ever-dwindling interest in, or appreciation of, serious literature, history, and art, which are more and more replaced, especially among the best-educated young people, by fascination with brutal and sentimental or escapist and mindless modes of entertainment; the decay of civilized life in the heart of our major cities, at once fueled by and manifested in the appalling incidence of drug consumption.

Never has there been so much evocation of "community," "bonding," "empathy," "nurture," and "gentleness," and never has there been so icy and thorough a disconnectedness between women and men, between generations, between fellow citizens and workers and neighbors. With the erosion of the supports in tradition, religion, and reason for shared ties of reverence and meaning, "individualism"—a word coined by Tocqueville as the name of the peculiarly American pathology he so presciently diagnosed—becomes more and more the hallmark of American existence.

As Christopher Lasch put it in a guest column in the *New York Times* (December 27, 1989), speaking of the "state of almost unbearable, though mostly inarticulate, agony" he finds "young people in our society are living in":

They experience the world only as a source of pleasure and pain. The culture at their disposal provides so little help in ordering the world that experience comes to them in the form merely of direct stimulation or deprivation, without much symbolic mediation. . . . We have failed to provide them with a culture that claims to explain the world or links the experience of one generation to those that came before and to those that will follow.

In reaction to the growing emptiness and isolation of existence, Americans tend more and more to manifest what the *Economist* has decried (in an unsigned editorial of July 28, 1990) as "decadent Puritanism": "an odd combination of ducking responsibility and telling everyone else what to do." The decadence, the editorial shrewdly observes, "lies in too readily blaming others for problems, rather than accepting responsibility oneself," in "a habit of blaming government and expecting help from government," in an educational tendency to replace the cultivation of self-discipline with the demand for unearned self-esteem. The "Puritanism" lies in an intensifying demand for "correct" thinking, especially in the realms of race, sex, health, and "multiculturalism." "A conformist tyranny of the majority," the *Economist* warns, "is creeping into America."

The Renewal of European Liberalism

Yet why should one think that this disquieting portrait of the American educational and cultural scene does not also indicate the future toward which Europe itself is hurtling? Do not many of the planners of the future European Community intend precisely to create a more efficient and effective, more advanced or sophisticated, version of American culture and existence? This indeed, or something close to it, is one possible version of the European unity that hovers before us on the horizon: a Swedish California from the Urals to the Atlantic, administered by a bloodless bureaucratic Areopagus.

It was in revulsion at this possible future that Nietzsche coined the term "good European," planting the words as a battle standard around which to rally the "free spirits" who would launch the counterrevolution against this ultimate degradation of the human spirit. Nietzsche saw before us the specter of a coming world, centered in Europe, of dwarfed homunculi living lives without dedication, without reverence, without shame, without rank, without the sense of tragedy and nobility bred only in suffering; he foresaw beings whom he termed "the last men," inhabiting in smug satisfaction a world devoid of shattering challenges and gripping spiritual competition; he predicted the emergence of quasi-humans whose passions were drowned in a tepid sea of self-centered calculation and superficial, self-excusing universal brotherhood, a sea that washed away the very possibility of essentially exclusive love and lasting friendship:

The time is come, for humanity to set itself its goal. The time is come, for man to plant the seed of his highest hope.

His soil is still rich enough. But this soil will one day be poor and domesticated, and no tall tree will anymore be able to grow out of it.

Alas! The time is coming, when man will no longer shoot the arrow of his longing beyond man, and the string of his bow will have forgotten how to whir!

I say to you: one must still have chaos in oneself in order to be able to give birth to a dancing star. I say to you: you still have chaos in yourselves.

Alas! The time is coming, when man will no longer give birth to any star. Alas! The time is coming of the most contemptible man, the man who can no longer have contempt for himself.

Behold! I show you *the last man.*

"What is love? What is creation? What is longing? What is a star?"—thus asks the last man, and he blinks.

The earth has become small, and on it hops the last man, who makes everything small. His species is ineradicable like the flea-beetle; the last man is the most long-lived.

"We have invented happiness"—say the last men, and they blink.

They have left the regions where it was hard to live: for one needs to be warm. One still loves one's neighbor and rubs against him: for one needs to be warm.

Becoming ill and harboring mistrust are in their eyes sinful: one goes one's way with caution. A fool, whoever still stumbles over stones or men!

A little poison now and then: that makes for pleasant dreams. And much poison in the end, for an agreeable death.

One still works, for work is a form of entertainment. But one is careful, lest the entertainment become too gripping.

One no longer becomes poor or rich: both require too much exertion. Who still wants to rule? Who still wants to obey? Both require too much exertion.

No shepherd and *one* herd! Everyone wants the same, everyone is the same: whoever feels they are different go voluntarily to the madhouse.

"In the old days the entire world was insane"—say the most refined, and they blink.

One is clever and knows everything that has ever happened: so there is no end of ridicule. One still quarrels, but one is soon reconciled—otherwise the digestion might be affected.

One has one's little pleasure for the day and one's little pleasure for the night: but one pays honor to health.

"We have invented happiness"—say the last men, and they blink.

And here ended the first speech of Zarathustra, which is also called "the prologue": for at this point the cry and delight of the crowd interrupted him. "Give us this last man, O Zarathustra"—they cried—"make us into these last men!"

(*Thus Spake Zarathustra*, Prologue, sec. 5)

So transfixed was Nietzsche by this nightmare possibility that he was seduced into a harsh hatred of democracy, of liberalism, of rationalism, of Christianity, and of humanism. Behind and between his lines lurks the dark shadow of fascism. Nietzsche was no fascist, and he would have recoiled from that movement with horror; he loathed anti-Semitism (the Jews were to be at the core of the new European nobility he envisioned), and he held nationalism, especially Bismarckian nationalism, in contempt. But he and some of his greatest followers helped spawn fascism, with their terribly intemperate and unsound identification of liberal democracy with its basest potential outcome.

We have survived the ensuing nightmare, a nightmare that rivaled any Nietzsche imagined, and we must fight against those who would belittle or obscure the renewed commitment to our common humanity, universal reason, freedom of speech and conscience, private property rights, and competitive representative government—the renewed commitment that is our greatest spiritual fruit of the holocaust.

The Western European democracies must summon the will and the wisdom to keep alive the deepest spirit of the North Atlantic Treaty Organization, while opening avenues along which, slowly but surely, the Eastern European peoples can find a way to join in the European Economic Community and eventually even in an enlarged and rededicated Grand Alliance. For although NATO was indeed born in response to the fear of Soviet communist imperialism, its deepest impulse was derived from Winston Churchill in his great speeches of 1938 outlining the strategy of a new European alliance based on "Arms and the Covenant." Churchill's presentation of what he called "The Choice for Europe" was meant to be a choice, not simply for the present or the near future, but for generations to come (Churchill 1941, 17–27). The strategy was one of international law backed up by a mighty sword in the hand of legal justice. The alliance was to be directed, not simply against Nazi Germany, or imperial Japan, or fascist Italy and Spain, or communist Russia, but against any and all dictatorial regimes that endangered the security of, or progress toward, liberal democracy. It was a defensive alliance against threats from left or right, whether ultramodern or atavistic. But as the world has been reminded in its struggle against Saddam Hussein, such an alliance requires more than adherence to law and principle: it requires the will to enforce law and principle. As Churchill said in his speech of 1938 on "Civilization":

There are few words which are used more loosely than the word "Civilization." What does it mean? It means a society based upon the opinion of civilians. It means that violence, the rule of warriors and despotic chiefs, the conditions of camps and warfare, of riot and tyranny, gives place to parliaments where laws are made, and independent courts of justice in which over long periods those laws are maintained. That is Civilization—and in its soil grow continually freedom, comfort and culture. When Civilization reigns in any country, a wider and less harassed life is afforded to the masses of the people. The traditions of the past are cherished, and the inheritance bequeathed to us by former wise or valiant men becomes a rich estate to be enjoyed and used by all.

The central principle of Civilization is the subordination of the ruling authority to the settled customs of the people and to their will as expressed through the Constitution. . . .

But it is vain to imagine that the mere perception or declaration of right principles, whether in one country or in many countries, will be of any value unless they are supported by those qualities of civic virtue and manly courage—aye, and by those instruments and agencies of force and science which in the last resort must be the defense of right and reason.

Civilization will not last, freedom will not survive, peace will not be kept, unless a very large majority of mankind unite together to defend them and show themselves possessed of a constabulary power before which barbaric and atavistic forces will stand in awe.   (Churchill 1941, 45–46)

If we are to adapt and apply Churchill's vision to our unprecedented situation, the Western democracies must revivify their understandings of, and commitments to, their highest purposes.

To this end, the Eastern Europeans, along with Asian heroes such as those who fell in Tiananmen Square, may have a very great deal to contribute. For it is in the East that the fervent revolutionary enthusiasm for the principles of liberal democracy and the free market has come to life once again. It is from the East, perhaps, that the sophisticated and jaded Western elites may be inspired by a desire to think through and thus recover, but also enlarge and enrich, the basic philosophic principles on which our constitutional and economic freedoms are based. It is from the East that the antidote may come for the debilitating relativism that now seeps its poison through the mass consciousness of the Western democracies. Pope John Paul II addressed to the young people at Jasna Gora (June 18, 1983) some winged words:

Perhaps at times we envy the French, the Germans, or the Americans, because their names are not linked to such a costly victory, because they are free so much more easily, whereas our Polish freedom costs us so much. I will not draw comparisons. I will only say that the thing which costs us so much is the very thing which is treasured. Let us not desire a Poland which costs us nothing.[5]

Yet these words of John Paul II—indeed, John Paul himself and everything he stands for—remind us that it may be doubted whether a collective rededication to the unflinching defense of our liberal principles is an adequate response to the dangers Nietzsche discerned, and to which the American predicament seems to lend more and more weight. I believe that if we are not in the long run to confirm Nietzsche's greatest fears, we must come to terms with, and act in response to, the deep truths underlying those fears. Among other things, we must recognize the possibility that fascism, or something like fascism—no doubt in a new, superficially softened, and perhaps even leftish guise—remains a continuing danger as a possible reaction to liberal democracy if, or insofar as, this system of government and way of life fails to avert its own degeneration toward the world described in Nietzsche's nightmare vision. For it may well be doubted whether human nature will tolerate for long the banalization of human existence. There is a searing insight in Nietzsche's oft-quoted aphorism: "Man will rather make the void his purpose than be void of purpose" (*Genealogy of Morals*, Third Essay, secs. 1 and 28).

5. Quoted from Vatican Radio in Jonathan Luxmoore, "Polish Catholicism under Fire," *Ethics & International Affairs* 1 (1987): 186.

The Question, and the Task, for Europe

What then might be the distinctive aims, in our present situation, of "good Europeans" who would chart a course for Europe—and eventually for the world—between the Scylla of rootless, spiritually empty, cosmopolitan individualism and the Charybdis represented by the fascist fate of Nietzsche's political message? This seems to me the most momentous question for good Europeans of our time. Given the significance of the answer for the entire world, Europeans will perhaps bear with non-Europeans who feel bound to try to make some cautious contribution to their reflections on the question.

It seems to me that Europeans ought to seek out and attempt to articulate their highest potentialities: not so as naively to make those potentialities directly into a program or goal for the immediate, or even foreseeable, future, but because some vision—rational and grounded in empirical reality, but nonetheless transcendent of the present—is needed to provide moral compass points. It is perhaps less misleading to speak of a vision of Europe's tasks or duties rather than of her potentialities; as Leo Strauss once wrote, "we cannot define our tasks by our powers, for our powers become known to us through performing our tasks; it is better to fail nobly than to succeed basely" (Strauss 1983, 147). Strauss was speaking of the tasks of individuals, but we can with great caution and some hesitation apply his statement also to nations, so long as we never forget the deepest truth of liberalism: that while human nobility must take root in attachment to public purpose, true human depth lies ultimately not in collectivities of any sort, but only in the individual human being, in gathering the forces of one's own soul. To quote Strauss again, "only individuals, and not nations, can engage in the quest for truth, and this quest unites individuals belonging to different nations"; this is what distinguishes "genuine cosmopolitanism from spurious and superficial cosmopolitanism" (Strauss 1959, 240).

I suggest that we might best begin by looking for guidance and inspiration to the greatest political philosopher of the liberal tradition, arguably the greatest political thinker the West has produced in the postclassical era: Montesquieu. Montesquieu was a truly good European, in every wise and humane sense of that term; but he is also the most direct philosophic link between America and Europe, for he exerted an unrivaled influence on the founding of the United States. He was the most profound philosophic source of European nationalism and at the same time the most profoundly cosmopolitan spirit that has ever walked the earth. He castigated the politically destructive moral fanaticism of both religious and atheistic zealots. He taught the foundation in justice for the subordination of religious institutions to liberal civil authority, while suggesting that no just and humane society could do without a properly tempered religious consciousness. *L'Esprit des lois*, with its infinitely capacious humanity, its manly but delicate nobility, and its supremely flexible but uncompromising rationalism, is the only work I know that might be said to convey the richness and unity of European liberalism that we are seeking to recover.

Montesquieu celebrated the English system of government, but at the same time warned against the colorless, deeroticized, individualistic, and materialistic, way of life protected and even fostered by that system. Montesquieu blazed a trail for the future of Europe that would lead, not to the anglicization of Europe, but to the cultivation, on the basis of a commitment to natural rights, of both a sober and tempered national diversity and invigorating competition among the distinctive and somewhat disharmonious historical geniuses of the various European peoples.

Obviously, we cannot simply return to the world Montesquieu confronted or to his precise prescriptions. But his way of conceiving the problem, and the promise, of a liberal, cosmopolitan *"Europe des patries"* (to borrow a phrase from Charles de Gaulle) can set us on the right track. The struggle against Marxism and fascism have taught us to treasure human rights and liberal constitutionalism. Human rights constitute the pediment, the basis of human security, dignity, and fraternity on which all decent European societies in the future must rest. But on this basis a new task arises: the challenge of elaborating an invigorating spiritual competition within the common European home among individuals representing mutually critical national and religious traditions.

If this competition is not to degenerate into a mere game, it must be serious. Ignorance or shallowness must hurt, must cause suffering that spurs us to self-consciousness. The stupefying pall of relativism must be shredded in the name of a common dialectical struggle for the truth about virtue, God, and existence. The highest task of good Europeans would then be not only to define the foundations of human nature, but to try make out something of its peaks and heights; not only to guarantee the dignity that is common to every human being, but to seek also to clarify and honor those qualities that distinguish and make truly admirable the few who can and should be beacons for the rest; not only to secure human rights, but, on the basis of those rights, to explore competing human virtues. No doubt high among those virtues will be the thoughtful compassion and generosity that ought to be exhibited in Europe's concern for the suffering mass of mankind dwelling outside Europe and North America, the vast majority of our fellows who lack the security and opportunity implicitly demanded by the most basic human rights. In this regard, Europeans will have to learn to avoid the pitfalls of both sentimental pity and obtrusive paternalism; they may be helped if they remember the challenging, "as yet unanswered, question" Nietzsche addressed to what he called "the moral fashion of a commercial society": the question "whether one is of *more use* to another by immediately leaping to his side and *helping* him—which help can only be superficial where it does not become a tyrannical seizing and transforming—or by *forming* something out of oneself that the other can behold in joy" (*Daybreak*, No. 174).

A Europe that set itself the goal I am now limning might find itself drawn back to the deepest wellsprings of its own diverse spiritual legacy. Europe might reopen, with a receptivity that has not been seen since Goethe, the great biblical and classical heritages of its thought and art and civic life: not as museum specimens, or as weapons of ideological propaganda, but as living texts of discordant authority, and hence of compelling engagement and serious intellectual struggle.

Unfortunately, we can look with only qualified hope to Western European intellectuals, too many of whom are infatuated by their own endless petty squabbles and evanescent ideological infatuations. It is therefore also to Eastern Europe, and to Russia—to the Russia of the great dissidents—that I would look for intellectual leadership in the new European vocation whose outlines I am attempting to discern. As Czeslaw Milosz observed in his essay "The Telltale Scar,"

All the suffering of millions of human beings terrorized by totalitarian governments would be sentenced to total oblivion if something precious is not saved from the disaster, namely, the discovery made by those people of a clear line dividing good from evil, truth from lie. Central European countries made this discovery even as the literati of America and Western Europe were treating the opposition of good and evil as a somewhat obsolete notion. (Milosz 1989, 27)

In Eastern Europe the divine spark has a presence that has for too long been missing in the West: thought is serious, evil has a meaning, heroism makes demands. Three reservoirs of human depth—love of country, religion, and art—still brim with juices of life that are becoming scarcer in the West. Only a fool would try to deny that the first two of these are also potentially Pandora's jars of war and suffering. Recent experiences in Russia are reminders of the risks of nationalist and religious strife. Nonetheless, it would be an even greater fool who denied that nationalism in some form—sullen, neglected, alienated, and ugly; or welcomed, tempered, enlightened, and guided by a Montesquieuian liberal rationalism that distinguishes love of country from hatred of what is foreign—may be the device of destiny in the coming century.

The amazing sort of love of country or patriotism that characterizes the awakening Eastern European democratic movements—amazing not least because it has somehow survived the crude manipulations and degradations of communist pseudo-patriotism and chauvinism—may have something important to teach Western liberals. The womb of human nobility is reverence; and for most men, most of the time, reverence is reverence for one's own heritage, one's own tradition, one's own past and its heroic exemplars. Patriotism thus understood is the essential bridge between the isolated or lost individual and the meaningful world of passionately thoughtful individuals seeking together, in harmony and in argument, the truth about the most important questions of human grandeur and decadence. Patriotism thus understood is the bridge from the state of nature to the "genuine cosmopolitanism" of which Strauss speaks. Distinguishing his love of country from what is all too often called "patriotism," Václav Havel put it this way in a 1988 interview:

I am Czech. This was not my choice, it was fate. I've lived my whole life in this country. This is my language, this is my home. I live here like everyone else. I don't feel myself to be patriotic, because I don't feel that to be Czech is to be something more than French, or English, or European, or anybody else. God—I don't know why—wanted me to be a Czech. It was not my choice. But I accept it, and I try to do something for my country because I live here.[6]

As Havel's formulation suggests, there is a link between healthy love of country and the healthy religiousness of which we see strong signs in the renascence of Eastern European freedom. The Roman Catholic faith, liberalized by decades of opposition to Marxist atheism, has lent to the Polish Solidarity movement a patience and an appreciation for self-sacrifice and self-overcoming that cannot help but remind even the most jaded secular Westerner of the enormous legacy of moral virtue and vision that we owe to the biblical traditions that dominate our common heritage (cf. Michnik 1979). From Poland and from Eastern Europe in general, we may learn again the benefits of making room in our public life for some divine presence, with the attendant suprahuman moral limitations and sanctions. One might add that if we do not learn this lesson, we may reap the whirlwind of crude

6. Quoted in "A Master of Parable," *New York Times*, December 29, 1989.

and fanatic reaction that seems always to follow attempts to exclude the sacred from a nation's collective self-consciousness. Lech Walesa has said more than once, and only half-jokingly, "If I did not believe in God, I would be a very dangerous man."

Today, it is in Eastern Europe that the decisive inner unities binding art and life—the unity between art and justice or political responsibility, the unity between beauty and morality, the unity between art and god—still inform the calling of the artist and still bless the response that calling evokes in large segments of the masses, who must be the audience for any truly vital art. It is in Eastern Europe that the artist seems still to recognize his task as mediator between mundane daily existence and those moments that arrest and transfigure the forces of mind and heart. The writers from the East remind us of the heroic moral demands that art can make, but of greater and more lasting significance is the reminder they have given us that the artist is both the conscience and the leader of the consciousness of peoples. As Milosz wrote in an early poem entitled "Dedication":

> What is poetry which does not save
> Nations or people?

Or, in his words written in 1950, and engraved thirty years later on the Solidarity monument in the Gdansk shipyard:

> You who wronged a simple man,
> Do not feel safe.
> The poet remembers.

As the example of Milosz makes obvious, this does not mean that poetry is "politicized." Quite the contrary: it means that poetry forces politics, and the rest of life, to look beyond the trivialities into which politics and ordinary life usually and necessarily find themselves slipping or confined. In bringing about this elevation, the artist invokes not only the tragic or sublime but also the comic muse—as has been demonstrated to such effect in works like Kundera's *Book of Laughter and Forgetting* and Havel's *Memorandum*. "It seems," Havel said in a 1985 interview, "that in Central Europe, what is most earnest has a way of blending, in a particularly tense manner, with what is most comic. It seems that it is precisely the dimension of distance, of rising above ourselves and making light of ourselves, that lends our concerns just the right shattering seriousness."[7]

In the East, art is not just a game; it is not a separate compartment of

7. Quoted in ibid.

life into which people step when they want high-level diversion, or into which they flee when they want to escape life and responsibility, above all the responsibility of citizenship. In the East, art is still intelligible in classical republican terms: as the heartbeat of life, and as the school of civic virtue.

The voices of the civic-spirited artists of the East recall us to the peroration of Churchill's address broadcast to Europe on January 20, 1940:

> Let the great cities of Warsaw, of Prague, of Vienna banish despair even in the midst of their agony. Their liberation is sure. The day will come when the joybells will ring again throughout Europe, and when victorious nations, masters not only of their foes but of themselves, will plan and build in justice, in tradition, and in freedom a house of many mansions where there will be room for all.
>
> (Churchill 1941, 216)

It is just barely possible that America might once again begin to learn from a spiritually renascent Europe what it means to look with an eye that intently searches for the truth rather than "appreciates aesthetically." From Eastern Europe we might learn again what it means to argue, not for the sake of victory or display, but with a thirst to know that scorns vanity, pretension, and popularity. From the spiritual stimulus that could conceivably emerge out of the ashes of the Cold War, America just might be drawn into a dialectical reaction that would wrench us from our spiritual doldrums—into a new, acutely felt need to define and defend what we believe to be admirable. It can surely do us no harm to begin to reflect on what sort of thinking and arguing would be entailed in trying to rise to such a challenge.

6 / The Need to Rethink Our Rights and Our Republicanism

The protection of human rights is the distinguishing glory of modern Western constitutionalism; and the American constitutional tradition can claim a place second to none in the steadfastness of its championing of the rights of the individual. Americans believe with good reason that the more seriously human rights are regarded, the more secure and elevated the human condition. In the past half century, we have learned through bitter experience that theorists, political leaders, and governments who resist or cast doubt on the centrality of human rights usually turn out, whether they intend it or not, to be sources of oppression and misery. Yet our justified confidence in the overwhelming prominence we give to rights carries with it grave specific dangers.

In the first place, we are prey to the temptation to believe that in individual rights all good things are, or ought, to be found: we slip too easily into believing that moral claims that cannot be formulated in terms of rights, or that are not reducible to or derivable from rights, are therefore unintelligible, if not bogus. Yet we are confronted time and again with moral questions, with moral dimensions of our existence, that cannot be done justice in terms of individual rights. The most massive reminder in the present situation is the abortion issue. More and more, sensitive men and women are aware that the questions posed by abortion—and by the family altogether—cannot adequately be articulated in terms of rights, contractual obligations, or even mutual respect, but require in addition an articulation in terms of duties, responsibilities, and a love or reverence that go well beyond individual rights and mutual respect for individual rights. The same sort of observation applies, if perhaps less urgently at the present moment, to questions of religion, statesmanship, citizenship, patriotism, education, and our posture toward the nature that encompasses and nurtures us all.

In the second place, our repeated discovery that the language and conceptual framework of individual rights is incapable of fully embracing some of the most important dimensions of our moral situation as human beings may lead us to react with an unhealthy disillusionment. Allied with other powerful and deleterious relativistic tendencies of contemporary thought, this experience tempts us to think that our commitment to human rights may, after all, be nothing more than our commitment: nothing more than the conditioned worldview we have inherited by chance or by some mysterious process of historical acculturation. In other words, we are all too easily left doubting whether there exists any genuinely rational argument underlying our most basic and treasured constitutional commitment. As a consequence, we may be induced to try to cram into the language and concept of rights whatever each of us supposes to be admirable or advantageous. Once set on these tracks, we tend to transform discussions of rights, and claims of rights, in the direction of an ideological warfare that slips further and further beyond the bounds of reasoned discourse and beyond the reach of the civic or humane fellowship constituted by such discourse.

To combat these dangerous proclivities, and, more important, to reinvigorate a reasoned commitment to rights more generally—to prevent the routinization and obfuscation of our commitment to rights—we need to return again and again to a rediscovery and reconsideration of the original arguments for a polity grounded in rights. By studying those arguments, by reenacting them ourselves, we are afforded the privilege of seeing the commitment to rights afresh, in its essentially controversial character. We are led to recognize again that, and why, rational arguments are necessary to *ground* the commitment to rights. We transform mere "commitment"—that is, conformity—into critical, and therefore independent, assent. In the best case, we cease to be slaves to an ideology or culture of rights and become free men and women who truly own our rights, and thus truly own our selves, because we truly know our rights and thus truly know who we are. The philosophers who first advanced, and the statesmen who accepted and modified, the arguments for rights-oriented civil societies were compelled to see the commitment to rights in a perspective whose breadth we can only with difficulty and with their help retrieve. They were forced to see more clearly and precisely the controversial character of the commitment to rights because they were rebelling against an earlier outlook, of great moral and intellectual power, that did not make individual rights central. They were obliged to come to terms with searching moral, religious, and philosophic critics from the past and in the present who were enlivened by an awareness that the commitment to rights was neither necessary nor as yet well established. The first theorists of rights could not help but recognize the limits of what could be expected from their new, controversial commitment to rights. They saw what would have to be left behind, or at least subordinated, in the new dispensation. Their hopes for and expectations of the new political and constitutional systems dedicated to the protection of individual rights were as a result more tempered than ours. In general, the statesmen, if not the philosophers, who founded the new constitutional systems were open to the idea that important residues of the earlier—and in their eyes to some extent nobler—traditions could and should be preserved within the new societies they were in the process of creating.

In the case of the Founders of the United States, this meant above all the preservation—or, indeed, the reinvigoration—of the great classical tradition of republican self-government. Rights and republicanism may be said to be the twin pillars of the American political tradition. These pillars are planted in the soil of our history so firmly and seem to reinforce each other so strongly, that it is hard for us at first to credit any suggestion that there may be some tension or problem in their coexistence. Yet as soon as we step even for a moment outside the U.S. constitutional tradition, we are compelled to acknowledge that the linkage between republicanism and rights is much more ambiguous in the historical record than it at first appears to Americans. Republicanism is a leading theme of Western political thought from its first recorded beginnings in classical Greece. But the idea of rights—meaning to say, *human* rights, *natural* rights, the "rights of man," rights understood to belong to all human beings as individuals, and understood to constitute the moral foundation of legitimate political authority—becomes a clear theme only in the mid seventeenth century in northern Europe, and especially in England.

What is more, this relatively modern rise to preeminence of the idea of rights by no means necessarily entailed a preference for republican government. James Madison, writing in the fourteenth *Federalist Paper*, underlines the fact that in arguing for republicanism, the Americans face the opposition and authority of "some celebrated authors, whose writings have had a great share in forming the modern standard of political opinions." A fountainhead of this "modern standard of political opinions" is Thomas Hobbes, who may justly claim the honor of being the most powerful and influential theoretical originator of the focus on individual rights. Precisely because he believes that individual rights are fundamental, Hobbes is no friend of republicanism. Hobbes argues forcefully that to secure individual rights, the best form of government is a centralized monarchy, whereas republicanism, generally speaking, tends to threaten individual rights.

At the head of Hobbes's arguments in chapter 19 of *Leviathan* is an analysis of the relationship between the public and the private interest as exhibited in the histories of republics and monarchies. Everyone who bears or shares in sovereign political authority, Hobbes begins by observing,

> though he be careful in his politic person to procure the common interest; yet he is more, or no less careful to procure the private good of himself, his family, kindred, and friends; and for the most part, if the public interest chance to cross the private, he prefers the private: for the passions of men, are commonly more potent than their reason. From whence it follows, that where the public and private interest are most closely united, there is the public most advanced. Now in monarchy, the private interest is the same with the public. The riches, power, and honour of a monarch arise only from the riches, strength, and reputation of his subjects. For no king can be rich, nor glorious, nor secure, whose subjects are either poor, or contemptible, or too weak through want or dissention, to maintain a war against their enemies.

Republics, in contrast, are compelled to demand from their leaders and citizens that they in some measure transcend, or even sacrifice, what appear to be their private interests. But given human nature, citizens will either circumvent this demand or seek some kind of compensation, and the result is inevitably hypocrisy, dishonest posturing, and covert exploitation of the public. These effects are intensified by the fact that republican policymaking entails, to a far greater degree than policymaking in a monarchy, endless public disputes within the pluralistic highest councils. Sooner or later the disputants start organizing factions and issuing rhetorical appeals to the populace, thus setting in motion the vicious spiral of hatred, fear, violent instability, and endless insecurity for every individual. "No tyrant was ever so cruel as a popular assembly." Hobbes aims his attack on republicanism in the name of rights against the moralistic ancient republican theorists, especially Aristotle, but he speaks with equal fervor against the radically different, and radically amoral, republican principles of Machiavelli and his followers, who revived admiration for the imperialistic republicanism of the Romans. The anti-Machiavellianism of Hobbes's thought is trumpeted on the first page of the epistle dedicatory to his first published work, *On the Citizen.*[1]

Later votaries of individual rights did not go nearly so far as Hobbes, but many—including notably Montesquieu and Hume—did raise doubts as to whether republics, with their natural proclivity to faction, tended to secure rights (or curb their own tendencies to violate rights) as effectively as well-designed monarchies like the English one—that is, monarchies whose *mixed* constitutions included the checking and balancing advantages of a religious establishment, a hereditary, and hence stable, nobility, and a powerful, but legally limited, popular assembly. This kind of doubt was one important source of some thoughtful Anti-Federalists' animadversions against any attempt to establish in the American context a consolidated national republic that would eclipse the state republics, with their smaller scale, greater simplicity, and closeness to the people. As the eloquent Patrick Henry put it in the Virginia Ratifying Convention on June 9, 1788:

Tell me not of checks on paper; but tell me of checks founded on self-love. The English Government is founded on self-love. This powerful irresistible stimulus of self-love has saved that Government. It has interposed that hereditary nobility between the King and Commons. . . . Here is a consideration which prevails, in my mind, to pronounce the British Government, superior in this respect to any Government that ever was in any country. . . . Have you a resting place like the British Government? . . . Where are your checks? You have no hereditary Nobility—An order of men, to whom human eyes can be cast up for relief: For, says the Constitution, there is no title of nobility to be granted.[2]

Similarly, John Francis Mercer, a veteran of the Revolution and a former member of Congress and governor of Maryland, from which state he was a delegate to the Constitutional Convention, turned against the Constitution, explaining his stand in part as follows (in his address to the members of the conventions of New York and Virginia):

The most blind admirer of this Constitution must in his heart confess that it is as far inferior to the British Constitution, of which it is an imperfect imitation[,] as darkness is to light—In the British Constitution, the rights of Men, the primary objects of the

---

1. Thomas Hobbes, *Leviathan, or, the Matter Forme and Power of a Commonwealth Ecclesiasticall and Civil,* ed. Michael Oakeshott (Oxford: Basil Blackwell, 1960), 122–25, 216–18, 221–22; *Behemoth, or, The Long Parliament,* ed. Ferdinand Toennies (London: Frank Cass, 1969), 23. Hobbes attacks the influence of Aristotelian republican theory, and, more generally, "the reading of the books of policy, and histories of the ancient Greeks, and Romans," as a cause of disloyalty to monarchs and hence as a threat to the security of individual rights: *Leviathan,* 214, 447–48; *Behemoth,* 3, 43, 56.
2. *The Complete Anti-Federalist,* ed. Herbert J. Storing (Chicago: University of Chicago Press, 1981), 5:233–34.

social Compact—are fixed on an immovable foundation and clearly defined and ascertained by their Magna Charta, their Petition of Rights and Bill of Rights[;] and their Effective administration by ostensible Ministers, secures Responsibility. . . . And after all Government by Representation (unless confirmed in its views and conduct by the constant inspection, immediate superintendance, and frequent interference and control of the People themselves on one side, or an hereditary nobility on the other, both of which orders have fixed and permanent views) is really only a scene of perpetual rapine and confusion. . . . may we never have cause to look back with regret on that period when connected with the Empire of Great Britain, We were *happy, secure,* and *free.*[3]

In contrast, the Federalists or proponents of the new Constitution were far less trusting of small-scale republics, and considerably more willing to take their chances with the possibility of creating a sound large-scale republic through proper institutional checks and balances. But they were by no means unanimous or unqualified in their support for republicanism, though they were less likely than the Anti-Federalists to express their grave doubts in public. That Alexander Hamilton was deeply moved by such doubts is clear from his remarkable speech at the Constitutional Convention on June 18. While "he was sensible" that, given public opinion in America, "it would be unwise to propose" a government "of any other form" than a republic, "in his private opinion he had no scruple in declaring, supported as he was by the opinions of so many of the wise & good, that the British Govt. was the best in the world: and that he doubted much whether any thing short of it would do in America." Hamilton joined in "the praise bestowed by Mr. Neckar on the British Constitution, namely, that it is the only Govt. in the world 'which unites public strength with individual security.'" And "as to the Executive, it seemed to be admitted that no good one could be established on Republican principles." Hamilton accordingly went on to propose "that we ought to go as far in order to attain stability and permanency, as republican principles will admit. Let one branch of the legislature hold their places for life or at least during good-behaviour. Let the Executive also be for life." On June 26, Hamilton "acknowledged himself not to think favorably of Republican Government," despite or because he "professed himself to be as zealous an advocate for liberty as any man whatever, and trusted he should be as willing a martyr to it though he differed as to the form in which it was most eligible."[4]

The doubts as to the harmony between republicanism and the securing

3. Ibid., 5:105–6.
4. *The Records of the Federal Convention of 1787,* ed. Max Farrand (New Haven: Yale University Press, 1966), 1:288–89, 424.

of individual rights (or liberty conceived in terms of such rights) cannot be said to be obviously contradicted by the history of republicanism prior to the founding of the United States—as the ninth *Federalist Paper* candidly concedes. Certainly, republican theory, as well as practice, prior to Hobbes—one might well argue, prior to the founding of the United States—can only with difficulty be associated with the idea of "human rights" or the "rights of man." It is doubtful, to say the least, whether any text that has come down to us from the Greco-Roman world ever mentions anything that can properly be translated as "human rights," "natural rights," or the "rights of man." Concern for fundamental rights, of a kind, does figure in classical republican political life and theory. But this is not the chief concern of the classical republic; and insofar as rights are of concern, the rights in question are mainly rights of *citizens* or specific groups of citizens (families, neighborhoods, classes). The rights protected in classical republicanism are typically of two sorts: rights defined by, and within, a particular legal and political order; and the rights of the whole political society, both vis-à-vis other societies and vis-à-vis individual citizens.

Belief in the sanctity of all human beings as such would seem to be a legacy of the biblical social and political tradition rather than the classical one. But the sanctity of mankind as the Bible conceives of it is rather different from either rights-oriented or republican conceptions of the sanctity of man and human society. The difference was understood by colonial Americans, as evidenced in John Cotton's noted pronouncement of 1636:

Democracy, I do not conceyve that ever God did ordeyne as a fitt government eyther for church or commonwealth. If the people be governors, who shall be governed? As for monarchy, and aristocracy, they are both of them clearly approoved, and directed in scripture, yet so as referreth the soveraigntie to Himselfe, and setteth up Theocracy in both, as the best forme of government in the commonwealth, as well as in the church.[5]

There are not even expressions in the Bible for "republic," "democracy," "human rights," or "natural rights." The Bible does indeed speak, and speak loudly, of justice or "righteousness" (and hardly ever of rights: see, for some rare examples, Ruth 4:6, Heb. 13:10, and Rev. 22:14). But the Bible understands righteousness fundamentally as obedience to a law that is not of man but of God. This law or legislation is from God not merely in the weak sense that it is the product of human attempts to take the divine as a

5. "Copy of a Letter from Mr. Cotton to Lord Say and Seal in the year 1636," in Thomas Hutchinson, *History of the Colony and Province of Massachusetts-Bay*, ed. Lawrence Shaw Mayo (Cambridge, Mass.: Harvard University Press, 1936), 1:415 (Appendix III).

standard. It is from God in the sense that it is, in fact, given by God Himself through his prophets. Divine law dictates mercy, humility, charity or love and loving-kindness, and above all a radical detachment from the things of this world and from trust in the things of this world—a detachment from merely human things—for the sake of God and an utter dependence upon God.

Thou shalt love the Lord thy God with all thy heart, and with all thy soul, and with all thy mind. This is the first and great commandment. And the second is like unto it, Thou shalt love thy neighbor as thyself. On these two commandments hang all the law and the prophets. (Matt. 22:37–39; cf. Deut. 6:5)

You shall be holy, for I, the Lord your God, am holy. You shall each revere his mother and his father, and keep my sabbaths: I the Lord am your God. Do not turn to idols or make molten images for yourselves: I the Lord am your God. . . . Love your neighbor as yourself: I am the Lord. You shall observe my laws. . . . The stranger who resides with you shall be to you as one of your citizens; you shall love him as yourself . . . you shall faithfully observe My laws: I the Lord make you holy. (Lev. 19–20)

If you reject my Laws and spurn My rules, so that you do not observe all My commandments and you break my covenant, I in turn will do this to you: I will wreak misery upon you . . . and if, for all that, you do not obey Me, I will go on to discipline you sevenfold for your sins, and I will break your proud glory. I will make your skies like iron. (Lev. 26)

Mankind is sacred, insofar as it is sacred, because it was created by and in the image of God: there is no "humanism" in the Bible.

Republicanism, it would then appear, is a nonbiblical genus of political society, of which one relatively new species (to which the United States belongs) is the republicanism that puts individual rights at the center of attention. What then *does* properly define the genus republicanism per se? What new qualification to historic republicanism was required, and what change in the original theoretical understanding of politics based on individual rights was needed, to make possible the new, close link between republicanism and rights we find in the American tradition? Is the new American synthesis of republicanism and individual rights altogether successful, or does there remain an important and troubling tension between the two? Do either of the elements, or does their synthetic combination in the American tradition, succeed in adequately coming to terms with the competing challenge posed by the biblical concept of human brotherhood ruled by divine, as opposed to merely human, law?

The Founders' Conception of Republicanism

We may begin the search for answers to these questions by looking more closely at how the Founders conceived of republicanism. The framers of the Constitution were so confident of the agreed meaning of "a republican form of government" that they included a guarantee of this form to every state without further explanation (Art. 4, sec. 4). What exactly was the meaning they seem to have thought would be generally understood?

Most who commented on this clause at the time of the framing conceived of the guarantee primarily as a bar to monarchy and hereditary aristocracy. More essentially or positively, they generally defined the guaranteed republicanism by the criterion of *popular sovereignty*, or majority rule, based on an underlying "social contract" or "compact" to which all citizens were presumed to have consented. This sovereignty of the people was understood to be properly expressed and channeled through representative legislative and executive institutions checked and balanced by the separation of powers, including an independent judiciary. As Madison put it in a famous passage of the thirty-ninth *Federalist*, a paper in which he explicitly refers to the Constitution's guarantee of the republican form of government,

If we resort for a criterion, to the different principles on which different forms of government are established, we may define a republic to be, or at least may bestow that name on, a government which derives all its powers directly or indirectly from the great body of the people, and is administered by persons holding their offices during pleasure for a limited period, or during good behaviour. It is *essential* to such a government that it be derived from the great body of the society, not from an inconsiderable proportion or a favored class of it.... It is *sufficient* for such a government that the persons administering it be appointed, either directly or indirectly, by the people; and that they hold their appointments by either of the tenures just specified.

Madison prefaces this passage with an admission, however, that the definition or criterion he here gives for republican government is controversial. In fact, he comes close to admitting that it finds at best only weak support in the previous tradition of political theory and history. He concedes, for example, that "Holland, in which no particle of the supreme authority is derived from the people, has passed almost universally under the denomination of a republic"; that the same is true of Venice, "where absolute power over the great body of the people is exercised in the most absolute manner by a small body of hereditary nobles"; that Poland and England have frequently been designated republics, despite the fact that their governments do not rest, except partially at best, on popular sovereignty (Poland, we may note in passing, included a guarantee of republican government in its Constitution).

Madison seems confident that his audience will agree on the "impropriety" of such undemocratic applications of the term *republic,* which "show," he claims, "the extreme inaccuracy with which the term has been used in political disquisitions." Indeed, throughout the *Federalist,* Madison sees a more plausible and urgent source of controversy to be those who insist on a criterion of republican government even *more* democratic or popular than his own. Against those who (either out of misplaced enthusiasm for "pure democracy" or a desire to discredit all democracy as unworkable) insist on identifying democracy with what he calls a "pure republic," in which "the people meet and exercise the government in person," Madison defends a *new* sort of representative democratic republic, resting on *"the total exclusion of the people, in their collective capacity,* from any share in" government (*Fed.* nos. 14, 63). This makes possible the famous "extended" republic whose basic principle and excellence as a cure for the fatal flaw of democracy—majoritarian faction and tyranny—Madison elaborates in the tenth *Federalist:* "Extend the sphere and you take in a greater variety of parties and interests; you make it less probable that a majority of the whole will have a common motive to invade the rights of other citizens; or if such a common motive exists, it will be more difficult for all who feel it to discover their own strength and to act in unison with each other."

Other prominent Federalists and Anti-Federalists were more candid than Madison as to the break with earlier republican tradition implied in this new American democratic or popular criterion for a republican government. The British Constitution, or more generally a mixed constitution that included monarchic and hereditary-aristocratic institutions together with a popular branch of the legislature, continued to be understood by some—most notably John Adams—as a kind of republic, albeit in a more traditional sense than what was becoming the standard American notion of one. The most learned Federalists and Anti-Federalists were ready to admit that the limitation of the term *republic* to governments resting ultimately on popular sovereignty or a social contract represented a democratic innovation. All were familiar with, even if they did not simply accept, the republican theory of Montesquieu, generally acknowledged as the greatest political theorist of the age. And the *Spirit of the Laws* (bk. 2, ch. 1) defines republican, in contrast to monarchic and despotic government, as "that in which the body of the people, *or only a part of the people* [my emphasis], has the sovereign power. . . . When, in a republic, the people in a body holds the sovereign power, this is a *Democracy*. When the sovereign power is in the hands of a part of the people, this gives itself the name *Aristocracy*."

Montesquieu's silence about the social contract, as well as his treatment of a strictly aristocratic government as a perfectly legitimate species of republican government, is an echo, if a muted and altered echo, of the great tradition of classical republicanism rooted in the political theories of Plato and Aristotle and in the practice of the cities of the Greco-Roman world. This classical republican tradition, as the Founders of the United States were to varying degrees aware, did *not* define republicanism in terms of a social contract or popular sovereignty, any more than it defined liberty in terms of individual rights. The classical republicans knew of the *idea* of a presumed social contract among individuals as the basis of legitimate authority; but Aristotle, in the preeminent classical republican discussion, rejects such a contractual grounding for civic justice and legitimacy as wholly inadequate:

Whoever takes thought for good laws gives careful consideration to civic virtue and vice. So that it is clear that it is necessary for every city that truly deserves the name, and is not one merely in a manner of speaking, to make virtue its care. Otherwise the community becomes just an alliance, differing from other alliances, with foreigners, only in the sharing of a location; and the law becomes a compact, as the sophist Lycophron has it—a guarantee to one another of the just things, not such as to make the citizens good and just. . . . So the city is not a partnership in a location, and for the sake of not committing injustice against each other and for transacting business. No: these things must necessarily be present if there is to be a city, but not even when all of them are present is there yet a city; a city is rather the partnership in the good life of households and families, for the sake of a fulfilled and self-sufficient existence. . . . And this, we declare, means living the happy and the noble life. Therefore the political community ought to be constituted for the sake of noble deeds and not for the sake of simply living together.

(*Politics* 1280b5–12, 30–35; 1281a1–4)

Similarly, the classical republicans were, of course, familiar with democracy, or government based on popular sovereignty, as one form of legitimate republicanism; but they can hardly be said to have regarded such government as the sole legitimate form of republicanism, let alone the best form. In Aristotle's classification of regimes, a classification that remained authoritative until the radical innovations of Machiavelli began to take hold, democracy was categorized as the least bad of the deviant kinds of government: democracy was classed as superior to tyranny and oligarchy, but inferior to mixed regimes, to aristocracy, and to monarchy.

It begins to appear, then, that we were mistaken in our initial inclination to suppose that republicanism is a genus, of which the new American type of republicanism, with its stress on rights, is a species. The difference between the new republicanism that came to the fore in the founding of the United States and the republicanism that comes down to us from the classics is a difference not between species but over the very definition and nature of the genus. The two types of republicanism dispute the basic principles of republicanism. But exactly what is the dispute, and how deeply does it run? If the classical understanding of republicanism, which had reigned in diverse forms for two thousand years prior to Machiavelli, did not conceive of republics in terms of the basic categories in which republics were defined by the new republicans of the eighteenth century, what then were the defining principles of republicanism in the classical understanding, and just how do these principles contrast with, and thus illuminate, the principles underlying the new American republicanism? To what extent does the republicanism of the Founders declare its independence from classical republicanism, and to what extent does it still hold in reserve a sustaining, if tenuous, lifeline anchored in that ancient vision?

PART III

Revitalizing the Intellectual Roots of Civic Culture

7 / Reinvigorating the Legacy of Classical Republicanism

Freedom and Equality

The massive primary concerns that preoccupy and distinguish republican government, in the classical view, are freedom and rule, conceived of as inseparable. For freedom in the republican sense entails some meaningful degree of self-rule; freedom seems incompatible with being ruled by others. To be free is to be, not an independent individual, but the citizen of a polity in which one has direct access to, or at the very least eligibility to participate in, sovereign office and the deliberations that authoritatively shape communal life.

This primary connotation of republicanism undergoes considerable transfiguration in the light of self-critical scrutiny. To begin with, of course, not everyone can rule all the time. Rule must be rotated. To be free is, then, to belong to a society in which one rules and is ruled in turn. To know how to rule as a republican, one must know how to submit to being ruled. One must know how to obey—not as a slave, under compulsion, but as a free citizen, animated by an inner and voluntary obedience. On closer examination, then, freedom is *not* incompatible with being ruled, but instead *presupposes* being ruled, and the capacities of character that make one a good—that is, truly obedient—follower. At the same time, knowing how to rule within a society where rule rotates means having the sympathy, rooted in experience, that allows one to treat one's subordinates as fellow citizens rather than as subjects. As Aristotle expresses it in his analysis of the meaning of republican rule:

There is a kind of rule according to which one rules over those who are similar in kind and who are free. This is what we call political rule, and it is necessary to learn it by being ruled—just as a cavalry commander is first a commanded cavalryman, a general is first subordinate, and similarly in the case of lower officers. Therefore this, too, is nobly said, that it is not possible to rule well without having been ruled. But the virtues of each position are different, and it is necessary for the *good* citizen to know and to be capable of being ruled and ruling; and this is the excellence of a citizen, knowing the rule over free persons from both perspectives.

(*Politics* 1277b7–16)

This excellence of citizenship is a standard by which all nominal citizens can and must be judged.

Citizens are and ought to be ranked—honored and dishonored—in accordance with their demonstrated capacity for free obedience. But if there are specific qualities of heart and mind according to which citizens are ranked in their capacity as *followers*, these qualities pale in comparison with the qualities by which citizens are ranked in their capacity as republican *leaders* or rulers. In a truly free and equal society, those who rule must *deserve* to rule. "Equality before the law" (*isonomia*) in the sense proposed by the Persian Otanes in Herodotus's famous debate over the best political system (*History* 3. 80–83) is an absurdity. Otanes's idea of "equality before the law" is a system in which all have equal "right" to rule, a system in which the most responsible offices are filled by lottery, a system in which no qualification or test is required for the privilege of voting on policy in a sovereign assembly; and this is as foolish or imprudent as the same Otanes's subsequent attempt, after his proposal fails to win support, to secure himself and his descendants from regulation by government or law. Otanes as depicted by Herodotus is the amiable, but all the more deluded, example of what we might call naive egalitarianism and libertarianism. As Isocrates, the greatest of all classical teachers of rhetoric, says in his famous oration in praise of the good old original democracy of Athens,

What contributed most to the noble management of the city was that, of the two recognized sorts of equality—the sort that apportions the same to everyone, and the sort that apportions what is fitting to each—they did not misunderstand which was most useful, but rejected as unjust the sort that holds in equal esteem the virtuous and wicked, and chose the one that honors and punishes according to the merit of each. Through this they managed the city, not selecting the rulers by lot from everyone, but selecting the best and the most capable for each task. For they expected that the other citizens would also tend to resemble those who supervised affairs.

(*Areopagiticus* 21–22)

Equality before the law (*isonomia*) in the reasonable or correct sense, equal republican access to or eligibility for office, turns out on analysis to mean equal opportunity to earn the trust of one's fellow citizens on the basis of proven merit and potential.

Civic Virtue and the Rule of Law

The "virtues" or qualities of character that ought to be taken into account in determining merit are in the main well known, in both their nature and their relative ranking, to all sensible citizens who have any experience of public life. At the foundation of the list are the virtues reasonably demanded of all citizens, followers as well as leaders. These include a sense of shame or reverence, courage, moderation or self-control, truthfulness, justice, especially obedience to law, and piety. Then there are the rarer excellences that begin to distinguish those who deserve their fellow citizens' respect and trust as candidates for positions of authority: generosity, noble ambition, pride, justice in the sense of a quasi-paternal concern for the common good, and, finally, reigning over all these more strictly moral qualities, a complementary intellectual insight, prudence, or practical judgment and wisdom (*phronēsis*) that crowns what we all call "statesmanship" (*politikē*). Continuing his definition of civic excellence in the passage we quoted a moment ago, Aristotle employs a striking image: "Practical wisdom [*phronēsis*] is the only virtue peculiar to the ruler; for the other virtues would seem to be necessarily common to the ruled and the rulers, while for the ruled there is not a virtue of practical wisdom, but in its place true opinion: the one ruled is like the flutemaker, the ruler is like the flute player or the user" (*Politics* 1277b25–30).

A sound republic will, then, be one in which the ruling offices are distributed as much as possible according to virtuous merit, and in which those who possess such merit are given the freest and fullest opportunity possible to exercise their capacities. Thomas Jefferson restated this basic classical republican thesis in his letter to John Adams of October 28, 1813:

I agree with you that there is a natural aristocracy among men. The grounds of this are virtue and talents. . . . There is also an artificial aristocracy founded on wealth and birth, without either virtue or talents; for with these it would belong to the first class. The natural aristocracy I consider as the most precious gift of nature for the instruction, the trusts, and government of society. . . . May we not even say that that form of government is the best which provides the most effectually for a pure selection of these natural aristoi into the offices of government? The artificial aristocracy is a mischievous ingredient in government, and provision should be made to prevent its ascendancy.[1]

But how do we distinguish between the false or conventional aristocracy based on wealth, name, prestige, good looks, luck, and so on, and the natural aristocracy based on moral and intellectual merit and accomplishment? The recognition of true merit and valid accomplishment depends on considerable merit and accomplishment in the selectors. Especially in politics, where experience is so important a teacher, and where deception and self-deception are so common and easy, the recognition of true merit depends on the maximum practical experience, combined with extensive education and presupposing great natural talent; and such education and experience require leisure, or liberation from money-making "business" and full-time labor. The best republic would therefore seem to be a strict or nonhereditary "aristocracy," as Aristotle goes on to call it in the chapter immediately after the chapter just quoted (*Politics* 3. 5). In principle, a strictly just aristocracy would be a regime in which (as in Plato's *Republic*) the meritorious few rulers, who themselves own very little private property, select their subordinates and replacements from the whole property-owning populace, to all of whom competition to test and display their potential merit is open on an equal basis—starting in the course of their publicly funded education in youth.

But in actual fact (as Plato's *Laws* demonstrates), the rule of the wise and virtuous must be qualified by the principle of popular consent—that is, by the principle of majority rule. To speak constitutionally, aristocracy must be "mixed" with democracy. But with what right? Precisely what principles justify the adulteration of the rule of the more public-spirited few by the power of the more selfish many (rich as well as poor)?

The primary and simplest, but for the classics most decisive, answer is that the majority are in virtue of their numbers superior in *strength* to the minority: the nature of political life is such that, in some measure, might makes right—or, at any rate, might cannot be denied a decisive voice. Still, as the reference to "equity" as well as "forgiveness" in the crucial passage in the *Laws* (756e-758a) indicates, the might or strength in question is a might or strength of human beings, not animals: it is the might of those who are concerned, not simply with sheer strength, but with the freedom and dignity that go with having some meaningful share in rule. The fact that some men are superior—sometimes vastly superior—in the moral and intellectual

    1. Lester J. Cappon, ed., *The Adams-Jefferson Letters* (Chapel Hill: University of North Carolina Press, 1959), 388. Cf. W. E. B. Du Bois's "Talented Tenth," reprinted in Du Bois 1988, 842–61.

qualities that constitute the capacity to be a statesman, to care for the community as a whole, does not utterly eclipse the more modest talents and attainments, and hence deserts, of the vast majority of ordinary folk in a decent republican society that makes provision for education, as well as for at least minimal relief from blinding poverty and at least minimal restrictions on acquisitiveness. The few who genuinely care for the good of the whole citizenry will, precisely out of this care, seek to give some opportunity for virtuous action, and hence some substantial political responsibility, to the majority. "Should the respectable rule and be sovereign over everything?" Aristotle asks; and responds: "But then all the others are necessarily dishonored, since they lack the honor that is political office. For we say offices are honors, and if the same persons rule all the time the others are necessarily dishonored. But then is it better that the one most seriously virtuous person rule? But this is still more oligarchic, since even more are dishonored" (*Politics* 1281a28–34).

Aristotle thus brings to light a fundamental ambiguity or difficulty in the meaning of the "common good," and in the meaning of virtue understood as dedication to the common good, in its highest and fullest manifestation. The common good is meant to be in some sense the good of all. It is meant to be a communal life in which all can share, and of which each can partake only by sharing. This communal life involves, obviously, the security and prosperity of all. But the good life for humans extends far beyond being taken care of like pets. The peak of this good life that is the common good is honorable activity in accordance with virtue, centered on justice or devotion to the common good. But this peak crowns a high and steadily narrowing pyramid. Men are unequal as regards the natural and acquired or practiced capacity for virtue; only a rare few seem fully capable of wise and just service to the whole, to others as well as themselves. In addition, the positions of responsibility that test wisdom and devotion become steadily fewer as they ascend to higher and fuller challenges. Yet insofar as virtue is constituted by service to the whole, or to others, and not just to the good of the virtuous, virtue itself seems to dictate that the virtuous few lower and broaden the peak: that they dilute their own fulfillment through virtue in order to afford opportunity to the less virtuous to develop and test their lesser degree of virtue. Yet does this not mean that virtue paradoxically requires the virtuous to act less virtuously, to retire from virtuous activity, or at any rate to make such retirement replace or constitute their activity? If this paradox is not in itself an insurmountable difficulty, does it not cast some doubt on the proposition that the common good is the good of the virtuous as well as of those they serve? Besides, does this retirement of the virtuous not entail considerable risk to the community as a whole? For it would seem obviously better for everyone if the community could be run by the wiser and more solidly trustworthy than by the less wise and less solidly trustworthy. But on the other side, it is dangerous for the city to ignore the majority's proud demand for a "share in the action." Still, insofar as this is a *proud* demand, and a demand that raises the claim of justice—and it always does—it is a demand that is compelled in one way or another to appeal, not simply to might or passion, but to virtue, to justice and desert. The majority may claim that it has an essential contribution to make in selecting or at least judging who is most virtuous, and in preventing the abuse of office by the imperfectly virtuous—for after all, those who do hold office most of the time are unlikely to be paragons. In the best sort of democracy, whose popular foundation is a hardworking, public-spirited yeomanry reluctant to spend its time participating in daily political affairs,

the offices will always be filled by the best, with the consent and without the envy of the people, and this arrangement will satisfy the decent and respectable. For they will not be ruled by those who are worse, and they will themselves rule in a just fashion because they will be subject to audit by others. For to be trammeled, and not to be able to do everything according to one's own opinion, is advantageous. For the capacity to do whatever one wishes is incapable of guarding against what is base in each of the human beings. The necessary result, then, is what is most advantageous in cities: the decent rule without lapses from decency, and the mass is not demeaned. That this is the best democracy is evident, and its cause is equally evident: the character of the people.[2]

This view of the claim of the majority only underlines, however, the degree to which consent, or majority rule, is a distinctly secondary and second-ranked principle of legitimacy. The principle that is first in rank, and hence in sovereignty, is *virtue*, including preeminently the virtue of justice or active concern for the common good; and consent must justify itself at least partly in terms of aspiration to and qualification for virtue. Strictly speaking, "popular *sovereignty*" is always an abridgment of civic justice—that is, of the sovereignty of the just, of those dedicated to and capable of serving the common good of the society.

The preeminence of virtue over consent, as well as the redefinition of freedom and rule in terms of virtue, becomes even more impressive when we give due weight to the observation that the virtues that qualify men for rule cannot adequately be comprehended simply as means to other ends.

2. Aristotle *Politics* 1318b33–19a6; see also 1292b25–30 and 1308b31–9a9.

The virtues do indeed function as means to lower ends, such as collective security and prosperity; and the duties the virtues dictate do indeed compete with and compel the sacrifice of private interests and gratification; but the virtues also shine forth as themselves central to the fulfillment and perfection of human existence. As Aristotle so eloquently teaches in the first book of his *Nicomachean Ethics*, virtue does not guarantee—and may not even wholly constitute—happiness; but it can be said to be the heart of happiness.

Serious and experienced moral citizens will tend not to dwell on the question of the relation between virtue and happiness; they will tend to try to do what is right for its own sake. But they are aware of the question, and when it is brought home to them, they will welcome the kind of answer Aristotle here suggests. Yet Aristotle, in suggesting this answer, does indeed compel his readers first to dwell on the question. He even reminds them that his contention, that virtue is the heart or core of happiness, is controversial:

The noble things and the just things, concerning which political science makes its investigation, are characterized by such great controversy and variation as to seem to exist by convention only, and not by nature; and the good things too have some such degree of variation, on account of their happening to be the occasion of harm to many. For some have been destroyed through wealth, and others through courage.
(*Nicomachean Ethics* 1094b14–19)

Some of the most arresting of the dialogues of Plato and Xenophon are set in motion by vivid reminders of how many people doubt, if they do not reject, the centrality of virtue to human happiness. And these doubts are rooted in observation of troubling facts.

There is in the first place the observation that the security, prosperity, glory, and even beauty of the republic as a whole, and of individuals, sometimes seems compatible with, and even to depend upon, actions and men who are not virtuous. Thucydides does not let us forget, any more than does Plato, that the splendor of Periclean Athens was founded on immoderate imperialism. Nor is it clear that the Sparta that presented itself as the alternative, which opposed and finally crushed Athenian imperialism, was itself an unambiguous agent of moral purity or even of republican liberation.

There is in the second place the observation that virtue is not natural; rather, it is dependent on early childhood habituation, which requires as a lifelong support the coercive, awe-inspiring, and frightening authority of the law, written and unwritten. Indeed, this support of the law and of legal sanctions seems required for all or almost all decent citizens throughout their lives. It is no accident that the greatest work of classical republicanism is called simply *Laws*; and in a fundamental passage of that work (875a-c), the Athenian Stranger observes:

It is necessary for human beings to establish laws for themselves and live according to laws, or they differ in no way from the beasts that are the most savage in every way. The cause of these things is this, that there is no one among human beings whose nature grows so as to become adequate both to know what is in the interest of human beings as regards a political regime and, knowing this, to be able and willing always to do what is best. For, in the first place, it is difficult to know that the true political art must care not for the private but the common—for the common binds cities together, while the private tears them apart—and that it is in the interest of both the common and the private that the common, rather than the private, be established nobly. Secondly, even if someone should advance sufficiently in the art to know that this is the way these things are by nature, and after this should rule the city without being audited, and as an autocrat, he would never be able to adhere to this conviction and spend his life giving priority to nourishing what is common in the city, while nourishing the private as following after the common; mortal nature will always urge him toward getting more than his share and toward private business, irrationally fleeing pain and pursuing pleasure, and putting both of these before what is more just and better.

But nowhere is the dependence of moral virtue on coercive law, enforcing communal morals through punishment, more vividly highlighted than in the closing pages of Aristotle's *Nicomachean Ethics* (1179b-end):

If reasonable discourses were sufficient by themselves to make men decent, "large fees and many" would they justly "reap," as Theognis says, and what would be needed is to provide such discourses. But now while they evidently do have the strength to arouse and encourage the liberal among the young, and to make a well-born character that is truly enamored of the noble become susceptible to virtue, yet they are incapable of arousing the many to gentlemanliness. . . . And it is necessary that the soul of the listener, just like the soil that nourishes seeds, be previously tilled with habits that lead toward enjoying and hating in a noble fashion. For one who lives according to passion would neither listen to nor comprehend the argument that turns away from passion. . . . But it is difficult to happen on a correct upbringing, with a view to virtue, from early youth, unless one is brought up under laws of this kind. Therefore the nurture and practices of the young must be regulated by laws. . . . But it is probably not sufficient to happen upon a correct nurture and upbringing while young: it is also necessary, when grown up, to practice and confirm by habit these same things. So we need laws for this as well, and in general regulating the whole of life. For the many are persuaded more by necessity than reason, and by punishments rather than by what is noble. . . . Now paternal authority has neither the strength nor the necessity, nor indeed, in general, does any one man's authority, unless he be king or some such. But law has a compulsory power, being a reasoning that comes from a certain prudence and intelligence. Human beings are resented when they thwart the appetites, even if they do so correctly; but the law is not hateful when it orders what is decent. Yet it is only in the city of the Spartans, along with a few others, that the lawgiver seems to have made nurture and conduct his concern.

The fact that virtue is not natural, in the sense of being spontaneous or easy or common, seems more than compensated for by the fact that it is said to be natural in the higher sense of completing or actualizing the natural human potential. Yet if moral and civic virtue is *law-bred,* to use the term Thucydides employs in his famous eulogy of Nicias (7.86–end), if moral and civic virtue depends on the external compulsion of law-enforced fear, shame, and honor, the question arises whether such virtue can be the true response to humanity's deepest natural needs. Above all, can virtue rooted in obedience to law be said to be virtue that completes man's nature as a rational being? John Adams was certainly correct to stress, in his *Defence of the Constitutions of Government of the United States,* that republicanism has always been closely associated with the rule of law; but it is doubtful whether he grasped the problematic character of this assertion in the context of classical republican political theory.

The rule of law is distinguished from, and said to be superior to, the rule of men. This distinction testifies to the unreliability or untrustworthiness of men unrestrained by coercion. Yet can law ever match or begin to match the flexibility, attention to particular cases, and synoptic capaciousness of a superior statesman's mind and vision? The speech of the Athenian Stranger in Plato's *Laws* quoted a moment ago continues, in a seemingly contradictory fashion, as follows:

Of course, if ever some human being who was born adequate in nature, with a divine dispensation, were able to attain these things, he wouldn't need any laws ruling over him. For no law or order is stronger than knowledge, nor is it right for intelligence to be subordinate, or a slave, to anyone, but it should be ruler over everything, if indeed it is true and really free according to nature. But now, in fact, it is not so anywhere or in any way, except to a small extent. That is why one must choose what comes second, order and law—which see and look to most things, but are incapable of seeing everything.

Similarly, Aristotle's classic and complex argument in *Politics* 3.16–17 for the rule of law is posed against, and illuminated dialectically by, an equally if not more powerful argument for the rule of the one truly superior man or kind of man, whose virtue and wisdom ought not to be trammeled by the necessarily bullheaded and crudely general strictures of law even at its best. Aristotle goes so far as to take serious note of the view that "to legislate concerning matters requiring deliberation is one of the things that is an impossibility" (*Politics* 1287b22–23). But here, as in the Athenian

Stranger's speech, the argument for law draws great strength from the recognition that men truly capable of ruling or living without being subject to law are extremely rare. The argument includes, that is, the recognition that most men who are conventionally or for most purposes called "virtuous" are at best imperfectly or incompletely virtuous—and hence in need of the threat of lawful punishment to keep them on the straight and narrow. Yet the rule of law cannot replace or escape reliance upon the rule of men, not only because men must apply and guard the laws, but, above all, because somebody has to make the laws. At the founding, the "lawgiver," in the supreme sense, is perforce someone who is unregulated by law. The founding calls for a man or men of pure virtue. But civic or moral virtue, as we have seen, is the product of lawfully sanctioned habituation in early childhood: does not the existence of a truly virtuous lawgiver presuppose an already established sound legal system in which the future lawgiver has grown up and learned virtue?

Divine Law

The fundamental problem is in one sense "solved," but in another sense deepened, by the introduction of divine law, or "natural law" conceived as reasonable edicts emanating from a divinely ordered cosmos. The classic text is again Plato's *Laws* (713e–716c):

There can be no rest from evils and toils for those cities in which some mortal rules rather than a god. . . . in public life and in private life—in the arrangement of our households and our cities—we should obey whatever within us partakes of immortality, giving the name *law* to the distribution ordained by intelligence. . . . Where the law is itself ruled over and lacks sovereign authority, I see destruction at hand for such a place. But where it is despot over the rulers and the rulers are slaves of the law, there I foresee safety and all the good things the gods have given cities. . . . For us, the god would be the measure of all things in the highest degree, and far more so than "man," as they claim.

What Plato's Athenian Stranger sets forth here with quasi-prophetic eloquence has been adopted and adapted by all subsequent classical republicanism. There has never existed any classical republic, or any authentically classical republican political theory, in history or in the literature, that has not been grounded on the establishment of a civil religion. Whatever its other tenets, such a religion must include the belief that the laws are sanctioned by, and in some measure derived from, superhuman intelligence and authority. The most vivid testimonies to this crucial element of classical republican thought are the great myths of the last judgment with which the *Gorgias* and the *Republic* conclude, and in which the civil theology elaborated in the tenth book of the *Laws* culminates. A more austere teaching on divine providence informs the Stoic doctrine of natural law, as presented most notably in the famous speech of Laelius in Cicero's *Republic* 3.33. The fragmentary remains of the Stoic texts make especially evident the fact that the appeal to divine providential sanctions goes hand in hand with an insistence on viewing the republic as situated in a larger, cosmopolitan or cosmic order. The source of such a conception is again the Platonic Socrates, who reforms and revises traditional poetic myths by putting them in the context of a stress on the mathematical moral structure underlying visible nature:

The wise say, Callicles, that heaven, earth, gods, and men are held together by community, friendship, orderliness, moderation, and justice; and for these reasons, my friend, they call this whole an order, a cosmos, not a disorder and intemperance. You, however, seem to me not to turn your mind to these things, even though you're wise about them, but it has escaped your notice that geometrical equality has great power among gods and humans, whereas you think one must practice getting more than one's share: for you neglect the study of geometry. (*Gorgias* 508a)

It is on the basis of this major strand in the classical republican literature that Calvin affirms, with only some exaggeration, that

if the Scripture did not teach that this office [of the civil magistrate] extends to both tables of the law, we might learn it from heathen writers; for not one of them has treated of the office of magistrates, of legislation, and civil government, without beginning with religion and divine worship. And thus they have all confessed that no government can be happily constituted unless its first object be the promotion of piety, and that all laws are preposterous that neglect the claims of God and merely provide for the interests of men. (*Institutes of the Christian Religion* 4.20.9)

It is this strand in the classical republican tradition that is reaffirmed by James Wilson in the conclusion to the second of his 1790 lectures on law: "Far from being rivals or enemies, religion and law are twin sisters, friends, and mutual assistants. Indeed, these two sciences run into each other. The divine law, as discovered by reason and the moral sense, forms an essential part of both."[3]

In short, it is this essential vein of the classical republican theory of law that brings the classical view into close proximity to the biblical view of politics. As I earlier remarked, the biblical understanding of political life

3. *Selected Political Essays of James Wilson*, ed. Randolph G. Adams (New York: Knopf, 1930), 257.

would seem at first to stand rather far from the classical republican one. But now we are in a position to qualify that first impression.

Despite the fact that there are crucial disagreements between the Bible and the Greek philosophers over the ultimate status of political life, and over the character and ranking of the specific virtues, the biblical theologians found much to welcome in classical republican thought. Above all, they approved of the classical republican commitment to law as the enforcer and cultivator of what the Greeks called moral virtue; they agreed as to the qualified subordination of the individual to the community, and of material welfare to spiritual welfare; and they acknowledged a kinship between their own thinking and the classical teaching on the superiority and transpolitical character of the contemplative life. On the other side, the followers of the Greek philosophers, though disclaiming direct prophetic inspiration for their teaching on the nature of law, nevertheless argued that the proper use of reason can disclose at least the decisive outlines of the true character of the divine legislative order. The great Islamic philosopher and theologian Avicenna, writing in his *Divisions of the Rational Sciences*, declared that "*the* treatment of prophecy and the divine law is contained in . . . [Plato's] *Laws*" (Mahdi and Lerner 1972, 97). Equally striking are the words of Maimonides, the greatest theologian of the Jewish faith:

In that which has occurred to me with regard to these matters, I followed conjecture and supposition; no divine revelation has come to me to teach me that the intention in the matter in question was such and such, nor did I receive what I believe in these matters from a teacher. But the texts of the prophetic books and the dicta of the Sages, *together with the speculative premises that I possess* [from Aristotle], showed me that things are indubitably so and so.

This chapter . . . is a kind of conclusion, at the same time explaining the worship as practiced by one who has apprehended the true realities peculiar only to Him after he has obtained an apprehension of what He is.[4]

Thomas Aquinas, while insisting that "divinely inspired Scripture is no part of the branches of philosophy traced by reasoning," nonetheless opens his *Summa theologica* with the question, "Is any other teaching required apart from philosophy?"—thus signaling the extent to which philosophy can rightly lay claim to very extensive understanding even in the realm of theology. It must not be forgotten that the very word *theology* is Platonic in origin (*Republic* 379a) and is never mentioned in the Scriptures.

The substantial differences between classical political philosophy and

4. Moses Maimonides, *The Guide of the Perplexed*, trans. Shlomo Pines (Chicago: University of Chicago Press, 1963), 416 and 618.

biblical thought were not so great, then, as to prevent the working out, by philosophers and theologians, of a variety of remarkably effective and convincing syntheses in each of the great religious dispensations, Judaic, Christian, and Muslim. As each of the great postclassical religions encountered the force of classical republicanism, each was compelled to reinterpret both itself and that republicanism so as to make the former seem the completion of the latter, the latter the preparation for the former. It was these various syntheses that the political theorists of the Enlightenment and the statesmen of the great revolutions of the seventeenth and eighteenth centuries faced when they looked back to the twin traditions from which they or their predecessors emerged.

For the founding generation of Americans, and the philosophers and theologians who influenced them, the most important such synthesis was, of course, the Christian one. The keystone of that synthesis was the idea of natural law. The authoritative elaboration of natural law is found in Thomas Aquinas, whose teaching was modified and adapted to the Anglican communion by Richard Hooker, and to other Protestant denominations by Calvin, Melanchthon, and lesser lights. It can be argued, as it was by this century's greatest Protestant historian of Christian social thought, Ernst Troeltsch (1976, vol. 2), that the essence of Thomistic natural law remains unaltered in these Protestant modifications. The same cannot be said, however, of the elaborate appeal made to Hooker's doctrine of natural law by James Wilson in his 1790 lectures inaugurating the first American law school. And yet even here, a key portion of the grounding of this most elaborate and authoritative original American philosophy of law remains the Thomistic doctrine as filtered through Hooker.

According to this doctrine, natural law is God's moral law promulgated to human beings through a specific faculty within their rational self-consciousness, a faculty whose action is the conscience. The conscience gives men an awareness of certain sacred restraints, formulable as moral rules, some of which provide a minimal foundation of categorical (absolute), prohibitive imperatives. These rules, both hortatory and prohibitory, are "natural" laws in two senses: first, they are knowable by mature, rational human nature, prior to revelation; and second, adherence to them fulfills the nature of the human soul, preparing that nature for the richer fulfillment that becomes available to it through the supernatural and suprarational avenue opened up by divine revelation. More specifically, the precepts of natural law fulfill the threefold character of the "natural inclinations" or natural directedness peculiar to humanity: preservation, the family, and the perfection of reason through participation in social life and through the life of the mind. The "human laws" enacted by men in positive constitutions and legislation ought to be guided by and (as much as possible within each circumstance) ought to bring to completion the dictates of the natural law. Human law almost always falls short of full excellence; but it must always remain at or above a minimal decency. Human law can never remain legitimate while violating the flooring of categorical prohibitions established by the natural law: prohibitions against theft, adultery, deceit or false witness, dishonor of parents, abuse of children, murder, and so forth. Above this flooring, the question of which laws are legitimate because conforming to, and illegitimate because in violation of, the norms of natural law depends to some extent on prudent judgment of the circumstances—historical, economic, military, and political.

Natural law thus provides a permanent, transcultural and transhistorical, but reasonably flexible, standard against which all human laws can be measured to test their legitimacy and true lawfulness. It is this standard that Martin Luther King, Jr., invokes in his great "Letter from Birmingham Jail" of April 16, 1963, responding to a criticism by a group of leading clergymen:

> You express a great deal of anxiety over our willingness to break laws. This is certainly a legitimate concern. . . . I would be the first to advocate obeying just laws. One has not only a legal but a moral responsibility to obey just laws. Conversely, one has a moral responsibility to disobey unjust laws. I would agree with St. Augustine that "an unjust law is no law at all." Now, what is the difference between the two? How does one determine whether a law is just or unjust? . . . . To put it in the terms of St. Thomas Aquinas: An unjust law is a human law that is not rooted in eternal law and natural law. Any law that uplifts human personality is just. Any law that degrades human personality is unjust. All segregation statutes are unjust because segregation distorts the soul and damages the personality. It gives the segregator a false sense of superiority and the segregated a false sense of inferiority.
>
> (Storing 1970, 121)

King then adds his own enrichment of the civic meaning of natural law in the American political context, defining the specific civic virtue involved in the breaking of an unjust law. In the passage just quoted, he speaks not of a "right" to disobey unjust laws, but of a responsibility or duty to do so. In subsequent paragraphs of his letter, he proceeds to clarify the nature of this duty by indicating the proper spirit, intention, and conduct that must inform a moral, as opposed to immoral, breaking of an unjust law. The proper spirit is one of highest respect for law, which implies dedication to the moral education, through law and lawfulness, of one's fellow citizens. The proper conduct is public conduct, carefully calculated with a view to such education of one's fellow citizens. King dismisses with contempt, and associates with his bitterest opponents, the claims of those who seek to defy or evade laws they regard as unjust merely in the name of personal beliefs. For models of the virtuous action he is defining, he appeals to the Bible, to the early Christians, to Socrates, and to the Revolution.

> I hope you are able to see the distinction I am trying to point out. In no sense do I advocate evading or defying the law, as would the rabid segregationist. That would lead to anarchy. One who breaks an unjust law must do so openly, lovingly, and with a willingness to accept the penalty. I submit that an individual who breaks a law that conscience tells him is unjust, and who willingly accepts the penalty of imprisonment in order to arouse the conscience of the community over its injustice, is in reality expressing the highest respect for law. Of course, there is nothing new about this kind of civil disobedience. It was evidenced sublimely in the refusal of Shadrach, Meshach and Abednego to obey the laws of Nebuchadnezzar. . . . It was practiced superbly by the early Christians. . . . To a degree, academic freedom is a reality today because Socrates practiced civil disobedience. In our own nation, the Boston Tea Party represented a massive act of civil disobedience. . . . you assert that our actions, even though peaceful, must be condemned because they precipitate violence. . . . Isn't this like condemning Socrates because his unswerving commitment to truth and his philosophical inquiries precipitated the act by the misguided populace in which they made him drink hemlock? (Storing 1970, 121–25)

The interweaving of human and divine law, lawgiving and prophecy, surely lends awesome force to truly moral law and to the virtues it sanctions. But sooner or later the need to appeal to such support cannot help but raise several difficult questions. Why does civic and moral virtue need such massive extrinsic support? What is the nature of divinity, and how do we know it? Can reason suffice to guide us in life by providing adequate answers to these questions?

Political Philosophy as a Way of Life

These grave questions, in which culminate or are summed up the whole gamut of difficulties that I have been attempting to outline, are the conundrums, arising directly out of serious reflection on the moral-political life, that open the door to political *philosophy* in the classical republican (Socratic) sense. Philosophy, in the classical republican sense, is not a method of thinking, a profession, an academic discipline, or a vague preoccupation with mystic or personal contemplation. Philosophy is above all a specific way of life, a specific form of human existence, a specific posture of the whole soul in relation to being as a whole. Socratic philosophy is the life, in

the words of Martin Luther King, Jr., just quoted, of "unswerving commitment to truth" through "inquiries." The political philosopher in this sense
is a man who intransigently raises, and, having raised, never ceases grappling
with, the question, "What is virtue?"—what is the nature, the essence, of
virtue, of true as opposed to apparent virtue, such as would explain its
relation to happiness, to God, to the law, to our human nature and its needs?
This question or set of questions does not meet with a speedy or simple
answer; rather, it opens up an alternative, more awakened, more fully rational, and hence more fully human and social, way of life that lies above
and beyond the life even of the lawgiver, not to mention the statesman or
the citizen.

The actual experience of this life, growing out of the gripping experience
of the awareness of our ignorance regarding the truth, or the true answers
to our most important questions about how we ought to live, leads us to the
discovery, Socrates insists, that human nature is so constituted as to find its
bliss in thinking and in the genuine self-knowledge that comes from thinking:

> Maybe someone then would ask, "Can't you go away, Socrates, and live keeping
> quiet and in peace?" This is indeed the most difficult thing of all to convince some
> of you of. For if I say that this is to disobey the god, and that it is on account of this
> that it is impossible for me to live in peace, you won't believe me, supposing that I
> am being ironic. If on the other hand I say that this happens to be the greatest good
> for a human being, each day to argue about virtue and the other matters about which
> you hear me carrying on dialogues and examining myself and others, and that the
> unexamined life is not worth living for a human being, when I say these things you
> will believe me even less. But that is the way things are, I claim, gentlemen, though
> to persuade [people] of it is not easy.   (Plato *Apology of Socrates* 37e–38a)

The philosophic life therefore exemplifies a kind of virtue that is truly
and radically nonutilitarian, inasmuch as it seeks no end beyond the practice
of virtue or excellence itself. This practice affords a life so rich, so electrifying
in its awakeness, so consuming in its endless preoccupation with unraveling
the mystery of human moral existence, that the philosopher finds himself
looking back on all political life and ambition as if upon life in a cave—to
recall Socrates' famous image, elaborated in book 7 of Plato's *Republic*.
Aristotle expresses the same point when he says that it is only by virtue of
our participation in the theoretical life and the theoretical virtues, above and
beyond the practical life and practical virtues, that we partake of the divine:

> Such a way of life would be superior to the way of life that is human. For it is not
> insofar as one is human that one will live this life, but insofar as there exists within
> [one] something divine. . . . It would seem too that each *is* this intelligence, if indeed
> this is the sovereign and best part; it would be strange, then, if one should choose

not to live one's own life, but the life of another. . . . The life according to the rest of virtue would be happy in a secondary degree. For the kinds of being-in-action in this respect are human: the just things and the courageous things and the other things pertaining to the virtues are things we enact in our relations with others, in contracts and services and all sorts of actions, and in passions where we observe what is due to each, and all these are evidently human things. But the happiness in accordance with intelligence is separate. . . . It would seem to need externals little, or less than that happiness which is in accordance with moral virtue. . . . For the purposes of action, much is needed, and to the degree that the action is greater and nobler, so much the more. But for one who is theorizing, there is no need of such things for the purposes of the being-in-action, but indeed they are, so to speak, impediments to theorizing at any rate. But inasmuch as he is human and lives together with others, such a man chooses to act according to virtue, and he will need such things for the purpose of his life as a human being. (*Nicomachean Ethics* 10.7–8)

Aristotle is by no means unaware of the initially paradoxical character, and the unquestionably disputable status, of this highest claim of classical republican thought regarding the superiority of the philosophic or theoretical life; he is therefore fully aware of the need to vindicate the claim by argument. Near the beginning of his *Eudemian Ethics* (1.5), he raises in a thought-provoking way the fundamental question of the best way of life:

The things ordered for the happy conduct of life being the three previously mentioned greatest goods for human beings—virtue, prudence, and pleasure—we see that there are three ways of life that all those who happen to have the means choose to pursue: the political, the philosophic, and the hedonistic. Now of these the philosophic means being concerned with prudence and theoretical speculation about the truth, the political means being concerned with noble actions (and these are the actions that proceed from virtue), and the hedonistic means being concerned with physical pleasures. Therefore each bestows the term *happiness* on something different, as was said earlier, and Anaxagoras of Clazomenae, when asked who was happiest, replied, "No one whom you would conventionally suppose, but someone who would appear strange to you." He answered in this manner because he saw that the questioner assumed that it was impossible to acquire this appellation "happy" if one were not great and noble or wealthy, whereas he perhaps thought that it was possible to call someone humanly blessed who lived painlessly, and purely as regards justice, or partaking of a certain divine theoretical speculation.

Having thus given us, by way of the pre-Socratic philosopher Anaxagoras, a more concrete indication of what he means by one who leads "the theoretical life," Aristotle proceeds, however, to indicate his own recognition of the continuing doubt as to the correctness of Anaxagoras's claim or presupposition: "Now with regard to many other things it is not easy to judge nobly, and especially is this the case with that which seems to everyone most easy, and available to every human being to decide—which of the things in life is choiceworthy, by the acquisition of which someone would fulfill desire." On the basis of this doubt, Aristotle announces his own distinctive philosophic path, and indicates the genealogy of this kind of philosophizing:

Let ours be the theoretical inquiry into virtue and prudence: the nature of each of them, what it is, and whether these are parts of the good life, either in themselves or in the actions that result from them; since these things are linked to happiness, if not by everyone, then by all those among human beings who are worth taking into account. Now the older Socrates thought that in fact this was the end, knowing virtue, and he inquired what is justice and what courage, and each of the parts of it.

"In doing so," Aristotle adds, "he acted reasonably; for he thought that all the virtues were scientific knowledge, so that knowing justice coincides with being just." To this proposition, however, Aristotle brings his characteristic reservation: "He sought what is virtue but not how and from what things it comes into being. Now while it is noble to know each of the noble things, with regard to virtue at least what brings the most honor is not knowing what it is but knowing from what it is." Aristotle makes it his business to add this most honorable supplement to the Socratic project. He does so while immediately making clear that his concern for making his philosophizing most honorable goes together with a desire to win the trust of men in general, and that he proceeds in this way on the basis of a very great sense of caution in view of the specific dangers of the enterprise of Socratic investigation into the nature of virtue:

And about all these matters one ought to seek to win trust through rational arguments, using as witnesses the examples that come to view. . . . The rational arguments in each investigation are divided between the philosophically spoken and the nonphilosophically. Therefore for the statesman as well, it ought not to be considered superfluous to engage in a theoretical inquiry of such a sort as will make clear not only what a thing is, but on account of what it is; for such is the philosophic investigation about each thing. Yet this requires great caution. For there are some who, on the basis of the opinion that what characterizes a philosopher is speaking with reason and saying nothing at random, put over arguments that are off the track and empty (doing this sometimes on account of ignorance, sometimes on account of boastfulness), with the result that men of experience and capacity for action are taken in by these people, who neither possess nor are capable of either architechtonic or practical intelligence.   (Eudemian Ethics 1.6)

There is then a serious potential disharmony, as well as a mutual need and benefit, involved in the relationship between philosopher and statesman or citizen. Philosophy, we have observed, comes into being as a puzzled questioning of the meaning and purpose of law or lawfulness in general.

This kind of questioning that the philosopher like Socrates engages in is of a much more thoroughgoing sort than the questioning or challenging of specific positive laws or dictates of assemblies and magistrates on the basis of a clear commandment of constitutional or natural law, or natural right—the sort of questioning in which the moral man of action like Martin Luther King, Jr., engages. It is one thing for Socrates, acting as a moral citizen in his executive capacity as a president of the Athenian Assembly, to risk death or imprisonment by defying the democratic majority. (In the Arginusae affair, Xenophon reports in his *Greek History* 1.7, when the majority proclaimed, " 'It is a terrible thing, if the people are not allowed to do what they wish,' . . . the presidents were frightened, and all agreed to put it to a vote except Socrates the son of Sophroniscus; this man said he would not, but would do everything according to law.") It is something altogether different for Socrates the philosopher to raise the question, "What is law?" This latter questioning Xenophon never presents Socrates as directly engaged in. Plato presents Socrates doing so only in a short dialogue (*Minos*) so obscure and unattractive that it is usually not even included in collections of translations of Plato's works: in that dialogue Socrates is depicted speaking in a most puzzling way, in private, with a single nameless and puzzled companion. (*Laws*, Plato's longest dialogue, does not directly raise the question, "What is law?" and is, furthermore, the only Platonic dialogue from which Socrates is absent.) If, or insofar as, Socrates does present his philosophic activity in the public forum—in his defense speech in court— he does so always by insisting that he is pursuing a divine commandment, if not a divine law.

Behind this cautious or conservative posture toward law lies the classical republican observation that the philosophic questioning of law as such, however positive or reinforcing it may be of law in the final analysis, is nonetheless necessarily disturbing to obedience to law. For such obedience is only rarely and partially a matter of reasoning. As Aristotle puts it in a remarkable passage (*Politics* 1268b22–69a28), a passage underlined by Thomas Aquinas in the *Summa theologica* (1–2.97.2), "The law has no strength to exact obedience other than habit [*ethos*], and this does not come into being except through lengthy passage of time." Aristotle expresses the basic point in another way through his insistence that moral and political deliberation is always about means, not about ends, or at least not about ultimate ends. Statesmen and citizens deliberate over policy with a view to some ultimate ends that are given prior to, and as the foundation for, deliberation. They do not ask whether a regime or society ought to survive, but how it may best be preserved; not what the virtues are, but how they may be fostered. Once the agreed-upon ultimate ends are questioned, the common ground for deliberation disappears; civil health has broken down; revolutionary strife is imminent. Therefore, apart from emergency conditions, such questioning properly belongs to a sphere other than the political. The true political philosopher, he who knows what he is doing when he takes up questions of philosophy, must then assume an awesome responsibility. He must possess, as Aristotle puts it in the passage previously quoted from the *Eudemian Ethics*, an "architectonic and practical intelligence": "for," as Aristotle says at the beginning of the *Nicomachean Ethics* 7.11, "He is the architect of the end, toward which we look when we call each thing bad or good without qualification." The political philosopher is neither a ruler nor a lawgiver, and still less an "ideologist" or "intellectual," but his inquiries cannot help but be of sovereign concern to the rulers and lawgivers of all societies in all times and places that his speaking and writing might touch.

On the level of public or legal policy, the classical republican political philosophers respond to the problem by favoring a cautiously prudential communal censorship. They do so especially with a view to the impact of speech and writing, especially serious writing, on the young; for in a healthy republic the young are involved in a most delicate and crucial civic education, aimed at molding character.

This classical republican position was restated for the English-speaking world in the new era of printing by the great poet and political theorist John Milton. Milton's *Areopagitica*, combining exquisite subtlety with passionate eloquence, explicitly echoes the great oration of Isocrates—that student of Socrates who devoted himself to applying Socratic philosophy in the teaching of rhetoric and the training of statesmen. Isocrates' *Areopagitica* is an exhortation to the Athenians to return from a permissive and expansive democracy to their earlier, more severe and traditional form of democracy. The oration takes its name from the Council of the Areopagus, which had been the Senate and the board of censorship that maintained the moral tone of that earlier free and democratic Athenian regime. Milton's *Areopagitica* is an exhortation to the English Parliament to abandon its newly instituted law of prior restraint through the licensing of printers and authors.

Milton argues that such a policy of prior restraint was never followed by the classical republics, even in their sternest days, and that the apparent favoring of such policy that might be read out of the seventh book of Plato's *Laws* is based on misinterpretation. Such a reading of Plato is too literal; it reflects a failure to appreciate the ironic and playful character of the Platonic dialogues. Neither the *Laws* nor the *Republic* should be read, Milton insists, as seriously proposing the establishment of the regimes and laws they elaborate. But this is not to say that there is no doctrinal political teaching in Plato, or that the teaching permits or endorses unlimited freedom of speech or writing. While in a healthy republic there should be no prior restraint on publication, all authors must be held accountable for the effects on morals and religion of their writings. Those writings judged by the republican citizenry or authorities to be deleterious can and should be publicly decried; in rare cases, they should be banned, or even burned, and their authors punished. Such judgment, to be sure, ought to be delivered with the greatest reluctance, circumspection, and deliberation, in light of the precious character of freedom of thought, in both its civic and its religious and philosophic consequences. It is because Milton takes thought and speech so seriously, because he attributes to them such power to shape the life of mankind for good or evil, that he takes the position he does—opposing censorship that would prevent the community from having the opportunity to judge, and advocating the censorship that follows upon considered judgment.

I deny not but that it is of greatest concernment in the church and commonwealth, to have a vigilant eye how books demean themselves as well as men; and thereafter to confine, imprison, and do sharpest justice on them as malefactors: for books are not absolutely dead things, but do contain a potency of life in them to be as active as that soul was whose progeny they are; nay, they do preserve as in a vial the purest efficacy and extraction of that living intellect that bred them. I know they are as lively, and as vigorously productive, as those fabulous dragon's teeth; and being sown up and down, may chance to spring up armed men. And yet, on the other hand, unless wariness be used, as good almost kill a man as kill a good book: who kills a man kills a reasonable creature, God's image; but he who destroys a good book, kills reason itself, kills the image of God, as it were, in the eye. Many a man lives a burden to the earth; but a good book is the precious life-blood of a master-spirit, embalmed and treasured up on purpose to a life beyond life. . . . Give me the liberty to know, to utter, and to argue freely according to conscience, above all liberties.[5]

The most important censorship is, then, self-censorship on the part of philosophers, the most disturbing, but at the same time most perspicacious, thinkers. Philosophers' activity, they well know, poses the danger of undermining the traditions, bonds, and healthy limits on thought that support the strongest lawful republican communities and the most lawfully dedicated

5. *John Milton: "Areopagitica" and "Of Education," with Autobiographical Passages from Other Prose Works,* ed. George H. Sabine (Northbrook, Ill.: AHM Publishing, 1951), 5–6, 49.

republican leadership. Decent citizens can be deeply disoriented by philosophy, and the insights and questions of philosophy can sometimes be misused for evil ends by unscrupulous men. The philosopher who is humanely and humanly wise must take responsibility for these dangers. He must philosophize in a manner, or communicate and publicize his philosophic speculation with a caution, that accords with the gravity of the threat his questioning might otherwise pose to republican freedom and virtue. The Socratic response is the "loving rhetoric" or "erotic rhetoric" Socrates teaches in Plato's *Phaedrus* and *Gorgias*, as well as the "Odyssean" rhetoric Xenophon describes Socrates as practicing in his *Memorabilia*, or recollections of Socrates (on which, Benjamin Franklin's *Autobiography* reports, Franklin modeled his entire adult life as writer and communicator).[6] This mode of public and private communication mediates between philosophic skepticism and civic commitment. Through this mode of communication, the Socratic philosopher leads a few of the young toward sharing his life and attempts to guide their less thoughtful, but nonetheless serious and teachable, comrades and elders toward a more clear-sighted, gentle or humane execution of their political duties.

This most radical dimension of classical republican political philosophy to which we are now attending casts an even longer shadow over our initial assumptions about, or impressions of, the virtues that qualify men to rule in a republic. Those men (the genuine philosophers) who are most truly qualified to rule—because they are the most fully aware of the problematic character of human existence, and because they are so preoccupied with virtuous activity and friendship that they are most immune to temptations to divert their lives from virtuous activity—practice a kind of virtue that leads them to wish not to have to assume the burdens of rule, and that in addition leaves them unapt to attract the recognition, or assume leadership, of large numbers of necessarily unphilosophic citizens. As Socrates explains to the surprised Glaucon in the first book of the *Republic* (347b–d),

The greatest of penalties is being ruled by a more wicked man if one is not willing oneself to rule. It is because they fear this, in my view, that good men rule, when they do rule; and at that time they proceed to enter on rule, not as though they were going to something good, or as though they were going to be well off in it; but they enter on it as a necessity and because they have no one better than or like themselves to whom to turn it over. For it is likely that if a city of good men came to be, there would be a fight over not ruling, just as there is now over ruling; and there it

---

6. Xenophon *Memorabilia* 4.6; *The Autobiography of Benjamin Franklin*, ed. Leonard Labaree et al. (New Haven: Yale University Press, 1964), 64–65.

would become manifest that a true ruler really does not by nature consider his own advantage but rather that of the one who is ruled.

The most appropriate public role of the philosopher is, in the best case (as adumbrated in Plato's *Gorgias*, depicted in Plato's *Laws*, and manifested in Aristotle's *Ethics* and *Politics*), to give some crucial general advice to conventionally decent, politically ambitious and talented men engaged in framing laws or in reforming republics under law.

This means to say, however, that those citizens who are rightly regarded, for most or all practical purposes, as "the serious ones," "the respectable community leaders," "the gentlemen," are revealed on closer and more precise analysis to be characterized by defective (if nonetheless considerable and rare) virtue. They now appear to be men who have not yet taken seriously enough the problems that appear in a careful, critical scrutiny of the life-experience of virtue as ordinarily or primarily understood. These men, even in the best case, are therefore not entirely reliable: their virtue is somewhat fragile, or exposed to bafflement, if not temptation. This difficulty is brought out with remarkable dramatic richness and imaginative vivacity in Xenophon's great political novel, *The Education of Cyrus*. It is brought out more briefly and incisively in the "Myth of Er" with which Socrates concludes Plato's *Republic* (see especially 619c–d). In this light, the republican "mixed regime" of which we spoke earlier takes on a claim that is in one sense stronger, in another sense more disappointing.

Given the fact that full or genuine wisdom, the wisdom that consists in self-knowledge and knowledge of ignorance, belongs to a rare few marginal philosophers like Socrates, who are neither easy to identify nor easy to draw into competition for rule, republican life is compelled in almost all actual situations to substitute some kind of approximation to wisdom or virtue. And on the other side, since popular consent is necessarily consent of the less wise or less reflective, it is always consent colored by deception and self-deception. The complex task of constitution-making and of ruling, in the classical republican understanding, is then the weaving together of the necessarily impure simulacra of the twin roots of political authority—wisdom and consent. As a result, the art of political or civic *rhetoric*, understood as the art of conveying noble and beneficial opinion—in the best case, true opinion—rather than knowledge, stands at the very forefront of classical republican theory. It is through "the noble art of civic rhetoric," whose highest aspirations are first sketched in Plato's *Gorgias*, and whose richest elaboration is Aristotle's *Rhetoric*, that the wisdom that is politically possible and the consent that is politically necessary are combined and elevated, under the somewhat distant guidance of philosophy. One may say that it is through their teaching on political rhetoric that the classical political philosophers attempt to make their biggest direct contribution to improving and guiding republican statesmanship and lawgiving. A sign of this characteristic thrust of classical republican theory is the fact that those individuals who most successfully combined classical republican theory and practice in their own careers were themselves great teachers of rhetoric (Isocrates, Xenophon, Cicero).

Nothing so clearly distances today's republican life from the republicanism promoted by the classical theorists as the contemporary attitude toward rhetoric. For we tend by and large to underestimate or hold in contempt the art of rhetoric. In our public life, *rhetoric* is more often a term of abuse than of pride; it tends to be identified with "public relations," "spin control," media manipulation, and deception. Equally unfortunate is the reaction caused by our revulsion at the perceived manipulative character of so much of our public discourse. Distrust and cynicism in the public at large can easily slip into rejection of every attempt to appeal to sentiment, passion, and imagination. Among some intellectuals (perhaps the most prominent figure here is Habermas), one hears the apolitical demand that political and public discourse be transformed into an utterly candid and factual and simply rational, not to say philosophic, discourse of a sort that is, in fact, quite inappropriate to any republican civic arena. Contemporary academic proponents of a return to greater emphasis on "civic deliberation" too often fail to observe the limitation on deliberation as regards ultimate ends: some go so far as explicitly to deny the Aristotelian insight into the essentially limited character of truly healthy civic deliberation. By bringing to republican public discourse such an inappropriate and apolitical standard, these intellectuals only heighten the obscurity that now surrounds understanding of the precise nature of the discourse and communication suitable to republican debate and oratory; in condemning the necessarily rhetorical character of republican debate and speech, they intensify the prevailing, debilitating incapacity to comprehend the unique character of republican communication.

The Socratic teaching on "the noble art of rhetoric" begins from an appreciation of the necessarily deep distinction between truly philosophic, simply rational or dialectical, argument and the kind of discourse, communication, controversy, and deliberation that is possible in republican life. A political rostrum is not and cannot be a classroom lectern; an assembly or council deliberation cannot be a philosophic seminar or symposium; the preamble to a piece of legislation or even to a constitution cannot be a treatise on political theory. The medium of republican political discussion is unavoidably characterized by severe limitations on strict rationality: by enormous and nigh-unbridgeable diversities of experience, education, talent, and need; by intense pressures of unpredictable occasion and time; by constraints entailed in the sheer numbers of participants; by the need to maintain consensus regarding essentially disputable and disputed basic opinions as to the goals of civic life. Given these constraints, collective civic consciousness is inevitably defined not by knowledge but by opinion. The highest reasonable goal of political communication must be, not truth simply, but true opinion. The medium of political discourse is inevitably a medium where reason must be advanced through an alliance with passion, with imagination, with musical grace—as well as with concision and forcefulness of speech. Accordingly, in Plato's *Gorgias* and *Phaedrus*, Socrates does not hesitate to include tragic and comic drama as well as lyric and epic poetry among the subdivisions of republican rhetoric. Insofar as the noblest rhetoric includes education in civic life, the poets who may touch us deeply beginning from our youth must be seen as having one of the highest rhetorical functions and responsibilities. The most delicate question for any truly self-conscious political speaker or writer will be the degree to which, in the circumstances, the public arena can be opened up to critical—albeit, even in the best case only approximately rational—argument.

The classics certainly did not disregard the dangers implicit in these observations. They did not deny some considerable truth to the pejorative connotations associated with "rhetoric." The study of rhetoric originated with the sophists, and among many, though not all, of them the "art" of rhetoric tended orginally to take the form of what Socrates in the *Gorgias* characterizes as the ignoble "knack" of rhetoric. That ignoble knack comprises the clever ability to win praise through flattering popular opinion; it includes the talented capacity to advance the selfish interest of the speaker through appeals to the passions that lull or deceive the critical reasoning capacity of the citizenry. But Socrates did not react to the sophists by trying to deny the penetrating insights that they had achieved, even if those insights had been abused. On the contrary, he learned from the sophists, and from their teachers the poets, that politics could not transcend appeal to passion and imagination.

The teaching on a noble art of rhetoric that Socrates adumbrated and Isocrates and Aristotle elaborated was a teaching on a mode of discourse that would appeal to popular passion without flattering it. The noble art of rhetoric aims to elevate rather than to gratify, to sober rather than to inebriate. The Socratic art of rhetoric seeks to bring into being a mode of civic communication that will awaken and channel popular imagination and fervor without enflaming that imagination and fervor. The followers of Socrates tried to initiate a system of education that would produce leaders and orators who would accept the responsibility of a potentially unpopular public vocation for the sake of devotion to the common good and buoyed by hope of eventual fame and grateful remembrance. In the *Gorgias*, Socrates points to a "chastizing" rhetoric that would place the orator in the situation of opposing or warning against the ever-present self-indulgent proclivities of the people gathered in crowds or mobilized through the force of public opinion. More concretely, in the *Gorgias*, Socrates appeals to the model of the anti-imperialistic, dour, and unpopular Aristides—"Aristides the Just"—in contrast to the more superficially splendid models of the imperialistic, growth-promoting Themistocles and Pericles.

By this very choice of examples, Socrates indicates the grave practical limits to any hopes he might be thought to have entertained for the successful reform of republican life in the direction he indicates. Obviously it is the Periclean rather than the Aristidean tendency that will generally remain most attractive to democratic communities. And as Socrates quietly indicates in other passages of the *Gorgias*, the triumph of Periclean or Themistoclean foreign and domestic policies finds very considerable excuse, if not justification, in the economic needs of the Athenian populace and in the situation of Athens in relation to an ever-hostile international environment. But a continual reminder, on the part of the philosophers and their students, of the Aristidean alternative may contribute to hemming in the more extreme inclinations associated with Periclean dreams and ambitions.

In their constructive teaching on rhetoric, as in their constructive civic proposals generally, the classical political philosophers showed themselves amazingly free of unrealistic or sentimental hopes for any drastic transformation of political life as it had been known and recorded for generations, and as it had been presented with unrivaled lucidity and scope in the pages of Thucydides. It is thus all the more appropriate for us to give thought to how modest ingredients of the classical conception might infuse a healthy tincture into our present day public life—especially when the ingredients in question are traceable in the original political visions of some of the Founders of the American political tradition.

8 / Rethinking the Foundations of Liberalism

On the basis of our examination of classical republicanism, we are now in a position better to appreciate the important continuities, as well as the much more important discontinuities, that define the new turn in political theory that achieved its greatest practical influence and success in the founding of the American republic. To be sure, it is not possible to embrace all the crucial sources of the American experiment by focusing solely on classical and liberal republicanism and the debate between these two fundamental versions of republicanism. The American conception of republicanism, dedicated to the securing of equal and universal individual rights, and characterized by new institutions intended to safeguard these rights, also has deep and substantial roots in the gradual evolution of European feudalism and English common law. The stress on property rights, and the prerogatives or dignity of property holders, bears unmistakable marks of the feudal lineage. The separation of powers, especially insofar as it is characterized by a tense balance between a unitary executive and a bicameral legislature, obviously derives to some considerable extent from the history of the struggles between kings, nobles, and commons or third estate. Religious toleration, with the attendant limits on government and respect for the sanctity of a suprapolitical sphere of worship, morals, and family life, is indebted to the centuries-long medieval struggle between clerical and secular authority. Yet lest we miss the forest for the trees, we must not underestimate the extent to which these traditional materials were exploited, recast, and in the final analysis profoundly transformed by the philosophic revolution of the Enlightenment:

the great wave of rebellious rationalism and political theorizing that took root with Machiavelli, Bacon, Descartes, Hobbes, and Spinoza, and reached its highpoint of world-historical power with Locke and his somewhat restive successors—John Trenchard and Thomas Gordon, Montesquieu, Hume, and Adam Smith.

As a vast historical movement, the Enlightenment was, of course, complex, diffuse, and diverse. But at its core, it was a rebellion in the name of true, rational insight into human nature and the norms derivative from nature against what was understood to be the political, moral, and religious darkness resulting from insufficiently critical tutelage to the classical and biblical conceptions of politics and the human condition. As John Adams put it in his *Defence of the Constitutions of the United States of America*:

The United States of America have exhibited, perhaps, the first example of governments erected on the simple principles of nature; and if men are now sufficiently enlightened to disabuse themselves of artifice, imposture, hypocrisy, and superstition, they will consider this event as an era in their history. . . . It will never be pretended that any persons employed in [framing the United States' governments] had interviews with the gods or were in any degree under the inspiration of heaven, more than those at work upon ships or houses, or laboring in merchandise and agriculture; it will forever be acknowledged that these governments were contrived merely by the use of reason and the senses.[1]

The political philosophers who spearheaded the new conception of republican life were by no means indifferent to either moral or intellectual virtue: Spinoza, the first political philosopher to outline a theory of authentically liberal democracy, was also the first thinker to elaborate ethics in a rigorously deductive, geometric system—a scheme that culminated in a newly grounded preeminence of the philosophic life. Locke was the first philosopher who made it his business to devote an entire treatise (addressed directly to parents) to the moral education of young children. But precisely these striking innovations signal a new and unprecedented conception of the relation between theory and practice. The new republican theorists insisted that the classical and traditional biblical approaches had profoundly misunderstood both the nature of, and the proper way to instill or promote, virtue.

For the classical philosophers, as we have seen, knowledge of moral and civic virtue derived primarily, not from science or philosophy, but from the commonsense opinions of experienced and respected practical men. The philosopher's role was to distill, clarify, and enlarge common sense in the

1. *The Works of John Adams*, ed. Charles Francis Adams (Boston: Little, Brown, 1850–56), 4:292–93.

light of a critical inquiry and speculative knowledge that differed from, but could not replace, common moral sense as the primary basis for the virtues of active political life. Indeed, given the unfinished and skeptical character of the philosophic quest, an important duty of the philosopher was to protect the sphere of commonsense moral awareness from the corrosive possibilities of a too-direct exposure to philosophic questioning.

For the philosophers of the Enlightenment, this divide between theory and practice was drastically narrowed, if not denied. Knowledge of civic and moral virtue was to be directly deduced from the science philosophers had at their disposal, on the basis of which common sense was to be radically revised. Since philosophers were now to play so directly and openly sovereign a role in humanity's moral life, there was no longer any good reason for them to remain in the background or to hide their lights under bushels.

Both the Bible and classical philosophy were criticized, in the first place, for their unrealistically elevated demands. The Bible had taught humanity to judge political life against a life to come after death and virtues (proclaimed, most notably, in the Sermon on the Mount and Deuteronomy) beyond the reach of earthly human nature, and to attain which men and women desperately needed supernatural grace and guidance. Classical republicanism had taught citizens to judge political life in the light of what were admittedly extraordinary personal excellences and utopian conceptions of perfectly just or ideal political orders that could never be expected to be attained on earth. Both had taken their bearings by the aspirations the moral and pious proclaim in their speech when they attempt to articulate their deepest human longings. Both had therefore doomed mankind, the new theorists contended, to disappointment, disheartenment, and impotent resignation; both had alienated humanity from political life as it actually is, and had thus veiled from humanity what political life might one day become. Indeed, one might with reason suspect that it was the purpose of both the Bible and the classical philosophers to draw mankind, or at least the best among mankind, away from political life, or at any rate away from the energetic political ambition that seeks revolutionary, progressive transformation of the human condition. The modern political theorists of the Enlightenment and after claimed (with some plausibility) to be much more public-spirited than their predecessors. The purpose of theory, they insisted, is not simply to understand the world, but to change it, to make it better—on the basis of a prior understanding of the truth about the human predicament.

With that end in view, they argued, one must turn away from the misleading, often high-flown, speeches of political actors, to the revealing deeds of their actual behavior. One ought to analyze that behavior, not from the abstract perspective of a neutral observer, but rather from the perspective of a civic doctor seeking to understand pathologies with a view to curing or at least ameliorating them. The massive symptom of the pathology of political life is the endless war over the ends or purposes or excellences or salvation to which the community should be dedicated. The intractability of these controversies points to the irresolvable character of the issues at stake. Let us therefore take a new tack, they suggested. Let us seek those constant needs, arising directly from the strongest and most universal passions, that are always seen to be at work in all men in all times and places, no matter what their other, more disputable, and "higher" goals may be.

The liberal political theory of rights thus began from a self-conscious radicalization of the problems of the morality of law and the lawfulness of morality that we have been following in classical republican thought. The forerunners and founders of the liberal conception of rights rejected—as unrealistic, unworkable, or contrary to nature—the classical republican attempts to contend with these manifest difficulties. The classics had called for subordinating the naturally self-regarding passions to self-transcending habit or convention. This habit and convention were said to be grounded in rational argument, but were admittedly given much of their real psychological force, for most men, by the fact that they were backed up by fear of divine as well as human punishment. The philosophers of the Enlightenment demanded that this whole approach be replaced by, or drastically subordinated to, a new proposal for a new kind of alliance between reason and passion.

Reason ought *not* to be viewed as somehow constituting the preordained end or purpose of human existence (whether in the synthesis of reason and passion known as moral virtue or in the philosophic life). Instead, reason ought properly to be seen as the marvelously effective *servant* of the passions. More precisely, reason is best understood as the servant of those strongest self-regarding passions that, when enlightened by their servant, point toward forms of competition and cooperation that bring about "the common benefit of each"—a strikingly paradoxical phrase coined by Machiavelli, in the proem to book 1 of his *Discourses on Livy*, and then taken up by Locke, in the eleventh of his *Questions concerning the Law of Nature*.[2]

The thinker at the origins of the new outlook is indeed Machiavelli.

2. John Locke, *Questions concerning the Law of Nature*, ed. and trans. Robert Horwitz, Jenny Strauss Clay, and Diskin Clay (Ithaca: Cornell University Press, 1990), 238–39: the phrase in the original Latin is *communi cujusque utilitati*.

Given the shocking boldness of Machiavelli's moral teaching, and the character of the "virtue" he tries to inculcate, it is little wonder that his most sober liberal successors disavow his paternity. They build, however, on Machiavelli's foundational innovations, even as they dispute and reform the political teaching he draws from those innovations.

Machiavelli's works bespeak neutrality in the age-old dispute between despotism and republicanism. This neutrality is evident not merely as between the *Discourses* and the *Prince*, but even more shockingly within each work. In retelling and examining the rise and fall of Appius Claudius, the failed subverter of the Roman republic at its finest hour, in *Discourses* 1.40–46, Machiavelli does not hesitate to show how Appius ought to have acted—and thus how a potential Appius in any future successful republic ought to act—in order to succeed in enslaving his republican country and his fellow citizens in a brutal tyranny. Machiavelli goes so far as to blame Appius for having failed in his plot to subvert the liberties of the Roman people. How is this seemingly inhuman detachment from love of freedom possible? On closer inspection, this neutrality reveals itself to be the result or expression of a drastic reconception of political life, both monarchic and republican.

At bottom, according to Machiavelli, there is no difference between a healthy republic and a healthy monarchy (tyranny), except in the appearance that appeals to those filled with adolescent moral and political naiveté. A healthy tyranny/monarchy is just a republic that has temporarily come under the domination of its strongest citizen, who will sooner or later have to give way to a rival. A healthy republic (like the Roman at its best) is a monarchy or tyranny with many rival potential despots, each of whom ought to be scheming and working to liquidate his competitors. In that way, a veritable dynamo of conquering power can be built up in either monarchy or republic; and those peoples are truly free, secure, rich, glorious, and long-lasting who thus prepare constantly for offensive war and seek every opportunity to expand their dominion. The model for Machiavelli is always the lupine Roman republic. In other words, politics at its best or truest is a wolf pack, or rather, to use Machiavelli's image—borrowed, he says, from King Ferdinand of Spain—a ceaseless contest between flocks of fighting birds of prey belonging to different and unequal species.

Perhaps no thinker has gone so far as Machiavelli in celebrating the beneficent effects of unleashed, ruthless human selfishness. No wonder his successors recoiled from the outcome of his thinking. Yet they could not help but be impressed by the thought-provoking daring and credibility of the fundamental first stages of his analysis. They sought, in different ways, to domesticate or humanize his basic insights. Locke and Montesquieu in particular succeeded in profoundly transforming Machiavelli's basic insights into the foundation for a new moral code.

The first step in constructing the new moral catechism is to bestow moral primacy on those passions that are by nature irresistible and therefore blameless. These are the passions by which all men are driven, the passions whose satisfaction all men cannot help but demand the freedom to pursue. As naturally irresistible, these passions express, or can be understood by reason to express, "*natural* rights." All men, as necessarily subject to these irresistible drives, can be said to have a reasonable claim to follow these drives. All men can be said to be equally endowed with inalienable "natural rights" to seek the reasonable or realistic gratification of these passions. More specifically, all human beings may be said to have natural rights to pursue security, along with liberty—and especially the economic liberty to labor and acquire for themselves material security. Again, all human beings naturally pursue happiness, although the content of happiness is so diverse and so elusive that it is a mistake to suppose that anyone can or ought to dictate to another his or her goal in this respect: human beings may be said to have a right, inherent in their nature, to pursue happiness as they see fit.

Yet a right, to be a moral right, must entail a duty in others to respect the right. How and when or where does duty enter the picture, especially given the obvious fact that the "natural rights" of which we are now speaking come into conflict? The natural or spontaneous relationship among men is that of a "state of nature," which is practically equivalent to a state of war or constant preparation for war. The state of nature is, of course, a *social* condition of a kind, but an unregulated social condition, "full of fears and continual dangers," as Locke says (*Two Treatises of Government*, 2.123). This state of nature can be overcome only if it is first recognized as such: only, that is, if reason admits and faces up to the ugly truth about the natural human social condition or tendency, and then proceeds to construct a remedy for the disordered and self-destructive spontaneous nature of mankind. Natural rights come fully into their own by commanding natural duties. These duties define, regulate, or limit the exercise of rights, insofar as reason discovers rules of behavior by which men may coordinate their pursuit of the objects of their strongest passions in such a way as to minimize destructive conflict and maximize mutually beneficial competition. In his speech to the Pennsylvania ratifying convention (November 24, 1787), James Wilson summarized the "principles and conclusions generally admitted" by Americans "to be just and sound with regard to the nature and formation of single governments, and the duty of submission to them" as follows:

> Our wants, our talents, our affections, our passions, all tell us that we are made for a state of society. But a state of society could not be supported long or happily without some civil restraint. It is true that, in a state of nature, any one individual may act uncontrolled by others; but it is equally true, that, in such a state, every other individual may act uncontrolled by him. Amidst this universal independence, the dissensions and animosities between interfering members of the society would be numerous and ungovernable. The consequence would be, that each member, in such a natural state, would enjoy less liberty, and suffer more interruption, than he would in a regulated society. Hence the universal introduction of government of some kind or other into the social state.[3]

The "natural" duties or "natural" laws, as the products of rational calculation carried out with a view to the objects of the basic passions, are secondary to, and derivative from, the natural rights or claims that are the direct rational expressions of the basic passions. Natural duties and laws are defined as those imperatives that dictate the best means to the securing and promotion of natural rights, above all the right to secure or comfortable self-preservation. "These dictates of reason," as Hobbes has it, "are but conclusions or theorems concerning what conduces to the conservation and defense of themselves" (*Leviathan*, ch. 15, end). Natural law or morality can thus become, to a degree that is unthinkable in the classical or the medieval outlook, a strictly deductive science issuing propositions as eternally valid as those of Euclid. "The laws of nature," Hobbes concludes, "are immutable and eternal"; and "the science of them, is the true and only moral philosophy" (ibid.). "I doubt not," says Locke, "but from self-evident Propositions, by necessary Consequences, as incontestable as those in Mathematicks, the measures of right and wrong might be made out" (*Essay concerning Human Understanding* 4.3.18). "Before there were ever any laws made," says Montesquieu at the outset of the *Spirit of the Laws* (1.1), "there existed the possible relations of justice. For some one to claim that there is nothing just or unjust except what the positive laws enjoin or prohibit, is the same as if to say that before someone had traced a circle, all the radii of a circle were not equal."

To take the preeminent example, reason deduces that there can be no security without cooperation in stable, law-governed society; and that there

---

3. *Selected Political Essays of James Wilson*, ed. Randolph G. Adams (New York: Knopf, 1930), 172.

can be no stable and lawful society unless men can trust one another to make and keep contractual promises, above all the fundamental promise that constitutes the "social compact" that creates the foundation of law. Therefore making and keeping such a promise is a virtue, a moral virtue, derived by reason from the fundamental natural right of self-preservation. So understood, the moral status of this virtue is not dependent on classical republican or biblical claims that it fulfills the health of the soul: such a consequence is not denied, it is simply dismissed as irrelevant to that aspect of the virtue of keeping promises that is pertinent to political life. Of course, one must hasten to add that the virtue of keeping promises therefore comprises only a conditional imperative, not a categorical or absolute imperative: there is a duty to keep one's promises where one can reasonably be assured that others will do the same; no one is obliged to keep a promise whose consequences place one in clear and present danger. The God of nature or of reason, the God whose moral message can be apprehended by unaided reason, would not and could not demand such a thing. In the words of John Locke, nature

has a Law of Nature to govern it, which obliges every one: And Reason, which is that Law, teaches all Mankind, who will but consult it, that . . . being all the Workmanship of one Omnipotent, and infinitely wise Maker; . . . Every one as he is *bound to preserve himself*, and not to quit his Station wilfully; so by the like reason when his own Preservation comes not in competition, ought he, as much as he can, *to preserve the rest of Mankind*, and may not unless it be to do Justice on an offender, take away, or impair the life, or what tends to the Preservation of the Life, Liberty, Health, Limb, or Goods of another.   (*Two Treatises of Government* 2.6)

The Educational Controversy Dividing the Liberal Tradition

Government is best understood as the rationally constructed artifice by which individuals contract with one another to create a collective police power that will limit everyone's pursuit of the objects of his or her passions so as to make such pursuit more secure for all. But how in practice is this police power to be organized and operated, and how in practice are the citizens' passions to be schooled in the new, enlightened self-interest guided by reason? Is this schooling, even at its most effective, adequate to create citizens with sufficient public spirit to keep lawful and free society functioning well? It is the great series of arguments and debates over the answers to these questions that animate and divide the history of modern liberal political philosophy.

Perhaps more than any subsequent thinker, Hobbes stresses the need for education—of an intellectual or scientific, rather than moral and habitual, sort. The citizenry must be enlightened as to the true, if somewhat frightening, principles of human nature. They must be brought to understand the strength and the selfish, competitive character of the passions; the subordinate, but decisive, guidance given by reason; and the artificiality, but by the same token the necessity, of law and politics as a cure for the sickness of man's natural condition. This teaching, as laid down in the philosophic treatises of Hobbes himself, is to be promulgated primarily in the universities to the clergy and the gentry. It is to emanate thence, via pulpits and schools and public orations and offices, to the great body of the people. The people will thus grasp the reasons for the onerous burdens and restraints imposed on their passions by law and government; they will understand why government must be authoritarian (in the best case, centralized monarchy), in order drastically to limit the natural drift of human selfishness and competitiveness toward civil war. The people will learn, in other words, that precisely their innate or natural equality requires, for their own protection, the drastic *in*equality of political power artificially instituted by their presumed consent in the social compact.

For seeing the Universities are the fountains of civil and moral doctrine, from whence the preachers, and the gentry, drawing such water as they find, use to sprinkle the same (both from the pulpit and in their conversation), upon the people, there ought certainly to be great care taken, to have it pure, both from the venom of heathen politicians, and from the incantation of deceiving spirits. And by that means the most men, knowing their duties, will be the less subject to serve the ambition of a few discontented persons, in their purposes against the state; and be the less grieved with the contributions necessary for their peace, and defence; and the governors themselves have the less cause, to maintain at the common charge any greater army, than is necessary to make good the public liberty, against invasions and encroachments of foreign enemies. (*Leviathan*, "Review and Conclusion")

Mass enlightenment or education in this new scientific and philosophic sense, emanating from the universities, remains a keynote of liberal thought. But it is very much supplemented and reformulated by Hobbes's successors in the light of their insistence on (1) the need for better fences against governmental oppression, and (2) greater concessions to widespread human pride or ambition. Both of these considerations, Hobbes's successors argue, dictate a much less restrictive distribution of political power than that proposed by Hobbes. The considerable increase in the numbers having some share in political power can be made workable or safe, the later liberal thinkers argue, by a much more elaborate division and channeling of both governmental powers and economic pursuits so as constructively to check and balance natural human competitiveness. Locke and Montesquieu propose a series of famous institutional schemes—representative government; federalism; separation of powers; "mixture," or regularized antagonism, of popular, hereditary-noble, and monarchic governmental bodies—by which even imperfectly enlightened selfish pursuits of power can be made to issue in constructive competition. Locke and Montesquieu further argue that the competitive, commercial or free-enterprise economic system, once liberated and protected, can wean even the most spirited men away from the thirst for militaristic vainglory and toward the creation of vast new sources of collective welfare, security, and comfort: "Commerce cures destructive prejudices; and this is almost a general rule, that wherever there are soft manners and morals, there is commerce; and wherever there is commerce, there are soft manners and morals. . . . The natural effect of commerce is to lead to peace" (Montesquieu *Spirit of the Laws* 20.1–2).

Devotion to commercial growth had been part of the modern innovation from the beginning. Both Machiavelli and Hobbes had stressed the importance of the sovereign's fostering of acquisitiveness and protection of trade and industry in order to build a strong and secure society. "Money the blood of a commonwealth" is Hobbes's slogan (*Leviathan*, ch. 24). But it was only with subsequent thinkers—above all, Locke—that the moral foundation for economic growth was made firm.

Even the most superficial acquaintance with the documents of the eighteenth century cannot help but impress upon the reader the primacy, in the minds of almost all the advocates of a rights-based politics, of the right to property. What is the principled basis of this primacy? Traditionally, the right to property and preoccupation with ownership, and especially accumulation, of material goods had been looked upon with grave reserve. The classics did indeed recognize the importance of property rights, especially in land, as a crucial impediment to tyranny.[4] But from both the biblical and the classical republican perspectives, money-making appeared to be a temptation to lose one's soul in what was spiritually barren, basely competitive, and crassly vulgar or illiberal. The virtues associated with money or material possessions were the virtues of giving, not getting: generosity and charity, rather than work, thrift, and business shrewdness. The latter were viewed, not as noble or free employments of the human spirit, but as unfortunate necessities. Citing the authority of the first book of Aristotle's *Politics*, Thomas Aquinas declared that trading, when carried on with a view to

4. See the discussion and references in Leo Strauss, *On Tyranny* (Glencoe, Ill.: Free Press, 1963), 71–72.

profit, rather than simply with a view to providing the household or city with the necessaries of life

is justly deserving of blame, because, considered in itself, it satisfies the greed for gain, which knows no limit and tends to infinity. Hence trading, considered in itself, has a certain debasement attaching thereto. . . . Nevertheless, gain, which is the end of trading, though not implying, by its nature, anything virtuous or necessary, does not, in itself, connote anything sinful or contrary to virtue; wherefore nothing prevents gain from being directed to some necessary or even virtuous end, and thus trading becomes lawful.

(*Summa theologica* 2–2.77.4; Dominican Fathers' trans.)

By the same token, private ownership was understood in terms of a prior and always preeminent public or communal ownership. Proprietorship was understood in terms of stewardship: as a custodial care of what belonged, in the final analysis, to the community or to God.

Two things are competent to man in respect of exterior things. One is the power to procure and dispense them, and in this regard it is lawful for man to possess property. Moreover, this is necessary to human life. . . . The second thing that is competent to man with regard to external things is their use. In this respect man ought to possess external things, not as his own, but as common, so that, to wit, he is ready to communicate them to others in their need. Hence the Apostle says, "Charge the rich of this world . . . to give easily, to share," etc. [1 Tim. 6:17, 18].

(Ibid., 2–2.66.2)

Hence, whatever goods some have in superabundance are due, by natural law, to the sustenance of the poor.

(Ibid., 2–2.66.7)

What we may call, somewhat anachronistically, capitalism—that is, the employment of money as an "investment" with a view to making more money—was judged severely by Plato, Aristotle, and Thomas Aquinas; and their worst strictures were reserved for what we would call banking, or what they called "usury": the loaning of money at interest. To quote Thomas once again, "to take interest for money lent is unjust in itself" (ibid., 2–2.78.1).

Nowhere did the modern advocates of the new republicanism find more to complain about in their predecessors than in this attitude toward honest love of gain. Generosity is a noble thing, they acknowledged; but it is also, they observed, a rare luxury in most men's lives. All men must, however, seek personal comfort, security, and happiness for themselves and their families. Men disagree sharply, of course, over what constitutes happiness; but they agree almost universally in the recognition that the quest for happiness requires power or wherewithal; and the most solid, useful, pacific, and mutually beneficial power men may seek in society is the economic power generated by participation in the free market. What is more, true liberty or independence requires an economic basis; therefore, only where a sizable proportion of the citizenry each owns its own land, or has access to gainful employment and material accumulations comparable to real estate in solidity and magnitude, will there prevail an empirical, and not merely abstract, independence and dignity of the average citizen. To protect liberty and dignity, as well as the pursuit of happiness, it is therefore necessary to protect and promote this reasonable, and thus natural, love of gain. The liberation and protection of this natural love entails the destruction of those historical and merely conventional barriers that have excluded the vast majority of men from access to the tools, freedom, capital, and opportunity to produce and acquire wealth. No reason derived from natural rights—which are equally and universally distributed—justifies restricting property to any group on any basis other than enterprise and inheritance.

The mention of inheritance calls our attention to the fact that Locke's and Montesquieu's teachings on the natural right to property envisage human beings not merely as individuals but as individuals united in families, and especially as individuals who are actual or potential parents, naturally striving to better the lot of their offspring. The protection of rights of inheritance, like the protection of family privacy, is a fundamental aspect of the original doctrine of natural rights. One of the most striking signs of the confused retreat from liberal natural rights that has afflicted the Marxist-influenced United Nations, as well as recently instituted constitutions in leading liberal democracies such as Canada, is the shameful dilution of property rights and inheritance rights of individuals and families. To take some remarkable examples, neither the United Nations International Covenant on Economic, Social, and Cultural Rights nor the Charter of Economic Rights and Duties of States enunciates any individual human being's right to any property or any state duty to protect any such right. The United Nations Declaration of the Rights of the Child recognizes no right of the child to own or to inherit any of the parent's property—not even the home and family belongings or clothing. In comparison to these grim silences, and the history of bureaucratic indecency in communist nations whose constitutions are silent about property and inheritance rights, Locke's compelling logic in arguing for the property rights of wives and children is precious.[5]

5. See esp. *Two Treatises of Government* 1.86–98, 2.77–83. The erosion of fidelity to the protection of individual property rights is clear if one contrasts Article 17 of the original U.N. Declaration of Human Rights (1948) with the later U.N. International Covenant on Civil and Political Rights, Article 17—and the erosion becomes even clearer if one contrasts both these documents with Article 17 of the Declaration of the Rights of Man and Citizen of 1789: "Property being an inviolable and sacred right, no one may be deprived of it, except when the

Yet inheritance laws may so seriously curtail the free competition of talent that they stifle opportunity for many; there must then be a prudent balance struck between the legitimate concerns of parents and the equally legitimate concerns of the community for the access of all to the means of material betterment: Locke attacks laws of primogeniture, and Montesquieu recommends laws equalizing inheritance among all children of a marriage. More generally, the property right is never understood by the originators of the doctrine of natural rights to be a right beyond regulation, even extensive regulation, by government in the name of the vast majority of the people: in Locke's words, men "enter into Society with others for the securing and regulating of Property" (*Two Treatises of Government* 2.120). Locke celebrates "that Prince who shall be so wise and godlike as by established laws of liberty to secure protection and incouragement to the honest industry of Mankind against the oppression of power and narrownesse of Party" (ibid. 2.42). But as this remark illustrates, the principle that ought to animate governmental regulation is itself taken from natural rights; the equal freedom or right to compete, and to develop fully the potential of one's talents for acquisition, is the goal of legitimate government economic regulation.

The vast inequalities that result are justified, Locke argues, by the empirical fact that in a society that liberates acquisitiveness even the lowest rungs advance to conditions of greater material welfare than that prevailing among the kings and rulers of societies that choke off, or are ignorant of, the blessing of free enterprise: among the American Indians who do not recognize the acquisitive property right made possible by the invention of money, Locke says, "a King of a large fruitful Territory there feeds, lodges, and is clad worse than a day Labourer in *England*" (ibid. 2.41). This of course requires that government step in to assist those who for whatever reason are trammeled by misfortune to such a degree as to be unable to gain a footing to compete in the free market: "Common charity teaches, that those should be most taken care of by the Law, who are least capable of taking care for themselves."[6] Yet common charity is regulated by the principles of natural rights; and Locke's suggested poor law reforms mandate rather severe incentives (including corporal punishment) for the working poor to get themselves, even, or indeed especially, at a very tender age (beginning at three years old!), off the dependent public dole and into government training for

public necessity, legally established, evidently demands it, and under the condition of a just and prior indemnification." For a fuller discussion, see Orwin and Pangle 1984, 1–22.

6. John Locke, "Some Considerations of the Consequences of the Lowering of Interest, and Raising of the Value of Money," in *Several Papers relating to Money, Interest, and Trade, etc.* (London: Churchill, 1696), 13.

hard, gainful, and hence potentially independent work. Montesquieu's views are characteristically more humane, while yet avoiding sentimentality:

> A man is not poor because he has nothing, but because he is not working. . . . In commercial countries, where many persons have nothing but their art, the state is often obliged to provide for the needs of the elderly, the sick, and orphans. A well-governed state takes this subsistence from the arts themselves: it gives to the sick and elderly the work of which they are capable; it teaches the children how to work, which is already a sort of work. A few alms given to a naked man in the streets in no way fulfills the obligations of the state, which owes to all citizens an assured subsistence, food, adequate clothing, and a way of life that is not unhealthy. . . . The riches of a state presuppose much industry. It is not possible in so many branches of commerce to avoid always having someone who suffers, or to avoid, as a consequence of the many branches, having workers who are temporarily in trouble.
>
> (*Spirit of the Laws* 23.29)

Yet precisely this passage highlights the fact that humane free enterprise by no means obviates—indeed, it in crucial respects increases—the degree of both political and economic inequality, and hence instability, among the citizenry. Given the principled universal equality, as well as liberty, at the foundation of the modern liberal political teaching about rights, what is to ensure that the mass of men will not grow restive under the highly unequal distribution that is the outcome of the protection of the equal liberties embodied in the natural rights? This question intensifies if we keep in view—as Locke especially insists we ought—the power of the selfish and domineering passions animating all men by nature. "The Natural Vanity and Ambition of Men," Locke avers, is but "too apt of it self to grow and encrease with the Possession of any Power" (*Two Treatises of Government* 1.10).

> I told you before that Children love *Liberty*; . . . I now tell you, they love something more; and that is *Dominion*: And this is the first original of most vicious Habits, that are ordinary and natural. . . . they shew their love of Dominion, [in] their desire to have things to be theirs; they would have *Propriety* and Possession, pleasing themselves with the Power which that seems to give. . . . we are all, even from our Cradles, vain and proud Creatures.
>
> (*Some Thoughts concerning Education*, secs. 103, 105, 119)

The question becomes acute when we recognize in addition—as Locke again stresses we ought—the threat posed by the human imagination, with its tendency to inflate and distort original, simple passions through religious, heroic, and erotic fantasies, hopes, and fears.

> The imagination is always restless and suggests variety of thoughts, and the will, reason being laid aside, is ready for every extravagant project; and in this State, he that goes farthest out of the way, is thought fittest to lead, and is sure of most

followers: And when Fashion hath once Established, what Folly or craft began, Custom makes it Sacred, and 'twill be thought impudence or madness, to contradict or question it. He that will impartially survey the Nations of the World, will find so much of their Governments, Religions, and Manners brought in and continued amongst them by these means, that he will have but little Reverence for the Practices which are in use and credit amongst Men.

(*Two Treatises of Government* 1.58)

Human beings, as individuals and in the mass, can be brought to their senses by grave threats or in times of emergency; but what is to keep them in their senses as the more routine years pass, especially in a flourishing commercial and liberal society? Such a society, we must add, will tend to accumulate ever-greater sources of administrative, economic, technological, and military power, whose irrational and destructive potential increases as the years go by. The problem of mass moral education remains pressing, despite—or even because of—economic progress.

In the case of Locke, the problem is especially striking. Lockean liberalism depends not only on the persistence of respect for rights of unequally distributed property, as well as respect for unending hard labor and the burdens of familial responsibility; in addition, by virtue of his doctrine of the popular right to revolution, Locke stands at the opposite pole from Hobbes among the founders of the tradition of rights-based politics. This Lockean principle, so highly celebrated by the American Founders, places in the hands of the majority the right and the duty to rise in violent and dangerous rebellion in order to depose a government that reveals itself to be aiming at the long-term enslavement and exploitation of the populace. But what will incline the people, or individuals among the people, to the heroism the exercise of this right may well entail; and what will prevent the people from abusing the right, in fits of mass hysteria or under the delusions bred by "soak-the-rich" demagogues? What, if anything, in the Lockean doctrine of natural rights, will tend to breed leaders like Martin Luther King, Jr., with his carefully considered appeal to the "conscience of the community" rather than to its passions?

Two answers are prominent in Locke's works. The first is a new popular religion: a Christianity reinterpreted and transformed so as to provide otherworldly sanctions for nothing more and nothing less than obedience to the laws of reason or nature dictated by Locke's liberal political philosophy. To the creation of such a radically liberalized Christianity, Locke devoted a large and very influential portion of his published writings. But, in the first place, there are insuperable tensions or contradictions between Locke's strictly theological writings and the arguments concerning human knowledge carefully elaborated in the *Essay concerning Human Understanding*. Chiefly as a consequence, Locke was a major source of religious skepticism in the eighteenth century, not only in Europe, as is stressed by Dugald Stewart in his great history of the Scottish Enlightenment (1854, 240–42), but in America. "It is unquestionable," James Wilson declares near the beginning of his second lecture on law of 1790, "that the writings of Mr. Locke have facilitated the progress, and have given strength to the effects of scepticism." But even more problematic is the inevitable observation that even, or precisely, within Locke's theology, the extraordinarily prosaic or mercenary, and almost transparently utilitarian, nature of the exhortation to newly "reasonable" piety renders rather questionable its capacity to bring authentic religious fervor to the support of the commands of Lockean reason. Locke's *Reasonableness of Christianity* concludes with the following amazing doxology (para. 245):

The portion of the righteous has been in all ages taken notice of to be pretty scanty in this world: virtue and prosperity do not often accompany one another, and therefore virtue seldom had many followers: and 'tis no wonder she prevailed not much in a state, where the inconveniencies that attended her were visible, and at hand, and the rewards doubtful, and at a distance. . . . The philosophers, indeed, shewed the beauty of virtue: they set her off so as drew men's eyes and approbation to her; but leaving her unendowed, very few were willing to espouse her. The generality could not refuse her their esteem and commendation, but still turned their backs upon her, and forsook her, as a match not for their turn. But now there being put into the scales, on her side, "an exceeding and immortal weight of glory," interest is come about to her: and virtue is now visibly the most enriching purchase, and by much the best bargain. The view of heaven and hell will cast a slight upon the short pleasures and pains of this present state, and give attractions and encouragements to virtue, which reason and interest, and the care of ourselves, cannot but allow and prefer. Upon this foundation, and upon this only, morality stands firm, and may defy all competition.

As Locke remarks at the end of his treatise on "reasonable" Christianity, "this is a religion suited to vulgar capacities."

The second, and more compelling, Lockean answer is a new stress on moral education, outlined in *Some Thoughts concerning Education*. The personality that is the goal of Locke's new system of character formation is considerably less austere, self-transcending, or public-spirited than the personality aimed at by the moral education envisaged in classical republicanism. Moreover, Locke views moral education as a private matter. He says almost nothing about education in his political treatises, *except* to note the importance of moral education and that it is a matter for parents to take care of. Government is within its rights when it provides basic technical public education, but when government attempts to take on direct responsibility for the character formation of its citizens, it encroaches on the sacred private sphere of basic individual rights to liberty and to the pursuit of happiness. Besides, Locke argues, parents—and tutors personally selected and hired by parents—are the most appropriate directors of their own children's spiritual development. But all this means that Locke's education is restricted to a small minority: to those few whose parents are financially able to afford the leisure and the tutors necessary for a fully elaborated education in the home.

It is not surprising, then, that Locke's greatest liberal successors, Montesquieu and Hume, look to less exclusive and more widespread sources for the popular education required if the new liberal institutions are to function well. Both Montesquieu and Hume place a new stress on the importance of subpolitical climatic and historical forces shaping what Montesquieu calls a "general spirit of a nation"—a national character that welds human beings of all social strata into collectivities rooted in shared traditions, habits, customs, opinions, and beliefs. Yet these "national characters," the result of generations of shared cultural and natural environments, may be either well-disposed or ill-disposed to assimilate the new liberal principles and the modes of behavior those principles require. Both Montesquieu and Hume tend, in other words, to bring out the question of the degree to which the successful operation of enlightened self-interest requires accidently preexisting habits, and inner sources of discipline, trust, honor, and fellowship, or social solidarity, that are not themselves necessarily or even usually the product of enlightened self-interest, and may very often in fact be directly opposed to such self-interest. Accordingly, both Montesquieu and Hume are less sanguine than either Hobbes or Locke as to the degree to which liberal political systems and principles are likely to spread and take root throughout the world. And both Montesquieu and Hume are more troubled than are Hobbes and Locke by the fragility of the institutional checks and balances, as well as the fragility of the nascent economic freedoms, that they see beginning to mark England, Holland, and even France in the eighteenth century. As regards the protection of liberty and rights in England in particular, Montesquieu and Hume stress the critical roles played by the religious establishment, the hereditary nobility, and the hereditary monarchy within the mixed constitution of England. They both—Montesquieu implicitly and Hume explicitly—indicate grave reservations about the doctrines of the so-

cial contract, the right to revolution, and even human rights. Both philosophers worry that incautious promulgation of such libertarian and egalitarian
teachings might tend to contribute to a breakdown of the traditional senses
of reverence, deference, fraternity, civility, responsibility, and allegiance that
have been built up over generations and that serve as the cement preventing
the disintegration and atomization of what these thinkers conceive to be,
after all, essentially artificial civil societies. It is not surprising that Hume's
History of England, his most popular and eloquent presentation of his political theory, became the bane of the American Founders. The spirit of Hume's
political teaching is succinctly conveyed by two passages from his *Essays:*

I must confess, that I shall always incline to their side, who draw the bond of
allegiance very close, and consider an infringement of it, as the last refuge in desperate
cases, when the public is in the highest danger, from violence and tyranny. . . . Besides
we must consider, that, as obedience is our duty in the common course of things, it
ought chiefly to be inculcated; nor can anything be more preposterous than an
anxious care and solicitude in stating all the cases, in which resistance may be allowed. . . . the maxims of resistance . . . it must be confessed, are, in general, so
pernicious, and so destructive of civil society.   ("Of Passive Obedience")

It is but a foolish wisdom, which is so carefully displayed, in undervaluing princes,
and placing them on a level with the meanest of mankind. To be sure, an anatomist
finds no more in the greatest monarch than in the lowest peasant or day-labourer;
and a moralist may, perhaps, frequently find less. But what do all these reflections
tend to? We, all of us, still retain these prejudices in favor of birth and family. . . .
Or should a man be able, by his superior wisdom, to get entirely above such prepos-
sessions, he would soon, by means of the same wisdom, again bring himself down
to them, for the sake of society, whose welfare he would perceive to be intimately
connected with them. Far from endeavouring to undeceive the people in this particular, he would cherish such sentiments of reverence to their princes; as requisite to
preserve a due subordination in society.   ("Of the Protestant Succession")[7]

The Boldness of the American Project

It is especially these conservative tendencies in the political theories of Montesquieu and Hume that impress upon us the daring, and by the same token
the problematic character, of the American attempt to join popular government and rights. The Framers' liberalism opposed or qualified previous liberal or rights-oriented theory and practice inasmuch as it was married to a
continuing dedication to popular self-government—seen partly as a means

7. David Hume, *Essays: Moral, Political, and Literary,* ed. Eugene F. Miller (Indianapolis:
Liberty Classics, 1985), 490–91, 504.

to securing rights, but partly as another end, as an essential additional manifestation of human dignity. From the point of view of Hume especially, one
would have to say that the Americans were willing or compelled to run
rather severe risks with the liberal protection of individual rights in order
to comply with what Madison calls "that honorable determination which
animates every votary of freedom to rest all our political experiments on the
capacity of mankind for self-government," a determination dictating that
American government be "strictly republican" (*Federalist Papers*, no. 39).

Paradoxically, the dangers to which Hume would point are compounded
by the fact that the American notion of self-government departs decisively
from both classical republican and Humean notions of balanced government, in the direction of the basically democratic principles of the social
contract: the American notion of republicanism introduces the egalitarian
and libertarian, or popular-sovereignty, principles of the underlying social
contract directly into the constitutional organization and administration of
the government. The most prominent Founders (apart from John Adams,
who in this key respect appears an anachronism) ignore or jettison, to a
large extent, the institutional cautions and qualifications that had been the
great theme of Hume, Montesquieu, Blackstone, and other eighteenth-century liberals. The Americans insist on a government not only of and for, but
to a considerable extent by, the people. To be sure, the Americans seek to
construct, on a strictly popular basis, institutions that will play a role akin
to the role played by the nonpopular institutions of the English mixed constitution. And of course the Founders retain the great principle of representative, as opposed to direct, democracy. But they make the representative
government much more directly responsible to, and much more directly
under the control of, the people than had been the case in any previous
representative systems. What is more, the system and the outlook the Founders set in motion has in the two subsequent centuries developed far in
an even more popular and individualistic direction than their original plan
envisaged.

At the same time, the degree to which the American republic is dedicated
to the protection and fostering of *individual*, or even private, rights and
liberties moves it to an outer orbit of the English republican tradition—the
twofold tradition looking back to John Milton, on the one hand, and Algernon Sidney, on the other. The Founders largely leave behind the austere
blend of Isocratean classical republicanism and Calvinist political theology
expressed so eloquently in Milton's *Areopagitica* and *Of Education*. They
stand closer to Sidney's *Discourses on Government*; but they eschew even

the softened militarism and imperialism of Sidney's much-mitigated Machiavellian vision, while laying aside Sidney's still-classical reservations, voiced in the name of the claims of virtue, against popular sovereignty. With a few striking exceptions, the Founders do not characteristically echo Sidney in speaking of the people's duty, under natural law, to elect their virtuous superiors as rulers or representatives (see Sidney, *Discourses concerning Government* 1.10, 13, 16).

And yet nevertheless, as republicans, Americans do continue to express from afar, as it were, a sense of deep kinship with the classical republican tradition. They give expression to a genuine admiration for the improbable self-overcoming exhibited by Plutarch's heroes and fostered by the cities those heroes inhabited and defended. What is more, the Founders restate, at important junctures, some of the principles of classical republican political teaching. The *Federalist Papers* are concerned with recruiting men of virtue for public office under the new Constitution. They appeal to the proud, watchful, and fair-minded spirit of the people as the final bulwark against tyranny. They rely on the sturdy self-sufficiency and independence of the yeomanry to make up the moral backbone of the population. But they integrate these classical or quasi-classical elements into a framework that makes very little provision for the inculcation, fostering, or even preservation, of these crucial excellences of character.

The contrast between classical and American republicanism as regards the relationship between constitutional law and virtue is seen most sharply if we juxtapose a key statement from Plato's *Laws* with the conclusion of John Adams's *Defence of the Constitutions of Government of the United States of America*. Plato's Athenian Stranger describes the relation between constitutional law or institutions and the moral character of the rulers as follows:

although the giving of laws is a grand deed, still, even where a city is well-equipped, if the magistrates established to look after the well-formulated laws were unfit, then not only would the laws no longer be well-founded, and the situation most ridiculous, but those very laws would be likely to bring the greatest harm and ruin to those cities. (*Laws* 751b–c)

John Adams, in contrast, concludes with this observation:

The best republics will be virtuous, and have been so; but we may hazard a conjecture that the virtues have been the effect of the well ordered constitution rather than the cause. And, perhaps, it would be impossible to prove that a republic cannot exist even among highwaymen by setting one rogue to watch another; and the knaves themselves may in time be made honest men by the struggle.[8]

The question looming in Adams's conclusion, the question that has bulked ever larger as our constitutional system has evolved, especially in the past forty or fifty years, is whether and how the system provides for the moral and civic education of a people that becomes more fragmented in every sense even as it is given more and more power and responsibility.

The form this question took in the founding period is instructive. For in the years immediately following ratification of the Constitution, a few of the Founders—most notably Jefferson, Wilson, and Washington, along with the lesser figures Benjamin Rush and Noah Webster—became increasingly uneasy at the absence of governmental concern, at the national or state level, for the establishment of educational institutions and programs aimed at civic virtue. In attempting to address the problem of preserving and fostering a reliable popular civic ethos, they tended to return again and again to two sources for guidance and inspiration: the classical republics and Protestant Christianity. They did so despite the fact that they tended themselves to be rather freethinking and were mostly opposed to any but the most minimal establishment of religion. They did so despite the fact that they or their colleagues directed severe criticism at the classical republics for their failure to protect individual rights, especially acquisitive property rights; for their anticommercial and Stoical or moralistic austerity; and for the religious "superstition" that, in the Americans' eyes, stained their councils and public actions.

In other words, Americans during the founding period tended to try to imitate or evoke, if only in diluted versions, the classical virtues, while subordinating, without altogether abandoning, the classical principles and practices that aimed at producing those virtues. The Americans celebrated the Revolution's spirit of brotherhood in arms, sacrifice of life, and martial manliness, while creating a society in which commerce was to reign supreme, explicitly displacing old-fashioned heroic republicanism. They tried to instill reverence for constitutional law and tradition, while insisting that the law could only draw legitimacy from its service to the welfare of individuals. They assumed the names of Plutarchian heroes as pen names, while deploring and distancing themselves from the decisive aristocratic dimension of Plutarchian republicanism.

The rather slender threads that once linked the new, rights-oriented re-

8. *The Political Writings of John Adams*, ed. George A. Peek, Jr. (Indianapolis: Bobbs-Merrill, 1954), 162.

public to the ancient republican tradition have become increasingly frayed and tenuous. The check these threads provided on the more powerful mainsprings of the American republic have become weaker and weaker. For several generations now, we have been witnessing and experiencing the process by which the American republic, led by its "advanced" elites, has been radicalizing and making ever more unqualified both its liberal or libertarian and its democratic or egalitarian nature. The changes in our public and our private life that have resulted are troubling. The question is not the survival of the system and the republic, at least in the foreseeable future; what is at issue is rather the shrinking of the spirit, the shriveling of the heart, the banalization of existence that seems to loom as we look about us.

Americans seem increasingly to confirm Tocqueville's warnings about the dangerous "individualistic" proclivities of democracy. In Tocqueville's analysis, the kind of democratic society we find in the United States exhibits a new kind of human isolation that must be understood in contradistinction to selfishness or egoism:

Egoism is a passionate and exaggerated love of self which leads a man to think of all things in terms of himself and to prefer himself to all.

Individualism is a considered and calm feeling which disposes each citizen to isolate himself from the mass of his fellows, and to withdraw into the circle of his family and his friends; with the result that, after this little society has been created for his use, he gladly abandons the greater society to look after itself.

Egoism springs from a blind instinct; individualism proceeds from an erroneous judgment rather than from a depraved feeling. . . .

Egoism is a vice as old as the world. It hardly belongs to one form of society more than to another.

Individualism originates with democracy, and it threatens to enlarge itself in proportion to the equalization of conditions.

Among aristocratic peoples, families remain for centuries in the same situation, and often in the same place. That makes all the generations contemporaries, so to speak. A man almost always knows his ancestors and respects them; he believes that he already sees his great grand-children, and he loves them. . . .

Since, in aristocratic societies, all citizens are placed in fixed stations, some above and some below, the consequence is that each of them always sees someone higher whose protection he needs, and perceives someone lower whose assistance he can claim. . . .

In proportion to the equalization of conditions, there are more and more individuals who, no longer rich enough or powerful enough to have much influence over their fellows, have nevertheless gained or kept enough understanding and property to be self-sufficient. Such folk owe no man anything and expect, so to speak, nothing from anybody; they form the habit of always thinking of themselves in isolation, and gladly imagine that their whole destiny is in their own hands.

Thus, not only does democracy make each forget his ancestors, it also hides from him his descendants and separates him from his contemporaries; democracy ceaselessly draws one toward oneself alone, and threatens finally to shut one up entirely in the solitude of one's own heart. (*Democracy in America* 2.2.2)

Are not successive generations of Americans finding it harder and harder to resist these disintegrating effects of which Tocqueville warned? Do we not seem, as a people, more and more cast adrift in a floating anomy of lonely crowds denuded of trustworthy emotional and intellectual sources of human fellowship and inspiration or aspiration? In darker moments, one cannot help but wonder with trepidation whether the country might not be entering upon an irreversible trajectory. Is our culture not gathering a rather frightening momentum? Throwing themselves into essentially unpleasant or stultifying work with a view to the accumulation of greater material satisfactions and petty signs of prestige, to which they become ever more grimly enthralled; seeking escape in mindless music, sports, travel, and short-lived, gripping diversions of all kinds; convulsed periodically with fantastic longings for revelatory erotic or religious experiences: may not future generations of Americans lead increasingly fragmented and purposeless existences in a world of unprecedented materialism, desperate personal isolation, and inner psychological weakness verging on collapse?

Or will perhaps the inspiriting rebirth of enthusiasm in Eastern Europe, for *both* individual rights *and* republican self-government—for freedom not only in a negative but also in a more positive, civic or virtuous sense, with all the challenges and responsibilities this implies—infect us here in America with a renewed aspiration to recover the full meaning of both our dedication to rights and our dedication to republicanism?

A judgment of modern democracy from the critical perspective of classical republicanism would not suggest a quixotic attempt to bring back the sort of civic life that characterized the *polis*, or for that matter even the New England township. Classical republicanism values above all the virtue of prudence or practical wisdom. This prudence consists in adapting the highest reasonable goals to circumstances, in the awareness that every conceivable political circumstance will be decisively deficient in more than one respect, and, what is more, in the clear-eyed recognition that even the best conceivable political system will be flawed, given the essentially disharmonious tension among the highest of the natural human needs and goals. It is in this sense that classical republicanism is indeed essentially and self-consciously "utopian."

The "utopian" is today frequently misunderstood. The word *utopia*, coined by the Christian Platonist Thomas More, means "good place / no place" (from *eu topos / ou topos*). As More's *Utopia* is meant to remind us, classical republicanism culminates in articulation of the best regime simply, the best regime by nature for human beings. But it conceives of that best regime as one fraught with fundamental contradictions, and, partly for this reason, as a regime whose actual coming into being is not only extraordinarily unlikely, but indeed, in the final analysis, impossible and *undesirable*. The best regime is *not* an "ideal." The purpose of elaborating the best regime is not to set forth a blueprint for action, but rather to place before the mind's eye the highest standard in the light of which to judge all historical situations. This standard breaks open the horizon imposed by the reigning regime's inevitable dogmas, while yet allowing one to resign oneself to the limits of reform in every actual regime. The point of reflection on the best regime is not, then, to attach our hopes to a hypothetical best regime, but rather to detach us, in some measure, from unreasonable hopes. Reflection on the "best regime" is meant to afford to the individual a source of wisdom about the human condition; and from that wisdom is meant to spring a tempering of both enthusiasm and despair.

In part, then, the teaching on the best regime is meant to loosen the citizen's total fidelity to the given regime or tradition in which he finds himself. Aristotle's famous discussion of the relationship between the good or "serious" human being and the "serious" citizen (*Politics* 3.4) brings out with remarkable clarity the fact that the truly good or serious human being will only rarely, if ever, be simply a loyal citizen. For the virtue of the serious citizen, in contrast to that of the good human being, is a relative virtue. What it means to be a serious citizen, at least in the ordinary civic sense of the term, is dependent on the regime in power: loyalty to the existing regime and reform that does not subvert the existing regime are at the heart of serious citizenship. At the heart of good humanity, however, is loyalty to the truth and to virtue grounded in nature, in what is right by nature, or in the unfinished quest for the truth about human nature. Still, this implies that the citizen striving to be a good human being, precisely because of a qualified loyalty to the existing regime, may be a better friend to that regime, if it is a decent regime, than its most passionate supporters. The good human being strives to correct or improve the regime, and not merely in the light of a standard provided by the regime. The good human being, one may say, strives to be a kind of conscience or gadfly to the regime in which he finds himself, and to which he is naturally attached—but with a reasonable, because reasoned, love.

We need to apply these general reflections in trying to understand the viewpoint from which classical republicanism would assess our liberal republican regime, and in trying to understand how we might best appropriate the critical viewpoint classical republicanism affords.

I am inclined to believe that our regime and tradition might well be judged a noble, if flawed, republican experiment, whose flaws and nobility both in key respects surpass those of the republics known to antiquity. Liberation of the vast majority from slavery, disease, and poverty; maintenance of stability, lawfulness, and dignity through the new design of political institutions; toleration, protection of personal and familial privacy, and compassionate social welfare are achievements that were all but unknown to classical republican history. At the same time, however, the vantage point of classical republicanism permits us to see that we may have to diagnose the dispiriting symptoms of disintegration all around us as substantially rooted in original deficiencies of the modern republican experiment.

Certainly the classical perspective encourages a reexamination of the importance of government, law, rhetoric, and public policy in cultivating the civic and moral virtues of republican citizenship. Yet classical prudence warns us to proceed in a manner that does not threaten the fabric and foundation of the regime into which we are attempting to introduce modest reform. The spirit of classical republicanism would counsel resuscitation of, and building on, those specific elements of classical republicanism that are most incontrovertibly present—even if in unobtrusive, and hence forgotten or submerged, ways—in the original aims and reflections of major participants in the founding of the United States.

We ought not to expect or seek the full and direct political participation that was once possible in smaller republican communities, but we could nevertheless invest as much responsibility as possible in local government. The twenty-first century is likely to be an age of experimentation with various forms of federalism, as the Soviet empire dissolves and the European community recreates itself, and the American legal and political system, rooted as it is in a great federalist tradition, ought to be prepared to profit from and contribute to these experiments. We could certainly try harder to compel centralized bureaucracies to bend before—and perhaps even to elicit or stimulate—diverse, and relatively autonomous, local civic initiative. In the private sector, greater attention could be paid to the possibilities of worker participation in the decisions that affect and guide the workplace in large corporations. Of course, with greater participation comes greater responsibility, not to say "headaches." But perhaps the shock administered to organized labor by the decline in union membership over the past generation might be the occasion for a reconsideration and broadening of the kinds and the range of interests unions might represent at the bargaining table.

It is true that local government and workplace democracy are inevitably and properly overshadowed by the drama of state, and especially national, politics. In a mass democracy, it is necessarily the tiny numbers of representatives clustered in the state and federal capitals who fight over, and then carry out, the policies that give direction and shape to our collective life as Americans. Most Americans will participate in these cockpits of republicanism only at a great distance, through a kind of vicarious partisanship. But this partisanship need not be as passive, or as episodic and erratic, as it so often seems to be today. Our conception of representative politics needs to be rethought after we have found our way back to the classical republican teaching on rhetoric, and then have revised and redrafted that teaching in the light of modern circumstances, dominated by the "media" and above all by television. Given the enormous significance of television for the communication that weaves us together as a citizenry, ought not more time be reserved for, and ought not more thought be given to, formats in which issues and leaders of the day might present themselves, or in which our civic traditions and historical legacy might be examined from diverse and competing points of view?

In the realm of economic policy, sumptuary laws could, of course, be reintroduced only through stupidly tyrannical measures; but tax and fiscal policy, and the economic practice and rhetoric of our political and business leaders, could more clearly keep our commitment to economic growth and opportunity limited by a respect for moderation, a distrust of luxury, a sense of stewardship, and cultivation of habits of liberality or charity. Along with more worker participation in company decisions, companies could exercise charity less by large grants to bloated bureaucratic foundations and more by initiating charitable projects that would depend on coordinated voluntary efforts on the part of workers at all levels, to some extent on paid company time. Such initiatives might prove to be the seedbeds for the development of a taste for wider civic participation on the part of many. In the realm of welfare policy, a classical republican perspective would, I believe, lead us to applaud the movement toward a welfare policy that pays much closer attention to the moral and educational effects of government assistance. Such a perspective would prompt strong attempts to build into assistance programs incentives for hard work, for the assumption of personal and familial responsibility, for rehabilitation and education; but the classical republican perspective would be distinguished by tougher-minded recognition that these programs will inevitably result in not a few unlucky or self-inflicted failures on the part of recipients and beneficiaries, and that much of the suffering induced by such failures is an essential negative consequence or sanction of policies aiming at genuine autonomy. For genuine autonomy and responsibility entail self-reliant acceptance of varying degrees of pain, poverty, and loneliness. "Life is unfair," as President Jimmy Carter reminded us in one of his more courageous public pronouncements. To become an adult citizen, in the classical republican understanding, is to accept that unfairness without whimpering and without resentment, and to husband one's moral indignation for responses to instances of clear and avoidable human unfairness. Even more legitimate, from the classical perspective, would be sanctions imposed by law for failure incurred through the consequences of laziness, self-indulgence, and irresponsibility on the part of welfare recipients.

Insofar as family policies were informed by a classical republican perspective, they would aim in a direction not unlike that so forcefully indicated by Mary Ann Glendon, in her revealing comparative study of family law (1987). Legislators and judges would keep more squarely in view the extent to which law "tells a story" of who we are and what we stand for as a people. One significant consequence might be a return to the notion of well-wrought preambles to legislation concerning fundamental moral issues: preambles that would crystallize, in a healing spirit, our national purposes even, or precisely, when those purposes emerge as the result of profound and painful compromises among bitterly divided, but finally reconcilable, fellow citizens. In the implementation of specific policies, the responsibilities of paternity as well as maternity, both legitimate and illegitimate, would be much more vigorously enforced through both criminal and civil law. Divorce, custody, and abortion law would focus preeminently on the interests, rather than the rights, of children, and on the responsibilities or duties, more than on the interests or rights, of parents. Of course, this means that local government and the community—meaning not merely the courts—would have to take on a considerably greater role in supervising the upbringing of our children: but what reasonable alternative exists? To be sure, every effort should be made to support the family bond and family responsibility. Parents ought to be involved as much as possible in the creation and administration of family and educational policy at the local level. No small contribution to supporting family responsibility might be effected by revisions of tax and welfare legislation providing for childcare—including support for mothers who stay at home—and enabling families to care for aged relatives, thus allowing more old people to remain safely outside custodial nursing homes. Policies encouraging and enabling the aged to work, and to assist in caring for their community's young children, as well as schemes for a national youth service program, are natural complements to this sketch of general suggestions for family policy.

In the realm of the arts and letters, we cannot and ought not to return to Miltonian legal censorship; but we could recall one another to the responsibility of self-censorship, as opposed to the indulgence of unrestrained self-expression. We could remind one another of the need to give careful thought to the civic and moral effects, especially on the young, of our literary, artistic, rhetorical, and theoretical publications and utterances. The National Endowment for the Arts could take much more seriously the duty to encourage art that speaks to and uplifts the mass of citizens, inculcating not irresponsible rebellion against the nation's traditions but renewed appreciation for those traditions in an age that is all too bent on uprooting tradition. Instead of catering to the dominant, left-leaning ideologies and cultural predilections of the artistic community, the Endowment might begin to think of challenging those ideologies and predilections, so as to awaken philosophic controversy and open up political diversity.

In the realm of speech and expression and modes of life more generally, a classical perspective might well incite an unapologetic movement to reclaim our public living spaces and our public realms of discourse in the name of civility and mutual respect, and with a view explicitly to favoring those whose speech and action, however controversial, truly make a contribution to enlarged and more thoughtful communal life. We can and must reject the notion that the citizenry and its representatives ought not to rank, in order of priority of access to public places and media, the various claimants to our attention and tolerance. A republican citizenry can, and in the final analysis must, judge and debate the difference between obscenity and artistic innovation, between profit-seeking advertising and forceful advocacy, between idiosyncratic personal freedom and the pitiable or threatening behavior of addicts and mental incompetents. We need to swing the pendulum back from a notion of liberty that becomes harder and harder to distinguish from license, as the occupants of our public buildings, parks, streets, schools, and airwaves allow their sense of civic responsibility to be eclipsed by their fervor for self-expression and their unreflective zeal for vaguely conceived private rights. Private rights are the foundation of personal dignity and autonomy; but this means that genuine, as opposed to sham, personal dignity and autonomy is the limiting purpose of private rights: and this essential core of a noble liberal vision needs to be rediscovered and proclaimed anew.

Without sacrificing any substantial part of our commitment to toleration, American courts and intellectuals might become much more aware than they now seem to be of the value of public respect for religious belief, and even shared foci of reverence made visible in the public arenas of the nation. The meaning of the constitutional prohibition on establishment of religion was controversial even among the Founders; but this means that there is legitimate room for us to decide among the Founders' competing conceptions, and to do so informed by a sense of the the need, in the present period of crisis in our educational institutions, for every possible help in restoring discipline, inspiration, and aspiration to our public schools.

These are no more than some selected examples of the sort of circumspective civic spirit that might emerge from a resuscitation and strengthening of the classical roots of our republican tradition. But no consideration of the sort of civic spirit the classical outlook might dictate can dispense with sustained consideration of the last topic I have touched on: education. For education, meaning formation of the heart or character as well as training of the mind or talents, is the central preoccupation of classical republican political theory. Yet to what extent can education in this moral or civic sense be said to be a proper concern of public education in a liberal democracy like the United States? What sort of footing or resonance does this sort of public educational concern find in authentically American reflection on education?

PART IV

Education: Civic and Liberal

9 / Retrieving Civic Education as the Heart of American Public Schooling

In his 1990 State of the Union Address, President George Bush restated the themes and commitments enunciated at the "Education Summit" he had held a half year before with the governors of the United States. He spoke of expanding programs to prepare disadvantaged preschool children to learn; he set as a goal a sharp increase in the percentage of students who complete high school; he spoke of the need to assess student performance at critical stages in education, in order to make "diplomas mean something"; he called for school discipline. Each of these goals is worthy and was worth stressing. But surely something was missing from this attempt to outline the goals of a proper educational policy. What was striking was how little the president had to say regarding the *content* of education. What was remarkable was his almost complete silence about which sorts of lessons were or ought to be considered truly important. On only one point was there specificity—and there the clarity was unmistakable: "By the year 2000, U.S. students must be first in the world in math and science achievement." There was indeed a single passing reference, in the context of a call for literacy, to the fact that education must somehow prepare Americans to be *citizens*. But otherwise the education being discussed might well be regarded as an education aimed simply at the acquisition of the skills needed to work and compete well in a modern, technological world economy.

Nothing testifies more vividly to the loss, in American democracy, of clarity about the most important goal of public education in a republican society. I say "the most important goal." For of course the concern for an education that prepares men and women to be effective, useful members of the work force is an essential and even a noble concern—if, or insofar as, it is placed in a proper republican perspective. After all, skilled workers can be well-trained slaves. What makes the difference between a well-trained, efficient slave and a free human being? Does not education of a certain kind play an important, even the critical, role in this regard?

To this last question, the classical republican tradition delivers a resounding affirmative answer. It is "liberal education" that makes the difference between a free human being and a slave. But what is "liberal education?" So fluffy and banal has this expression become in our time that we need to exert some effort to recover the original meaning of this "liberal" educational ideal, as first articulated in Plato's *Laws* and *Republic*, and rearticulated in Aristotle's *Politics* and Xenophon's *Education of Cyrus*. To quote Plato's Athenian Stranger, what divides a liberal education from an education that is, however sophisticated and elaborate, nevertheless "vulgar, illiberal, and wholly unworthy to be called education" is this: liberal education is "the education from childhood in virtue, that makes one desire and love to become a perfect citizen who knows how to rule and be ruled with justice" (*Laws* 643b–644a).

Education in republican citizenship, an education that induces a passionate, loving commitment to civic participation in a just political order, does not exhaust the meaning of "liberal education" in the original, Platonic sense; but it is the heart of what Plato primarily means by "liberal education." The most important stages of such an education, the Athenian Stranger goes on to argue, are the early stages: when habits, tastes, and aspirations are formed; when heroes and objects of emulation and reverence are set before the imagination's eye; when a communal sense of shared destiny is shaped; when gratitude to the past and responsibility for future generations is instilled; when capacities for collective deliberation and action, for leadership and loyalty, are discovered, tested, and celebrated. The curriculum for this kind of education should be centered on poetry, music and dance, song and saga, history and drama, and, above all, religion.

This early civic and moral and religious public education is aimed mainly at formation of character, at the education of the heart rather than of the mind. This means to say that Platonic "liberal education" has another, higher dimension. This higher dimension, in its strictest sense, is philosophy; and in his discussion of the education of philosophers in book 7 of the *Republic*, Socrates identifies education in philosophy strictly speaking as "dialectics." But he simultaneously makes it clear that dialectics cannot be

directly cultivated by public schooling. At most, public schooling can cultivate the soil or prepare the ground in which individuals, in informal groups
of friends, can nourish true philosophic education. Yet Plato's Socrates also
shows that philosophic education, understood as centered on dialectics, presupposes an earlier moral and civic commitment that does depend, to a large
extent, on the less intellectual civic dimension of liberal education. Why so?
Why does philosophic education in the Socratic sense depend so much on
civic education? It is only on the basis of the earlier formation of passionate
moral commitments that the quest for *the truth* (which Plato's Socrates
makes clear is an essential presupposition of true dialectics, as opposed to
"eristics," or sophistry) can be launched. It is this moral seriousness that is
the foundation for the basic distinction between citizens and philosophers
devoted to the truth, on the one hand, and mere intellectuals, or traffickers
in ideas who are infatuated with the sound of their own names, on the
other. Hence, from the Socratic point of view, there is every reason to focus
attention on civic and moral education.

Now it is only fair to note that the president's State of the Union Address
did, contrary to initial appearances, and unlike the declarations made at the
time of the "Education Summit," make room for some substantial and serious reference to liberal education in this classical republican sense. But what
is remarkable—and yet so familiar to, and indeed characteristic of, our
world—is that the president treated the themes of moral education, not in
the context of his discussion of public schooling, but rather in his peroration,
where he dwelt on the themes of "faith and family." There the president
exhorted grandparents, "our living link to the past," to "tell the story of
struggles waged, at home and abroad. Of sacrifices freely made for freedom's
sake." He reminded parents that "your children look to you for direction
and guidance." "Tell them," he urged, "of faith and family. Tell them we
are one nation under God. Teach them that of all the many gifts they can
receive, liberty is their most precious legacy. And of all the gifts they can
give, the greatest—the greatest is helping others."

In a tradition that reaches back to Pericles, the president invoked the
morally educative, rhetorical authority of his supreme magistracy. In a tradition that is distinctly modern, and is deeply imbedded in the United States,
the president kept these higher and more important themes of education out
of his discussion of the institutions and policies of organized public schooling. The philosophic basis for this distinctively liberal or modern educational
vision is to be found in the treatises of John Locke, above all others. Yet if
it is the strongest, Locke's is nevertheless not the sole great voice that speaks

from within the original American conception of moral education. In order to retrieve and reconsider the American conception in all its rich and potentially fruitful controversy, we need to move from a summary view of Locke's notions to a survey of the founding generation's diverse reactions to, and modifications of, those Lockean notions.

As observed in the previous chapter, Locke speaks repeatedly of the importance of moral education for the success of a free civil society, while yet insisting that moral education is "the duty and concern of parents" rather than of government. Locke teaches one to be deeply uneasy about government-sponsored moral and civic education, because religion tends to be at the heart of such education; and Locke aims to provide the foundation for a *liberal* political society characterized, not merely by a separation of church and state, but by an unprecedented privatization, an extreme disestablishment, of religion.

But it is not only Locke's concern with liberating individual souls from the coercive hand of governmental authority that leads him to recommend private education at home; for Locke is as severely critical of *private* schools, or academies, as he is of public or state-supported schools. In order to see the full significance of Locke's attack on schooling in the name of education, we need to bear in mind the sharply contrasting position of Milton, whose essay on education, published when Locke was a young man, continued the classical republican educational tradition and applied it to the English-speaking world. Milton positively advocates *collective* education, in which young men leave their private homes to live together in troops or platoons housed in barracks. The value of learning to live and act together with others in a *team* spirit is regarded as an essential preparation for the duties of citizenship and militia service. In Milton's proposed English academies, to be erected in every city, an hour each day was to be devoted to swordsmanship and wrestling, with a view to moral as much as to physical education: "to inspire them with a gallant and fearless courage, which being tempered with seasonable lectures and precepts to them of true fortitude and patience, will turn into a native and heroic valor, and make them hate the cowardice of doing wrong."[1] For Milton envisages a republic with a citizen militia rather than a standing professional army. This facet of Miltonian or classical republicanism lives on in the second article of the U.S. Bill of Rights, guaranteeing "the right of the people to keep and bear arms" on the grounds that "a well regulated Militia" is "necessary to the security of a free State." The

1. *John Milton: "Areopagitica" and "Of Education," with Autobiographical Passages from Other Prose Works*, ed. George Sabine (Northbrook, Ill.: AHM Publishing, 1951), 69.

right to keep and bear arms is no part of Lockean natural rights, and in his educational treatise, Locke says nothing about preparing the young for military service. What is more, he draws attention to the pernicious influence crowds of inevitably rude and rowdy boys have upon one another's character development as reasonable, peace-loving, and industrious beings. He argues for the advantages that might accrue from an educational reform that would assimilate the education of boys to that traditionally bestowed on *girls*; indeed, his whole treatise may be said to intend the transformation of boys' education on the model of that of girls. Locke describes in glowing terms the control that might be achieved over boys' environments if they were brought up, as their sisters traditionally were, in the bosom of the private home, under the loving and painstaking supervision of the parents, and with the assistance of a carefully selected and well-paid private tutor.

Locke tried to persuade the upper classes to devote much more of their time, money, and thought to the upbringing of their children than was the custom in his or earlier times. One might say that Locke makes the challenge of educating, of governing or ruling, one's own children (the heirs to one's own property) an attractive and more natural supplement to, or even re-placement for, the classical challenge of a public life participating in political rule. Locke directed his message to the upper class because he saw no pros-pect, in the foreseeable future, of families in a lower station possessing the leisure and financial resources required to carry out the time-consuming, difficult, and complex labor that he conceived to be necessary for a truly sound and effective moral education. But Locke makes it clear that he hopes and expects that a reform, under his auspices, of upper-class education, character, and outlook will have a profound long-run impact on the way of life of the whole nation: speaking of his treatise, he says in the Epistle Dedicatory, "I would have every one lay it seriously to heart," though, he adds, "that most to be taken care of, is the Gentleman's Calling. For if those of that Rank are by their Education once set right, they will quickly bring all the rest into Order."

The *goal* of Lockean moral education is an enlightened self-interest grounded in rational self-control. The self-control is buttressed, and the self-interest is enlarged, by a sense of dignity, rooted both in shrewd management of private property, and in the unheroic, but solid, good name or recognition bestowed by one's similarly rational and independent-minded neighbors.

The primary *task* dictated by this goal is instilling into children a capacity to master their "natural inclinations"—their "natural *wrong* inclinations" as Locke puts it. According to Locke, the human being is naturally inclined to a lust for power and dominion that tends to violent conflict; and nowhere is this clearer, Locke suggests, than in little children, especially "at play." Human beings need to acquire, artificially, the inner rule of reason if they are to escape from a kind of chaotic, mutually threatening sociability (the "state of nature," which reproduces itself on every playground in the world); but human nature is such that it does not automatically possess, or even naturally grow toward, such self-rule by reason.

The defects or disorders of the mind to which education must respond are not ascribed by Locke to sin or to the Fall, and, accordingly, Locke never suggests that the remedy for them is to be found in fear of God, or hope and prayer for divine grace and redemption, or admission of guilt of any sort. In his very brief discussion of the child's religious instruction, Locke stresses that the child should at all costs be prevented from fearing God in any way. The proper remedy for the *natural* disorder of the soul is an artificial implantation, beginning when very young, of habits of self-control, resting initially on fear of the parents, and eventually on a reconstruction of the natural lust for power, together with a modulation of the natural desires for liberty and pleasure. What can give rationality or virtue its greatest strength in the human heart are "*Esteem* and *Disgrace*," which "are, of all others, the most powerful Incentives to the Mind, when once it is brought to relish them" (*Some Thoughts concerning Education*, sec. 56). The mind can be brought to such relishing because the natural desire for power can easily be linked to prestige, whose conventional character allows it to be shaped by the environment of praise and blame. In a rational Lockean environment, praise and blame will always be closely correlated with the display or lack of display of reasonableness. Children, Locke says, "love to be treated as Rational Creatures sooner than is imagined. 'Tis a Pride should be cherished in them, and as much as can be, made the greatest instrument to turn them by" (ibid., sec. 81).

Lockean education culminates in the inculcation of the social virtues, which represent the rational, constructed or artificial, antidote to the naturally vicious and irrational proclivities of human sociability: "Children who live together," Locke says,

often strive for Mastery, whose Wills shall carry it over the rest: Whoever begins the *Contest*, should be sure to be crossed in it. But not only that, but they should be taught to have all the *Deference, Complaisance and Civility* for one another imaginable. This when they see it procures them respect, Love and Esteem, and that they lose no Superiority by it, they will take more Pleasure in, than in insolent Domineering. (Ibid., sec. 109)

Justice, in the strict sense, depends on the respect for private property, and since children can, strictly speaking, own no property, they can know no justice. Still, they can be brought *toward* a sense of justice, or toward understanding of and respect for others' property, through being shown in a vivid way the meaning of labor (Locke says children should manufacture all their own toys, with the help of their tutors and parents) and by being taught the goodness of the virtue of generosity, and the evil of the vice of covetousness. Appealing to love or to sacrifice is *not* the proper method of instilling the virtue of generosity. Generosity is not charity, and Locke does not suggest children be taught charity. One succeeds in making children reliably generous by showing them that they will eventually profit and acquire more if they are first generous: "let them find by Experience," writes Locke,

that the most *Liberal* has always most plenty, with Esteem and Commendation to boot, and they will quickly learn to practise it. . . . This should be encouraged by great Commendation and Credit, and constantly taking care, that he loses nothing by his *Liberality*. Let all the Instances he gives of such Freeness, be always repaid, and with Interest. (Ibid., sec. 110)

The keystone of the social virtues is what Locke calls *civility*—a word to which he gives a new centrality and significance. *Civility*, as Locke uses the term, does *not* refer to political leadership, statecraft, or even citizenship: it is a *social* rather than a civic or political virtue, embodying an egalitarian sentiment of humanity. Indeed, while Lockean civility is observant of conventional distinctions of rank and station, this social virtue replaces the Christian or biblical virtue of humility in the lists as the opponent of the vice of vainglory—and also of the vice (which Aristotle, of course, called a leading virtue) of aristocratic *pride*. "We ought not," declares Locke,

to think so well of our selves, as to stand upon our own Value; and assume to ourselves a Preference before others, because of an Advantage, we may imagine, we have over them; but modestly to take what is offered, when it is our due. . . . Civility of the Mind . . . is that general Good will and regard for all People, which makes any one have a care not to shew, in his Carriage, any contempt, disrespect, or neglect of them. (Ibid., secs. 142–43)

The New American Conception of Civic Education

By the middle of the eighteenth century, the influence in America of Locke's educational treatise, partly by way of intermediaries such as John Clarke and Isaac Watts, was massive. Testifying vividly to this state of things is the most remarkable American contribution to the discussion of education in midcentury, Benjamin Franklin's *Proposals relating to the Education of Youth in Pennsylvania* (1749), coupled with his "Idea of the English School" (1750).[2] Franklin cites Obadiah Walker and Charles Rollin as well as Milton, but it is manifestly taken for granted that *the* supreme educational authority for Franklin and his readers is John Locke. Nevertheless, however numerous and substantial the explicit borrowings from, and implicit dependence on, Locke's theory of education and of human nature, we cannot fail to notice that Franklin's whole project departs in a decisive respect from Locke; and the nature of the departure may be said to be archetypical of the distinctively American path in education.

Franklin's project was the establishment of a school, an academy, representing the avant-garde of a grand new army of private (and, eventually, public) secondary schools to which Americans were to entrust the education of the leading citizens of the future. In the near term, Franklin's proposals met with only limited success; but the founding of Phillips Andover Academy in 1778 initiated a period of steadily growing enthusiasm for boarding-school academies whose curricula and vision of educational goals were in considerable measure shaped by the spirit of Franklin's suggestions.

As they followed Franklin's lead, Americans who spoke out about education became increasingly conscious that in advocating and designing formal schooling, they were shaping a new synthesis of Lockean and classical educational principles. Franklin's proposal for an academy includes among its curricular guidelines a strong recommendation to exploit the opportunity the audience of boys assembled together affords for education in the civic capacities of oratory and debate. The schoolroom should be the place where young future citizens and leaders learn the difference between sophistry and reasoned republican eloquence. But while reaching back to the Isocratean tradition, Franklin adds a new story to the classical edifice. The founder of American civic journalism emphasizes that perhaps the most important rhetoric in a modern republic is journalistic rhetoric: "Modern Political Oratory being chiefly performed by the Pen and Press, its Advantages over the Antient in some Respects are to be shown" (4:104). The text Franklin recommends as a model for the new study of journalistic republican rhetoric is the *Spectator*. Franklin links to the study of rhetoric the public reading of political texts, and especially newspapers, and calls for the cultivation of a

2. *The Papers of Benjamin Franklin*, ed. Leonard W. Labaree et al. (New Haven: Yale University Press, 1959–), 3:395–421 (*Proposals*) and 4:101–8 ("Idea"). Quotations in the pages that follow are from this edition of the two works.

vivid oral reading voice among the boys as a way of equipping future citizens with the power to bring to life and to disseminate the written word, in circles as small as the family and as large as public meetings in chapels or taverns:

For want of good Reading, Pieces publish'd with a view to influence the Minds of Men for their own or the publick Benefit, lose half their Force. Were there but one good Reader in a Neighbourhood, a publick Orator might be heard throughout a Nation with the same Advantages, and have the same Effect on his Audience, as if they stood within the reach of his Voice. (4:104)

Moreover, Franklin evidently means to have the envisaged academy encourage youngsters to enjoy and learn from participating in the give-and-take of public argument, especially in debates that intensify the drama of important contemporary occasions in the life of the community or the broader world, raising issues of political theory:

On *Historical* Occasions, Questions of Right and Wrong, Justice and Injustice, will naturally arise, and may be put to the Youth, which they may debate in Conversation and Writing. When they ardently desire Victory, for the Sake of the Praise attending it, they will begin to feel the Want, and be sensible of the use of *Logic*, or the Art of Reasoning to *discover* the Truth, and of Arguing to *defend* it, and *convince* Adversaries. This would be the time to acquaint them with the Principles of that Art. Grotius, Puffendorff, and some other Writers of the same Kind, may be used on these Occasions to decide their Disputes. Publick Disputes warm the Imagination, whet the Industry, and strengthen the natural Abilities. (3:413–15)

To some extent, it is true, American concern with formal schooling in the late eighteenth century builds on the peculiarly strong traditions of public schooling of the New England states, especially Massachusetts and Connecticut; but a closer look shows the very limited degree to which this is the case, at least as regards the spirit set in motion by Franklin. The cultivation of Puritan religious spirituality, as well as the cultivation of Quaker spirituality, which was more familiar in the existing schools of Philadelphia, ceases to be a goal of Franklin's educational scheme. This is not to say that the new academic notion entails the total expulsion of religion from schooling. But Franklin treats religion as a necessary supplement to, rather than the inspiration and guiding light of, morality. And the religion in question is what he calls "publick" or civil religion: that is, the minimal popular creed that history has shown to be essential for social health.

After the ratification of the Constitution and the enactment of the Bill of Rights, the question of whether the republic was to establish a system of public schooling took on a new urgency, in a few minds. Benjamin Rush and Noah Webster, following to some extent the trail blazed by Franklin, tried to promote state-supported school curricula and textbooks that would marry a nonsectarian Protestant Christian public spirit with the ethos of self-government and commercial and agrarian enterprise that was the moral core of the new republic.

But no one devoted as much effort and thought to the attempt to establish public schools as Thomas Jefferson. Jefferson parted company with Rush and Webster inasmuch as he was disinclined to base civic spirit on what Franklin had called "public religion." Instead, Jefferson sought public schools and textbooks that would inculcate a new, purely secular, moral code of liberal, agrarian or yeoman, citizenship. A crucial ingredient of the Jeffersonian program was the notion that the government of the schools could be placed in local and parental hands. Jefferson hoped to exploit concern with educating children, male and female, resident within each local "ward," as he called his envisioned subdivisions, so as to draw the boys' and girls' "parents, guardians, or friends" out of their purely private economic and familial spheres. He hoped to plant a kernel from which a more generally active, participatory republican spirit could grow at the local level, leading to the creation of "wards" as the critical, subcounty units of government: "Begin them only for a single purpose," Jefferson confided to his comrade Joseph Cabell in a famous letter on the "wards" (February 2, 1816), "they will soon show for what others they are the best instruments." In other words, the Jeffersonian educational vision brought concern for early childhood civic education into an organic unity with concern for the civic education, through practice and habituation, of adults.[3]

It is indeed striking to compare our contemporary leaders' declarations of the goals and purposes of public education with Jefferson's most authoritative statement on the subject, his remarkably subtle Preamble to the 1779 Virginia Bill for the More General Diffusion of Knowledge. The Preamble begins with a ringing appeal to the "natural rights" belonging to "individuals," protection of which is *the* purpose of, and criterion for, good government. But Jefferson moves at once to the need for popular education in political science, or knowledge of the "forms of government," especially through the study of history—not economic or social, but *political* history—and foreign affairs. This education is an education not simply of indi-

---

3. The letter to Cabell is quoted from *The Life and Selected Writings of Thomas Jefferson*, ed. Adrienne Koch and William Peden (New York: Random House, Modern Library, 1944), 662. The other quotations in this paragraph are from Jefferson's "Bill for the More General Diffusion of Knowledge," in *Crusade against Ignorance: Thomas Jefferson on Education*, ed. Gordon C. Lee (New York: Teachers College Press, Columbia University, 1961), 83–92. Quotations from the bill in the following pages are from this text.

viduals but of individuals united in "the people at large." It is the people who possess—but only as an educated community—the "natural powers" that can best safeguard against tyranny:

Whereas it appeareth that however certain forms of government are better calculated than others to protect individuals in the free exercise of their natural rights, and are at the same time themselves better guarded against degeneracy, yet experience hath shewn, that even under the best forms, those entrusted with power have, in time, and by slow operations, perverted it into tyranny; and it is believed that the most effectual means of preventing this would be, to illuminate, so far as practicable, the minds of the people at large, and more especially to give them knowledge of those facts, which history exhibiteth, that, possessed thereby of the experience of other ages and countries, they may be enabled to know ambition under all its shapes, and prompt to exert their natural powers to defeat its purposes.

But informed popular watchfulness by no means exhausts Jefferson's civic educational purpose. In the second half of the Preamble, he proceeds from the common education of all citizens to the uncommon "liberal education" of the rare few—especially among the poor—"whom nature hath endowed" with the superior intellectual and moral qualities that make them eligible to be entrusted with legislative and administrative responsibility in the representative form of government that marks the semi-aristocratic American regime:

And whereas it is generally true that the people will be happiest whose laws are best, and are best administered, and that laws will be wisely formed, and honestly administered, in proportion as those who form and administer them are wise and honest; whence it becomes expedient for promoting the publick happiness that those persons, whom nature hath endowed with genius and virtue, should be rendered by liberal education worthy to receive, and able to guard the sacred deposit of the rights and liberties of their fellow citizens, and that they should be called to that charge without regard to wealth, birth, or other accidental condition or circumstance; but the indigence of the greater number disabling them from so educating, at their own expence, those of their children whom nature hath fitly formed and disposed to become useful instruments for the public, it is better that such should be sought for and educated at the common expence of all, than that the happiness of all should be confided to the weak or wicked: be it therefore resolved [etc.]

Jefferson's civic educational theory is here adumbrated with impressive succinctness: natural rights belong to individuals, who can only secure those rights by being transformed, through education, into a "people" with the "natural powers" to protect themselves against oppression. But the people must hold those powers largely in reserve, since they must in practice "deposit" the protection of their rights and liberties in the hands of civic leaders and administrators. These latter ought to be distinguished by a natural moral and intellectual superiority—a superiority that, however, requires a "liberal education" if it is to be realized.

Jefferson neither ignored nor underestimated the importance of vocational and technical education, or of giving, as he put it in his later Rockfish Gap Commission Report, "to every citizen the information he needs for the transaction of his own business; to enable him to calculate for himself, and to express and preserve his ideas, his contracts, and accounts, in writing."[4] But Jefferson always insisted on putting in the foreground or at the summit of declarations of educational goals the moral and civic dimension of education. As he went on to say in the Rockfish Gap Report, the higher goal is

to enable the citizen to improve, by reading, his morals and faculties; to understand his duties to his neighbors and country, and to discharge with competence the functions confided to him by either; to know his rights; to exercise with order and justice those he retains, to choose with discretion the fiduciary of those he delegates; and to notice their conduct with diligence, with candor, and judgment; and, in general, to observe with intelligence and faithfulness all the social relations under which he shall be placed.

The specific civic spirit aimed at by Jefferson and other educational theorists among the founding generation involved, of course, both a passionate patriotism and a sense of fraternity or solidarity with fellow citizens in past and future generations, as well as the present one; but both the patriotism and the fraternity were of a new sort, deeply planted in the soil of personal and property rights of individuals. Love of country was to be love, not simply of the land and people and traditions, but love of the carefully articulated principles of political theory Americans drew from Locke and Montesquieu, mingled with reverence for the heroes who were most clearly dedicated to those specific principles. Care for one's fellow citizens was to express, not so much selflessness or even self-transcendence, as the rational understanding that the rights of each depended on the rights of all. The heart of the matter is well expressed by Jefferson's young disciple Samuel Harrison Smith, concluding his essay on education, which in 1795 shared with another Jefferson disciple, Samuel Knox, the prize of the American Philosophical Society:

The citizen, enlightened, will be a free man in its truest sense. He will know his rights, and he will understand the rights of others; discerning the connection of his interest with the preservation of those rights, he will as firmly support those of his

4. "Report of the Commissioners Appointed to Fix the Site of the University of Virginia," in *Crusade against Ignorance*, 114–33; passages quoted are from p. 117.

fellow men as his own. Too well informed to be misled, too virtuous to be corrupted, we shall behold man consistent and inflexible. Not at one moment the child of patriotism, and at another the slave of despotism, we shall see him in principle forever the same.[5]

In the essay he published in 1787 supporting ratification of the Constitution, Noah Webster spoke with rather startling clarity about the degree to which the new American republic departed from traditional notions of civic solidarity and education:

Virtue, patriotism, or love of country, never was and never will be, till men's natures are changed, a fixed, permanent principle and support of government. But in an agricultural country, a general possession of land . . . may be rendered perpetual, and the inequalities of commerce, are too fluctuating to endanger government. An equality of property, with a necessity of alienation, constantly operating to destroy combinations of powerful families, is the very *soul of a republic*. . . . But while *property* is considered as the *basis* of the freedom of the American yeomanry, there are other auxiliary supports; among which is the *information of the people*. In no country is education so general—in no country, have the body of the people such a knowledge of the rights of man and of the principles of government. This knowledge, joined with a keen sense of liberty and a watchful jealousy, will guard our institutions.[6]

That Webster by no means intended to belittle the importance of patriotism in the context of an education centered on knowledge of rights, especially property rights, and politics rooted in such rights, is made clear in his later essay "On the Education of Youth in America." "Every child in America," he there says,

should be acquainted with his own country. . . . As soon as he opens his lips, he should rehearse the history of his own country; he should lisp the praise of liberty and of those illustrious heroes and statesmen who have wrought a revolution in her favor. A selection of essays respecting the settlement and geography of America, the history of the late revolution and of the most remarkable characters and events that distinguished it, and a compendium of the principles of the federal and provincial governments should be the principal schoolbook in the United States. These are interesting objects to every man; they call home the minds of youth and fix them upon the interests of their own country, and they assist in forming attachments to it, as well as in enlarging the understanding.[7]

Webster adds further specificity to his curricular ideas when he speaks of the sort of knowledge that ought to be diffused in the American republic:

5. Samuel Harrison Smith, "Remarks on Education," in Rudolph 1965, 220–21.
6. "An Examination into the Leading Principles of the Federal Constitution etc.," in *Pamphlets on the Constitution of the United States Published during Its Discussion by the People, 1787–88*, ed. Paul Leicester Ford (Brooklyn: n.p., 1888), 57–58.
7. Quoted from Rudolph 1965, 64–65.

not only "a knowledge of spelling books and the New Testament," but "an acquaintance with ethics and the general principles of law, commerce, money, and government is necessary for the yeomanry of a republican state." The degree to which Lockean principles of individual rights are here being merged with and elevated by classical republican principles of education and citizenship becomes visible when Webster adds the reflection that "in Rome, it was the common exercise of boys at school to learn the laws of the twelve tables by heart, as they did their poets and classic authors. What an excellent practice this, in a free government!" This remark, like Webster's remark above on what ought to be the character of "the principal schoolbook in the United States" was far from a speculative utterance: he authored and published a series of such books that met with fantastic success. Selling literally millions of copies, and remaining for generations the core of American school curricula, these lively little books testified to the truth of Webster's prediction that political theory and history, along with moral theology, could be made memorably attractive to young future citizens.

Shining through the writings of those early Americans who reflected deeply on the nature of a modern republican civic education, there is discernible a special notion of popular self-respect. Those early American educational theorists held in their mind's eye the ideal of a widely diffused sense of dignity rooted in real independence of spirit as well as property, and real understanding of the moral and political principles that undergirded such spiritual and material independence. They hoped to cultivate a sense of self-respect, and a reverence for one's own rational laws and institutions, that would avoid both the childlike awe or adoration characteristic of paternalistic aristocracy and the vulgar incapacity for reverence, the mass self-congratulation, of populist democracy. "The people," John Adams wrote in a 1785 letter on civic education, "must be taught to reverence themselves, instead of adoring their servants, their generals, bishops, and statesmen." Reaching back, characteristically, to Plutarch's evocation of ancient republicanism for illustration, Adams added:

If Thebes owes its liberty and glory to Epaminondas, she will lose both when he dies, and it would have been as well if she had never enjoyed a taste of either. But if the knowledge, the principles, the virtues, and the capacities of the Theban nation produced an Epaminondas, her liberties and glory will remain when he is no more. And if an analogous system of education is established and enjoyed by the whole nation, it will produce a succession of Epaminondases.[8]

8. *The Works of John Adams*, ed. Charles Francis Adams (Boston: Little, Brown, 1850–56), 9:540.

The extraordinary difficulty, or delicacy, of the task becomes clearer when we see that what is sought is at one and the same time a self-consciously sovereign people, vigilant against governmental usurpation of liberty; and a people "inviolably respectful of lawful authority," as Washington put it in his first annual message to Congress, requesting (unsuccessfully, alas!) funding for public education. What is needed is a noncontradictory, but nonetheless paradoxical and difficult, combination of pride and humility.

The first American republicans spoke repeatedly of the significance of the education of women for the breeding of such popular sentiments. Both Locke and the classical republican philosophers had stressed the absolute importance of early childhood moral education, and hence the absolute importance of the education of mothers; and the Americans adopted this proposition. It was Noah Webster, again, who put the theme in its clearest light, in his essay "On the Education of Youth in America":

In a system of education that should embrace every part of the community the female sex claim no inconsiderable share of our attention. The women in America (to their honor it is mentioned) are not generally above the care of educating their own children. Their own education should therefore enable them to implant in the tender mind such sentiments of virtue, propriety, and dignity as are suited to the freedom of our governments. Children should be treated as children, but as children that are in a future time to be men and women. . . . In order to prevent every evil bias, the ladies, whose province it is to direct the inclinations of children on their first appearance and to choose their nurses, should be possessed, not only of amiable manners, but of just sentiments and enlarged understandings. (pp. 68–69)

But it is not only in the context of their fundamental role in shaping the characters of children that women's own education shows itself to be of awesome importance:

Their influence in controlling the manners of the nation is another powerful reason. Women, once abandoned, may be instrumental in corrupting society, but such is the delicacy of the sex and such the restraints which custom imposes upon them that they are generally the last to be corrupted. . . . A fondness for the company and conversation of ladies of character may be considered as a young man's best security against the attractiveness of a dissipated life. For this reason, society requires that females should be well educated and extend their influence as far as possible over the other sex. (p. 69)

From these observations, Webster moved to an insistence on the need for a reform of women's education with a view to developing in women a new sense of civic mission:

A distinction is to be made between a *good* education and a *showy* one, for an education, merely superficial, is a proof of corruption of taste and has a mischievous influence on manners. The education of females, like that of males, should be adapted to the principles of the government and correspond with the stage of society. Education in Paris differs from that in Petersburg, and the education of females in London or Paris should not be a model for the Americans to copy.   (pp. 69–70)

Webster further observed that this extensive new educational task could not safely be trusted to private resources, whether tutors or family, because those were too likely to be still imbued with the traditional notions of women's roles as viewed in an aristocratic or monarchic society. But Webster himself did not draw out the conclusions implied in these observations so fully or so clearly as did Benjamin Rush in his "Thoughts upon Female Education, Accommodated to the Present State of Society, Manners, and Government in the United States of America" (1787). Rush began from the observation that if mothers were to inspire a sense of dignity in a society where independence was grounded on competence in economic matters, and where most families required the close cooperation of husband and wife in managing family finances and property, then women must be educated so as to be competent in such matters. Accordingly, women were to study English; bookkeeping and arithmetic; geography; the history of the nation, including especially its struggle for freedom; and the principles of modern political theory. Some women at least were to gain "a general acquaintance with the first principles of astronomy and natural philosophy." While praising training in vocal music and especially preparation for church singing, and allowing training in dancing ("in our present state of society and knowledge, I conceive it to be an agreeable substitute for the ignoble pleasures of drinking and gaming"), Rush advised against expensive and time-consuming training in instrumental music. In the place of this aristocratic adornment, he sought to substitute the cultivation of a habit of serious reading: "How many useful ideas might be picked up in these hours from history, philosophy, poetry, and the numerous moral essays with which our language abounds . . .!"[9]

The attention of our young ladies should be directed as soon as they are prepared for it to the reading of history, travels, poetry, and moral essays. These studies are accommodated, in a peculiar manner, to the present state of society in America, and when a relish is excited for them in early life, they subdue that passion for reading novels which so generally prevails among the fair sex. I cannot dismiss this species of writing and reading without observing that the subjects of novels are by no means accommodated to our present manners. They hold up *life*, it is true, but it is not yet *life* in America.

9. These and the following quotations are from the text in Rudolph 1965, 27–32.

"It will be necessary," Rush concludes, to "connect all these branches of education with regular instruction in the Christian religion." For Rush opposes many of his contemporaries in insisting on the need for a common religion as a common foundation for morality; and in this regard women have a uniquely important role to play, given that "the female breast is the natural soil of Christianity." The reading and study of the Bible is "improperly banished from our schools," and most improperly of all from schools for girls.

Benjamin Rush's vision and views found their most powerful advocate in a woman born the year that he delivered the address later published as "Thoughts upon Female Education": the great Emma Willard, to whom American education, and the distinctively American tradition of teachers' education, owes so much. In 1819 Willard presented a long-meditated and well-honed proposal for the creation of a system of state-supported seminaries for women to the governor of New York for transmission to the legislature. In essence, the "Address to the Public, Particularly to the Members of the Legislature of New York, Proposing a Plan for Improving Female Education," drew together the arguments of Rush, Webster, and others, and took them one further crucial step. For Willard argued that the education begun in the home by mothers educated in state seminaries must continue in state-established primary schools; and in these primary schools the most apt and available teachers would be women, not men. In other words, Willard spearheaded what was to become the most striking new feature of school education, a feature almost completely unforeseen by Americans in the founding period: the transformation of the educational profession, particularly in the primary grades, by the overwhelming predominance of women as teachers—as moral teachers and exemplars. When Willard's petition and proposal failed, she went on (in 1821) to establish the Troy Female Seminary, the first permanent collegiate-level school for women in the United States: an institution that pioneered, with enormous success, the unprecedented notion of educating women for a learned profession—to wit, teaching.

Emma Willard thus contributed perhaps more than did any other American of her time to the amelioration of the gravest practical problem recognized and lamented by almost all those who wrote about the future of schooling in the country: the shortage of dedicated, exemplary professional teachers, caused by the low salaries and limited esteem accorded men who entered the profession.

Still, the curricular substance of Willard's educational vision, like that of the earlier Founders from whom she drew inspiration, met with only very partial success. This guiding conception of school education, following Franklin in uniting Lockean and classical principles in an uneasy, but coherent, synthesis, was largely discarded, and at a rather early point in the development of America's political culture. But perhaps the time has come for a careful reconsideration of the possibility of resuscitating the goal of their educational proposals, and even the applicable parts of the curricular means they suggested. To be sure, changes reflecting the transformations that have occurred in American society would be required. America no longer exhibits even the degree of religious consensus that Rush believed he had to work with; and the rural and landowning backbone of the yeoman society Jefferson and Webster looked to has disappeared. But as the recent words of President Bush's State of the Union Address indicate, the nation still recognizes the need to communicate to our children a reverence for the past that incorporates us into a society whose freedom is more than the freedom of individuals hermetically sealed into the personal sphere, the present time, the immediate place. There still lives a heritage of civic virtues, virtues of gratitude and of generosity, of struggle at home and abroad, of sacrifice for freedom rather than mere enjoyment of freedom, of faith in the one God whose oneness inspires and helps weld our oneness as a nation. And there still lives the confidence that these virtues can be taught, in part through "telling the story." May it not be time to make a more deliberate and determined effort to make this telling—and, in addition, practices or habits reflecting what has been told—a central part of the curriculum of our public schools?

To this kind of suggestion I foresee a powerful objection, coming especially from thoughtful conservatives. What reason is there to suppose that we can entrust so important a task to the teachers of today—whose spirits have been formed in substantial part by a higher education many of whose guiding lights are anything but sympathetic to this kind of rootedness in, and reverence for, republican tradition, patriotism, piety, property rights, and family? Will not the effectual upshot be just more subtle indoctrination in the corrosive intellectual and moral fashions that pervade the academic elite and seep thence through every college classroom? Will not moral education be conveyed through "values clarification," with its hidden agenda of apparent skepticism, actual relativism, and hidden, only semiconscious, but all the more dogmatic, radical egalitarianism and individualism? Will not history be taught in such a way as to debunk or even defame the Founders, and all subsequent leaders who did not rebel against the American tradition as a racist, capitalist, sexist, Eurocentric conspiracy to dominate and exploit the "forgotten of history"? Will private enterprise, will the rootedness of human dignity in private property that has so indelibly marked the American republican tradition, be treated with anything like the respect it deserves? Will not every American war and war hero or ordinary soldier be treated as the veterans of the Vietnam War have generally been treated—pitied, where they are not contemned, their military achievements forgotten, where they are not excoriated? Will not the religious traditions of America be treated as the last gasps of benighted ages and darkened minds? Will the American family and American womanhood be celebrated for the hard and self-abnegating choices they made as they bowed to the stern laws of nature and the harsh edicts of destiny—or will their strength in adversity be seen as the stubbornness of "false consciousness under oppression"? In how many advocates of contemporary feminism do the principles and commitments of a feminist like Emma Willard still live?

I cannot offer reassuring answers to these questions. But I think Aristotle is correct in insisting that private and familial moral or religious education lacks the authority to sustain itself without direct public reinforcement: I do not think we can leave things where they are and expect them not to get worse. As is evident even from such superficial indicators as opinion polls, the mass of the American citizenry, and especially those who choose the burdens of parenthood, seem more sensible, more responsible, and wiser in civic matters than the elites who dominate the universities; and teachers in the public schools, since they tend to live among ordinary folk and only spend a few years under the direct tutelage of the higher education establishment, remain somewhere in between. On the whole, I am inclined to think reasonable the hope that primary and secondary schoolteachers are not as alienated from the educational principles I have sketched as is sometimes suggested by the pronouncements of their "spokespeople." At the very least, I think we have to hope that men and women who devote their lives to teaching will be willing to listen to and reflect upon calls for a return to our civic educational heritage, enlarged and enriched by a new infusion of classical republican inspiration.

But the universities, I must concede, are as Hobbes suggested the fountainheads of opinion in an enlightened society such as ours, where ideas and scientific learning, or the claim of scientific learning, wield such authority. Besides, to say that the people are less corrupt than the academic elite is not to say that the people are uncorrupt. And what is peculiar to our elite corruption (as Tocqueville, again, so presciently predicted) is that it consists in large part of flattery of "the people," or of democracy and egalitarianism, as well as individualism. This flattery works, although not as well as its disappointed purveyors expect. It works slowly, because the people in their lack of sophistication remain impressed by important traditional sources of contempt for the people or for populism—especially for the people and their judgment when they judge en masse. The people tend not wholly to trust those in government, partly because the people elect those in government and know something about how one gets elected in a mass democracy in which ancient traditions of republican and biblical virtue have worn thin. On the other hand, the people tend to trust professors, partly because they still think learning is linked (as indeed it ought to be, and still is in a minority) to moral sobriety and civic wisdom, and partly because they do not select professors and have no idea how they are selected. The people are all the more susceptible to the claims of authority advanced by the professors, especially since those claims present themselves as "progressive" and "anti-elitist," while promising "liberation" from onerous, old-fashioned demands or duties of family, country, God, nature, and the truth.

From these reflections I draw a practical, if perhaps somewhat disheartening, conclusion: the reform most needed as regards the spirit of education is the reform of the spirit of higher education, since it is higher education, or the practitioners of higher education, whose outlook is likely to come to dominate in the long run.

10 / Against Canons and Canonicity: Dialectic as the Heart of Higher Education

In turning to higher education, we are brought face to face with the full complexity and challenge of the idea of liberal education. For while higher education is indeed important as a continuation of, and source of teachers for, the liberal civic education that ought to begin at the lower levels, higher education as we know it in the modern university has other and more direct functions and goals. At its "highest," higher education aims at liberal education in a second sense, a sense that encompasses, but goes beyond, citizenship education. But just what this transcivic goal of higher education might be has become increasingly difficult to articulate in contemporary America. The problem is not simply the steady pressure on the universities to provide very sophisticated vocational preparation and technical scientific expertise. This pressure, after all, is inevitable and by no means altogether improper in the context of modern democracy. We need highly skilled lawyers, engineers, doctors, social workers, and technicians and scientists of all kinds. But to keep the pursuit of technical expertise within its proper bounds, there is required a counterpressure exerted by a reasonably clear articulation of the hierarchy of goals in the modern university. This articulation is the responsibility, above all, of the "humanities," including the more "humane" branches of the social sciences. Unfortunately, however, among the custodians of the humanities in today's universities there reigns profound confusion or despair regarding the very possibility of articulating a clear conception of "humanity" in its most "liberal" or liberated spiritual fulfillment. I suggest we try to recover our bearings by returning, again, to the original, Socratic articulation of liberal education—but now to the transcivic dimension of Socratic liberal education.

Socratic Dialectic

Liberal education in its highest and fullest sense is the education that truly liberates; and Socrates calls such an education "philosophy." But by "philosophy" Socrates means something rather different from most of what is taught in philosophy departments nowadays. Philosophy in its strictest sense Socrates identifies as *dialectic*. To understand what Socrates has in view, we may best start from the observation that *dialectic* is the name for the art of friendly conversational argument, or "dialogue," animated by a passionate, "erotic," thirst for the truth—a thirst rooted in an acute awareness of our ignorance about the most important things. The true art of dialogue culminates in the capacity to guide a conversation, by question and answer, by mutual cross-examination, from the relatively superficial and careless or easygoing to the ever-more-probing, more disquieting, more synoptic, and more precise. Appealing to the connotations of the Greek word for carrying on a dialogue, Socrates insists that "dialectic," or the art of conversation, includes a strong original connotation of accurately distinguishing the kinds or classes into which all particulars fall. This activity of separation and conjunction lays bare the natural articulation of things.[1] Much or most conversation is concerned principally with individuals, and is as such undialectical; dialectical conversation is concerned with universals. Dialectical conversation ascends from the individual to the general, from the present to the permanent.

According to Plato's Socrates, dialectic, and the reasoning peculiarly characteristic of dialectic, seeks and obtains a form of knowledge that is superior to scientific or deductive knowledge of the sort found in all the other arts or sciences—including mathematics, physics, psychology, theology, and metaphysics. For all other sorts of reasoning either ascend inductively to, or proceed deductively from, ultimate first premises, or what Socrates calls "hypotheses." But neither induction nor deduction by themselves deal adequately with the ultimate first principles or foundations. Indeed, the most fundamental of premises are usually not even recognized as such, because they are so deeply imbedded in the ground of thought. Dialectic and dialectic alone is the reasoning that can bring these most profound premises to the

1. Plato *Phaedrus* 264e–268b; Xenophon *Memorabilia* 4.5 and *Oeconomicus* 8.9.

glare of critical scrutiny, and, on the basis of cross-examination, provide such grounding as is possible for them to have. In the *Republic* (511b and 533b–c), Socrates says that the knowledge "reasoning itself grasps through the power of dialectic" is a knowledge attained by

making the hypotheses not first principles but instead really hypotheses, stepping-stones and springboards as it were, so as to arrive at the nonhypothetical, that is, at the first principle of the whole. . . . For all the other arts are all directed toward the opinions and desires of human beings, or toward generations and destructions, or toward care of things that grow and are put together. And the rest, which we affirm do lay hold of something of being—geometry and the arts that follow upon it—we see are as if dreaming about being, but are incapable of seeing in awakeness, so long as they use hypotheses and leave these unstirred, while not being able to give a reasoned account of them. For when the first principle is what is not known, and the conclusion and the intermediate steps are woven from what is not known, what device is there for making such agreement science? . . . the dialectical path alone proceeds in this way, doing away with the hypotheses on the way to the beginning so as to make it firm.

How can Socrates make such an amazing claim concerning the foundational function and power of the unprepossessing art of question and answer? An adequate explanation would require a full understanding and treatment of the core of Socratic philosophizing. Here we can only take the first steps.

Some helpful light is contributed by Aristotle, when he bestows a similar rank and function on dialectic in one of his treatises on logic (*Topics* 101a37–b4). Dialectic, Aristotle there says, is used

with a view to the first principles in each science. For from its own first principles, any given science is incapable of saying anything about them, since the first principles are the first of all; it is instead necessary to proceed by way of the generally accepted opinions [*endoxa*] about each of them. But this task is either uniquely or especially the province of dialectic. For to it, as the art capable of thorough scrutiny, belongs the path to the ultimate foundations of all paths of knowledge.

What Aristotle would seem to have in mind may be formulated as follows. All technical and scientific thinking derives ultimately from prescientific thinking. All scientific awareness of the world presupposes, and must build from and upon, a prescientific awareness of the world that is the awareness of "common sense," the awareness of the world in which we live as perceiving, reasoning, acting, caring, deliberating, reflecting human beings. The commonsense world is dominated or formed by generally accepted opinions. But scientific thinking is continually at risk of forgetting or obscuring its own humble, but inescapable, origins in the "life world." Scientific thinking is likely to assume that the movement or ascent from the prescientific to the scientific provides a sufficient criticism of the prescientific. But this assumption is false. The ascent to science can be a rigorous, well-grounded ascent if and only if all the presuppositions inherited from or incorporated into science from the world of common sense have been made fully conscious, and, in addition, have been exposed to a thorough critical scrutiny—a scrutiny that does not presuppose the validity of the ascent, for which the scrutiny alone can provide the foundation. In other words, radical reflection on the prescientific presuppositions of science in general, and of any science in particular, cannot be based on the assumption that the science is valid—for the validity of science, its ground, is what is in question. It was this classical proposition that was rediscovered in the most important insight of Edmund Husserl and his "transcendental phenomenology" aiming at "philosophy as rigorous science." But it may be doubted whether Husserl perceived clearly enough which are the most important, and yet the most unobtrusive, of the presuppositions of the "life world" that must be made the subject of a prescientific, but rationally rigorous, critical scrutiny. In the *Republic*, Socrates offers a decisive suggestion as to what the most important of these opinions are and why they are held in so unselfconscious a way. According to Socrates, the preeminent theme of truly self-conscious dialectic is the examination of the good, and of opinions about the good. This is accomplished by way of an examination of the noble and just, and opinions about what is noble and just. Socrates emphatically disclaims knowledge in this matter, and explicitly declines, in the *Republic*, to deliver even his considered opinions (506c–e). But he offers images and metaphors that adumbrate his opinions. He dares to say that his interlocutor should affirm that the good is an essential cause or source of knowledge and even of truth, in a manner analogous to the way in which the sun is an essential cause or source of seeing by way of light: "affirm that this that provides the truth to the things known and that gives the power to the one who knows is the concept of the good; and being the cause of science and of truth, think of it as itself knowable" (508e).

Let me try to explain something of what Socrates may mean, in a manner appropriate to our present concerns. All human thinking is the thinking, not of "pure minds," but of human souls. The human soul is motivated by desire, by love, by need. As Aristotle puts it in his treatise *On the Soul* (433a15–18): "The object at which desire aims is the cause of motion, and it is on account of this that thought is set in motion, because it is the object at which desire aims that is the original cause of thought." The world that we know or can know is the world that is of concern to us; it is the world inevitably shaped to some crucial extent by our concerns, or the world of which our concerns are among the preeminent constituents. All scientific "facts," we may say, are objective observations or propositions about the world we experience; these propositions can ultimately be understood as the objectively verifiable answers to questions; but the questions are prompted by our concerns, and the observations are directed by our concerns. The questions and the observations are determined by what we value: by our sense of what is important, what is trivial, what is dangerous, what is needed, what is interesting, what is attractive or beautiful or "elegant," what "makes sense." Every deductive art or science ultimately rests on some presupposed judgments about what is good, judgments that the art or science itself accepts without demonstration and, what is more, often or usually without sustained reflection.

This is most obvious in the teachable or objective practical arts. Take the typically Socratic example of shoemaking. The expert shoemaker's wonderful knowledge of leather is radically dependent on the standards for discriminating among leathers in light of the goodness of comfortable, protective, and supportive shoes. This premise as to the good determines both the knowable properties of leather and the categories through which and into which the expert classifies leather. Shoemaking does not demonstrate that it is good for feet to be shod, and thus protected and comforted; it assumes this proposition. One can question whether it is not better to toughen one's feet and, at the price of some risk or injury, to become more self-sufficient by going barefoot—as Socrates did. One might suppose that the podiatrist has a sufficient answer to Socrates; but the podiatrist assumes that what is good for the physiology of the foot, or the body, is good simply. The podiatrist as podiatrist does not raise the question of the relation between the good of the foot and the good of the whole human being, body and soul. Even the science of medicine in its furthest and grandest reaches—let us say psychiatry—does not pursue in a radical, thorough manner the inquiry into the nature of the soul, because psychiatry does not pursue in a thorough way the question of the existence and nature of the divinity to which the soul may be akin.

It is, indeed, the question of divinity that may be said to overshadow every science, even or especially the so-called "pure sciences." For Socrates certainly does not neglect what would be termed today "pure science." He insists that a thorough familiarity with what is close to what we would today call number theory, geometry, and physics (in which Socrates includes especially astronomy and music theory)—is an essential prerequisite to authentic dialectic (*Republic* 522–33). Socrates' concern with the scientific prerequisites for true dialectics is part of his emphatic warning against premature introduction of the young to dialectical cross-examination. That warning has two interrelated parts.

On the one hand, there is the consideration to which we alluded in the previous chapter: those who have not acquired in their youth a rich and compelling moral education in artistically and poetically inspired republican virtue will lack the moral seriousness—the intensity of concern, but also the practical sobriety and realism—that will strongly incline them to stick with the examination of their opinions, once they have begun to recognize the questionableness of all received moral opinions. When the morally immature, when the politically inexperienced, get a taste of dialectical arguments, Socrates says, "they abuse them, as if it were a game, always using them to contradict; and, imitating those who refute, they themselves refute others, like puppies who enjoy pulling and tearing apart whoever is around"; but the mature person "imitates the one who is willing to carry on a dialogue and to inquire into the truth rather than the one playing and refuting for the sake of a game" (*Republic* 539b–c).

On the other hand, however, moral maturity and political experience are not enough unless one has experience of solid and objective truth, as opposed to opinions that are pleasing or ancient or backed up by consensus and the power of poetry and religious faith. For once opinion as such, even the most revered or universally accepted opinion, is seen to be truly dubious, the soul may well recoil from dialectic as from a sort of nihilism unless the soul has firm and firsthand experience of what it means to possess clarity and grounding in truth based on knowledge as opposed to opinion. It is the teachable, demonstrable, arts and sciences—and especially the mathematical sciences—that afford a taste of this experience in the most vivid and authentic way. The sciences must be studied, Socrates concedes, with a view to their social usefulness; but their chief purpose from the point of view of the highest education is to give the young a powerful experience of what it means to possess intersubjective, universally and permanently valid, principles that describe the *necessities* governing the *nature* of things. The mathematical sciences draw the eye of the soul up and out of the changing particularity of history and empirical experience, showing the intellect's capacity to see underlying principles that are invisible to the eye, but demonstrably at work always and everywhere in the manifold of temporal and spatial experience.

Yet by themselves the sciences in no way guarantee the progression beyond science toward dialectic. Left to themselves, the sciences can confirm the soul either in its moral skepticism or in its moral absolutism. Only if the searing challenge of passionate, "erotic," dialectical questioning concerning the good and the noble is brought to a properly prepared soul will the true potential for liberation be realized.

That potential is heightened if, in the course of studying the sciences, the students are forced to reflect on their activity of study, and if they are made aware of the necessarily partial character of every science. Each science is a kind of speciality: each studies, not the whole of being or of what exists, but a part of the whole. The difficulty this partiality or specialization entails becomes especially clear, Socrates suggests, when the study of astronomy is undertaken in the awareness that the motions of the heavenly bodies may not be permanent—that is, when the question of cosmology or cosmogony, the origins of the visible universe, is raised (*Republic* 529c–530b). The science of astronomy studies the movements of the heavenly bodies, but in doing so it is compelled to make some assumptions, to leave open certain radical questions, about the original cause, about the "demiurge of heaven" (530a). Astronomy itself cannot study that cause or demiurge. Yet each science, including astronomy in its most comprehensive sense, seeks or claims to arrive at universally and permanently valid principles governing the part that has been taken as the subject matter of the science. This effort presupposes the permanent and universal character of the part, or indeed of the whole, since the part is derived from or takes its place in the whole. How does the scientist as scientist know that the regularities he uncovers are not temporary, or interruptible, creations of a mysterious and miraculous divinity or divinities who have intervened, and may intervene in the future, to change or suspend and violate all these regularities? The student of science who becomes troubled by this sort of question would seem to exhibit a critical aspect of the "synoptic" questioning that Socrates says is the surest test of the dialectician, as opposed to the mere scientist (537c). This synoptic uneasiness is compounded or deepened, or revealed in its full scope, by the following even graver difficulty.

Every scientist as scientist proceeds on the assumption that it is good or right or permitted to seek scientific knowledge; he assumes that the degree of self-reliance and inquiry and awareness that he seeks is not forbidden and will not be punished severely. He assumes that his enterprise does not violate the wishes and commands of divinities who seek to maintain humanity in a state of innocence. But it suffices to recall Hesiod's account of the Promethean theft of fire, or the biblical account of the Tree of Knowledge, to see that this assumption is radically questionable. How does the scientist know that it is good or right, rather than evil or base, to pursue rational knowledge of nature? How does he dispose of Hesiod's claim to have had a direct revelation from the Muses? How does he dispose of the biblical account of the Fall?

Socrates forcefully compels us to realize that the question of the good, or the examination of opinions about the good, involves the question of God or the gods: he does so by using metaphors that suggest that the ultimate good may be a god, or godlike, and that God or the divine may be a maker of the whole. Or as he also says, dialectic involves "divine theorizing" (*Republic* 508a–509d, 517d). Socrates seems to suggest that rational clarity about the divine can be the result of dialectical inquiry into our opinions about the good and the noble and just. What he has in mind becomes a bit clearer when he stresses that the opinions we most need to examine are the authoritative ones manifested in law and recorded in the sacred texts; divinity, one might say, makes its most accessible and awesome claim on our attention by way of the sanctioned commandments it imposes, by the morals and the way of life to which it authoritatively directs us. If so, then the question of the existence and nature of the divine cannot be settled by the other sciences, but only by dialectical inquiry into the good and the noble, an inquiry that presupposes some decisive insights afforded by mathematics and astronomy. As Socrates heard from the "most beautiful and most wise" Kleinias, "the geometricians and the astronomers and the calculators (for they are also a sort of hunter; since they are not makers of diagrams, but seekers of the things that are) don't know how to use what they get, but only how to hunt, and turn over their findings to the dialecticians to make use of—or at least those who are not totally mindless do so" (*Euthydemus* 290c).

Let us sum up what we have gathered thus far as to the nature of Socratic dialectic. True or full knowledge is self-knowledge, critical knowledge of the animating normative principles that drive and govern or define all our knowing and all our action. The path to true knowledge, or the beginning of what Socrates calls philosophy, is a deep immersion in both civic virtue and mathematical science, followed by a radical moral self-criticism, a radical questioning of one's deepest commitments and attachments, a radical scrutiny of one's first premises, and hence of one's morals, politics, and religion. This dialectical activity Socrates calls the "education" (*paideia*) which is truly identical with "liberation" (*lysis*). For he insists, in his most famous metaphor, the metaphor of "the cave" as the "image of our nature

in its education and lack of education," that we necessarily begin as en-
chained slaves (*Republic* 514–15):

> "See human beings as if they were in an underground cavelike dwelling, having
> its long entrance open to the light across the whole width of the cave; and as if they
> were from childhood in the cave, in chains that held their legs and necks in such a
> manner that they remained looking only forward, unable because of the chains to
> turn their heads around. Their light is a fire burning far above and behind them; in
> between the fire and the enchained is an elevated path, along which see a little wall
> constructed, just like the partitions puppeteers set in front of human beings, over
> which they show the puppets."
>
> —"I see," he said.
>
> "See also human beings carrying along this little wall all sorts of artifacts, which
> project above the little wall, both statues of men and other stone and wood figures
> and all sorts of works, and, as is to be expected, some of the carriers make sounds
> and others are silent."
>
> —"A strange image," he said, "you tell of, and strange enchained ones."
>
> "They are like us," I said. "For in the first place, do you think such people have
> seen anything of themselves and of one another except the shadows cast by the fire,
> the shadows falling upon the wall of the cave facing them?"
>
> —"How could they," he said, "if they were compelled throughout their lives
> never to move their heads?"
>
> "What about the things being carried by? Isn't it the same with these?"
>
> —"How not?"
>
> "Now if they were able to carry on dialogues with one another, don't you suppose
> that they would believe that these very things were the beings?"
>
> —"Necessarily."
> . . . .
> "In every way then," I said, "such persons would believe the truth to be nothing
> other than what is in fact the shadows of artificial things."
>
> —"Quite necessarily."
>
> "Consider now," I said, "what sort of a thing their liberation and the healing
> from the chains and the folly would be, if some such thing as the following were to
> happen to them by nature: When someone was liberated and compelled suddenly to
> stand up and turn his neck around and walk and look toward the light, in pain as
> he did all these things and incapable, on account of the dazzling lights, to make out
> those things whose shadows he saw before, what do you think he would say if
> someone told him that before he saw nonsense, but now he saw more correctly
> because he was somewhat nearer to what is and more turned toward the beings—and
> indeed, while pointing out to him each of the things passing by, asked and compelled
> him to answer what it was? Don't you suppose he would be at a loss and think that
> the things he saw before were truer than the things being shown to him now?"

At the very least, Socrates' metaphor is meant to teach us this: our human
condition, to begin with, is by nature always that of spiritual bondage within
a cavelike horizon almost totally dominated by artificial moral, religious,

and political beliefs so deeply rooted, so attractive, so comprehensive, so seemingly diverse and antagonistic, as to be almost impenetrable to the inhabitants of each cavelike age and culture. We are brought up, we acquire our humanity, not simply by nature but by lawful conventions and beliefs working on and overlaying nature. Conventions and laws in the fullest sense are not merely the fundamental rules enforced in courts, but are, above all, the great explanatory systems we nowadays refer to as "ideologies," but which Socrates speaks of as "poetry." A few rare human beings with fantastic imaginative and imitative gifts dominate the spiritual existence of the rest: these are the great founders of civilization, along with their most astute disciples. These are the poets, like Hesiod and Homer; the prophets, like Moses and Mohammed; the lawgivers, like Cyrus and Lycurgus; the so-called ideologists in modern times. Socrates leaves moot the question of the extent to which these "puppeteers" of culture have themselves been outside the cave or visited other caves: the answer may vary widely from one cave, and one puppeteer, to another. Socrates surely does not condemn these puppeteers, or suggest for one moment that there can ever be any society that is not in fact a cave dominated by puppeteers: he goes on to affirm that the society he has been elaborating in the *Republic*, the best or most just society imaginable, is also a cave. In outlining the "noble lies" required for the education of the children, Socrates has been fictively presenting himself as if he were an advisor to poetic puppeteers.

Paradoxically, the artificiality through which human beings become humanized is not itself artificial, or an accident; it is rooted in nature. Socrates introduces his metaphor by unambiguously declaring that this is the metaphor "of our nature" (*tēn hēmeteran phusin*: 514a). Human nature necessarily dictates that the "dwelling" or "home" (*oikēsis*) of human beings as political beings is a kind of cave. Human nature is such that it requires artifice and law and convention in order to grow or to realize its natural potential. We all are necessarily brought up having our minds ordered and predisposed by terminologies, categorizations, beliefs, and prejudices that we, and most of our teachers, mistake for the natural or necessary ordering of human existence. We question and we doubt, but our questions and doubts express the sort of skepticism expected from "right-thinking" people: our skepticism hides a deeper dogmatism, upon which it is based—a dogmatism so deep that we are scarcely aware of it. What we suppose to be "radical" criticisms of the contemporary powers that be are in fact only radicalizations, more extreme versions, of those very powers. For example, within today's American liberal-democratic cave, the most widely persuasive critiques of democracy will be the ultrademocratic, egalitarian, and the ultralib-eral, libertarian critiques. An education that is, in the Socratic sense, truly liberal—that is, truly liberating—must strive to bring into question these seemingly "necessary givens," these moral chains, that enslave our souls.

But how can this be done? How can we even begin to step outside our own souls, our own upbringings, our own heritages, our own epochs or cultures, our own deepest moral presuppositions? The problem, as Socrates' metaphor makes abundantly clear, is indeed an immense one—possibly, in the final analysis, insoluble. Certainly the metaphor is much less illuminating as to the method of the escape or liberation than it is as to the enchainment. Socrates seems to postulate a sort of deus ex machina, an unaccounted "liberator" who "compels" prisoners, one at a time, to undergo, unwillingly and in agony, the shattering process. Yet in the nonmetaphorical portion of his discussion, Socrates describes the first steps of a public education of selected students. Here he stresses that the higher, scientific branches of public education should in no way be compulsory (536d–e). As we have seen, Socrates commends the study of the sciences as essential preludes to dialectic; but he makes it clear that the sciences, taken all together and at their best, are only "preludes to the song itself that must be learned," that they cannot by themselves "sing the song" of dialectical liberation. By speak-ing of "song" and eschewing compulsion, he makes dialectic sound more attractive; but on the other hand, he stresses at the end the very grave dangers dialectic, or the attempt to educate in dialectic, may pose to the student, to society—and to philosophy itself, insofar as its reputation suffers as a result of being confused with those who abuse or misunderstand dialectical educa-tion. This grim warning of danger is practically his last word on liberal education. We are reminded that Socrates was convicted and executed by the Athenian democracy as a corrupter of the young.

Since Socrates' discussion of the process of education in dialectics is so hesitant or obscure, let us turn from what he says to what he does, and, to begin with, to what he does in the drama of the *Republic*. There we see him educating, or trying to begin educating, a group of young men. His discus-sion certainly poses some very grave and searching criticisms of the way of life prevailing in the Greece of his time, and, indeed, of the ways of life that have prevailed in all recorded times and places. These criticisms do not arise "out of the blue." Two "debates" are especially striking as affording starting points for Socrates' critique of the prevailing ideals. The first is a debate Socrates has with a foreign sophist who is present at the conversation: Thra-symachus. This man disposes of a very well-developed critique of conventional morality and republican politics. Beneath his critique, at the theoretical foundation, are discernible the categories developed by the "pre-Socratic" philosophers, whose works exposed the religious, moral, and political assumptions of Greek republican life to rather severe criticism. The second debate is with books: the works of Homer, which are subjected to a detailed and repeated critical scrutiny. The Homeric poems have rightly been called the Bible, or the canon, of the Greeks. They are certainly the most authoritative, sacred or canonical, texts for Greek life, and are so in part because of the wealth and depth of the human wisdom they contain.

These two sorts of debate or critical encounter are characteristic. Socrates is depicted as having a strong penchant for confronting and questioning foreign or alien thinkers—the sophists—whose claims and way of life challenge the conventionally or traditionally acceptable. He is only somewhat less visibly portrayed as being in the habit of studying, sometimes in reading groups with students or friends, the great texts of his predecessors, both poets and philosophers. In the dialogues, we usually of course see only the results of Socrates' study of the texts. But Xenophon does on one occasion present Socrates talking about his favorite pursuit (*Memorabilia* 1.6). When cross-examined by the sophist Antiphon, who criticizes Socrates in the presence of some of his followers for the poverty into which his pursuits lead, Socrates replies:

Now for my part, Antiphon, just as someone else may be pleased by a good horse or dog or bird, so I am pleased even more by good friends; and if I have something good, I teach it to them, and I introduce them to others, from whom I believe they will derive some benefit as regards virtue. And the treasures of the wise men of old, which they left behind by writing them in books, I open up and explore in common with my friends, and if we see something good, we pick it out and consider it a great gain if we can become beneficial to one another.

This statement by Socrates, seen in the broader framework of the model he provides, as educator and as searcher, may be said to be the beginning or source of the *proper* notion of what has come to be called "Great Books education." It seems to me that this Socratic model can and should be the paradigm for higher liberal education in our postmodern age. It seems to me that by reflecting on the Socratic idea of an education that is a true liberation, and by trying to apply that idea in our very different circumstances, we can at least gain some clarity about our goal: we can at least set before our mind's eye the aspiration that ought to be the inspiration of "liberal education" in the universities of the dawning century.

The Great Books as the Key to Dialectical Liberation in Our Time

A liberal education that is truly liberating in the Socratic sense is an education that brings us face to face with disturbing challenges to our deepest and apparently surest moral commitments. It is an education that compels us to rethink our most cherished convictions—to their very roots, thereby to rediscover and refertilize, and, if need be, replant, those roots. The aim of such a probing, if sympathetic, scrutiny of our treasured beliefs is not, of course, to subvert those beliefs; the aim is to transform our beliefs from mere opinions into such grounded moral knowledge as is available to human beings. The knowledge in question is partly inspired by, but is not the same as, the knowledge achieved in the mathematical sciences. Dialectic provides us with awareness of the genuine strengths of our principles, precisely by forcing us to deal with the most telling actual and potential challenges to those principles. The aim of dialectical education is to leave the subjectivity of "values" behind, by reenacting for ourselves, accepting or modifying, and therefore making truly our own, the great reasonings, the great choices rooted in argument, that ushered in our modern civilization. This kind of approach to the truth, or what Socrates calls his "human wisdom," is the opposite of all dogmatism. Such human wisdom or understanding always includes some skepticism, even as regards our most precious beliefs, because it always includes an acute awareness of the limits of our knowledge as well as firsthand experience of the power of the arguments that can be mustered against our beliefs.

In the present time and place, this means that we need to encounter disquieting critics of democracy, of human rights, of individualism, of toleration, of the free market and economic growth, of sexual liberation and sexual equality, of secularism, of monotheism, of modern science (including everything from atomism to evolution), of creativity, of art conceived of in terms of "the aesthetic." To achieve this sort of bracing confrontation, we cannot possibly rest satisfied with the sorts of challenges that originate in our own age and culture, because what we seek is precisely critics whose spiritual footholds are outside our cave, outside our own time, outside the basic matrix of our moral outlook.

Yet we must avoid the temptation of supposing that liberation means losing ourselves in the merely exotic, the strange, the provocative. Our goal is neither titillation nor escapism nor romanticism. It may help a bit to study the silent and deeply mysterious cultural artifacts of alien peoples, or the ways and beliefs of cultures that have no relation to our own; but such study will not suffice as the core of a liberating education. Such artifacts and cultures, however rich, are too distant and inarticulate to provide serious and lucid alternative conceptions of the good that we might find ourselves compelled to embrace and in whose terms we might have to begin to reorient our lives.

A revealing and helpful symptom of liberation, indicating that we may be on the right track, is our initial anger or moral indignation at the worldview we have encountered: for that indignation is a sign that we have run up against a real challenge, one that does not fit our accepted notions of what is right, and yet that we cannot view from a cool distance, laugh off as absurd, or shrug off as "historical."

In short, we seek serious and thoughtful critics whose arguments draw us, and are intended to draw us, into a true dialogue, in which the very meaning and purpose of our lives is at stake. We seek critics who challenge us to the core, compelling us to rethink our own foundations, and eliciting from us some genuine, if grudging, admiration for the alternative they represent or pose.

Now such critics, and such confrontations, are to be found especially through the simultaneous study of two sorts of great books: on the one hand, those, like the ancient Greek and Roman, or the medieval Muslim, Judaic, or Christian books, which elaborate a rich and philosophically well defended non-liberal and non-democratic conception of law, freedom, virtue, beauty, and love; on the other hand, those books that are the most original, the broadest, and the deepest sources of our own scientific, liberal, and democratic worldview. In almost every case, these latter primary sources of our own spiritual horizon will be found to have blazed their new path by way of a shattering argument with the previous, and especially the Greco-Roman and biblical, authoritative traditions.

For Americans, this implies that we should emphasize, on the one hand, those works that laid down the original stratum of our deepest presuppositions as regards justice, science, religion, art, and morality: for example, in political philosophy, the *Federalist Papers* and Montesquieu; in philosophy of science, Bacon and Descartes; in theology, Spinoza and Locke; in literature, Defoe and Fielding. And on the other hand, guided by these books that laid down our spiritual foundations, we should bring them into confrontation with the great opposing works and authors against which they directed their epoch-making innovations. The *Federalist Papers* and Montesquieu speak with severe, if sympathetic, criticism of the classical republics portrayed in Plutarch, Thucydides, and Xenophon; Bacon carries on a continuous argument with Aristotle's antitechnological, teleological conception of science and its relation to nature and society; Spinoza and Locke engage in a cautious, but searching, critique of the Bible and its great medieval interpreters like Maimonides and Thomas Aquinas; Defoe's plumbing of the depths of individualism in *Robinson Crusoe* is partly inspired by, and written in direct and sharp contrast to, Ibn Tufayl's *Hayy the Son of Yaqzan*. These are, of course, only selected illustrations—strategic points of entry, if you will, to the sorts of juxtapositions and arguments that would allow us to begin to examine our most basic presuppositions from a radically critical perspective.

This does not mean to say that every great work of the past must always be studied in juxtaposition or debate with some other work: liberal education has no place for such wooden didactic formulas. There is, indeed, much to be said for giving a single great and time-tested work the stage simply by itself, for an extended number of classes, in which teachers as well as students attend as faithfully and docilely as possible to the work's own articulation of the proper beginning point and the fundamental problems. It is possible, after all, to begin one's liberation by simply picking up and starting to read with questioning alertness and care any one of a number of the Great Books: in a sense there are as many entry points as truly great books. It is amazing to discover the extent to which some of the greatest books are the products of very great teachers—teachers fully capable of initiating the truly open or candid reader, step by step, into a new world of dramatic antagonism among unexpected human possibilities. I think at once of Thucydides' presentation of the great quarrel between the Spartan and Athenian regimes and ways of life, or Dante's imaginative pilgrimage, or the intellectual odyssey of Tolstoy's Pierre Bezuhov.

Yet it is also true that to leave it at this is greatly to underestimate the obstacles that stand in the way of our beginning to *listen*, with thoughtful wonder, to the books—instead of rushing to impose upon them our questions, our framework, our current preoccupations. I have some reservations about, though I certainly do not contemn, Great Books programs that approach the books as "a great conversation" into which any one of us can enter without more ado. It seems to me there is a danger in ignoring the distance that separates us, to begin with, from those who may have escaped in some measure from their caves. I would argue that a dialectical education through the great books must always take into account our own historical and cultural starting point—that of those studying the books—as the point from which our liberation is sought. This entails continuing reconsideration on the part of students and faculty of the reasons for reading the great books.

The conception of Great Books education that I am here propounding does not have as its guiding aim the cultivation of some sort of aesthetic appreciation for the books as cultural icons; the classes I have in mind on the great books do not resemble trips to a museum. The point is not to learn *about* the books; the point is to learn *from* them. But still less am I speaking of a treatment of the great books as comprising a sacred canon that presents some kind of unified doctrinal teaching; the classes I have in mind on the great books do not resemble religious observances or indoctrinations. What unifies the Great Tradition stretching from Socrates to Nietzsche is not a set of doctrines but a series of great debates around a small core of permanent questions; the agreement, such as it is, is on the search, defined by the questions and their permanently paramount importance for man as man, in all times and places. What qualifies a book to be called "great" is whether and to what extent it joins in this debate: that is, whether and to what extent it transcends, without neglecting, its time and place, moving from its rootedness in a specific culture or historical situation to awareness and discussion of the universal dimensions of the issues and debates.

Those who talk of the great books as a "canon" are in my experience almost always those who wish to discredit the books as independent vehicles for liberation and inspiration. To talk of the great books as "canonical" is to assimilate liberal education to religious indoctrination, carried out by scholars portrayed as high priests or propagandists. Such talk—ubiquitous, for example, in the American Council of Learned Societies January 1989 Report, "Speaking for the Humanities"—conjures up the notion that struggles over the curriculum are inescapably ideological, akin to struggles over theology curricula in the Middle Ages or the Reformation. The great books themselves are seen as mere "texts," without substantially ascertainable messages of their own, texts whose "interpretation" always and inevitably represents the imposition of the reader's or interpreter's framework. The entire question of education then becomes the question of which interests and power structures will control the agenda of "values" that is to be foisted onto the texts. And since all texts are treated the same—as mere hermeneutic vehicles for "encoded" values, or propaganda—it appears absurd to suppose that mere acclaim through the ages, or the testimony of other searching thinkers, or the breadth and depth of the questions addressed in a work, ought to "privilege" one text over another.

Behind all this cant about the "canon," there lies, to be sure, a profound

philosophic challenge: the challenge found in the hermeneutic reflections of
Nietzsche and Heiddegger, whose questioning of all previous conceptions of
readership, intentionality, and authorship deserves a careful and sympathetic
hearing in any study of the great books. The dialectical venture ought not,
and cannot, stop short of the most recent and most radical antagonists of
Socratism. But the profound meditations of Nietzsche and Heidegger will
always be reduced to fashionable chatter unless and until their thought is
grappled with at the high level at which they present it. They presuppose—or
at any rate surely do not discourage or seek to erase—a liberal education in
the Socratic spirit. It is no accident that among the most important works
of Nietzsche and Heidegger are searching dialogues with Socrates and Plato.
Nietzsche's essay "On the Advantages and Disadvantages of History for
Life" (rediscovered, as it were, by Heidegger in *Being and Time*) has as its
most urgent task the rejuvenation of a truly respectable encounter with the
great thinkers of the past, and especially the Greeks, in the face of what
Nietzsche sees (as Heidegger did later) to be the debasing historicism of late
modern scholarship, derived in a degenerated fashion from the master edifice
of Hegel's philosophy of history. Hegel still insisted—indeed, he insisted far
more than any previous thinker—on the ultimate autonomy of reason: Hegel
dared to proclaim the ultimate triumph of reason over subrational circumstance. But the historicism that devolved from the reaction to Hegel is a
historicism that both Nietzsche and Heidegger regard as the death knell of
liberated thinking. For it reduces the books and the thoughts of even the
towering figures of the past to mere reflections of their age, their culture,
their class, their gender, and so forth. Such historicism reinforces the chains
weighing down the human spirit by declaring in advance the impossibility
of any escape from the cave. Such historicism confirms the enslavement of
the human spirit, by teaching the fruitlessness of even the attempt to transcend one's time, place, and circumstances in the quest for what Nietzsche
still calls, following Socrates, "the natural," "the eternal," "the eternal basic
text of natural man" (*Beyond Good and Evil*, sec. 230). Instead of academic
historicism, Heidegger calls for what he calls "confrontation" with the great
books:

Confrontation [*Auseinandersetzung*] is true criticism. It is the highest and the only
way to a true estimation of a thinker. For the task confrontation undertakes is a
meditation on the thinker's thought and a following of it in its actual strength, not
in its weaknesses. And with what purpose? So that we ourselves become liberated,
through the confrontation, for the highest activity of thinking. . . . to experience,
what contemplative consciousness is, and what it means to be at home in genuine
questions.   (*Nietzsche* 1:13–15)

Similarly, Heidegger scorns any "experiential" or "aesthetic" approach to the great works of the past, and invokes as *the* standard for criticism and appreciation the approach to literature and art of the ancient Greeks:

> It was the good fortune of the Greeks that they had no "experiences" [*keine Erlebnisse*], but instead a knowledge so underivative in its growth, a knowledge so clear, and a passion for such knowledge so strong, that in this clarity of knowing they had no need for "the aesthetic." The aesthetic makes its appearance, among the Greeks, in that moment when the great art, and the great philosophy that accompanied it, come to their end. (Ibid., 1:95)

Nietzsche and Heidegger went back to the Greeks ultimately for the sake of demolishing the Platonic-Aristotelian foundations of the West. But in order to achieve this demolition, they had first to expose those foundations; and they knew that to accomplish this exposure they must treat Greek thought and the classical texts with alert attention to every detail, no matter how unobtrusive. In the search for "the eternal basic text of natural man," they thus allow us (and intended to allow us) a startlingly fresh and untraditional glimpse of a non-Nietzschean, non-Heideggerian alternative.

The question of nature, of human nature and its place in the larger whole of nature, is indeed the question of questions. Obviously, then, any attempt to make the great books again the core of the undergraduate curriculum, in the name of an aspiration to genuinely Socratic dialectics, compels healthy reconsideration of the essential linkage between the sciences and the arts. On the one side, as we saw in our discussion of Socrates, a genuine grasp of the meaning and character of truth requires all students to acquire a serious taste, at least, of mathematics and natural science. On the other side, any genuinely rigorous science must become far more self-conscious than contemporary science is about its own philosophical-historical genealogy. Professors of science must be provoked by reconsideration of the decisive historical debates in the metaphysical, theological, and moral evolution of science in the West. Examples of the subjects for rethinking that a Great Books curriculum might offer both the scientifically sophisticated and the amateur include the debate between Aristotelian and Epicurean physics; Galileo's challenge to late Aristotelian science; Leibniz's challenges to both modern and ancient science; the pathbreaking physico-theological treatises of Newton; and the break with Newtonian science in the late nineteenth and early twentieth centuries.[2]

2. Jacob Klein's *Greek Mathematical Thought and the Origin of Algebra* (trans. Eva Brann [Cambridge, Mass.: M.I.T. Press, 1968)] might well serve as a model of the kind of rethinking that ought to be held up as a goal.

The Special Demands on Political Science

But if the study of the great books is to retain its center of gravity, it must not lose sight of the political and moral questions—the questions as to the highest norms that animate and focus all serious human efforts. This means that in the university as presently constituted, political science departments must shoulder a special burden of responsibility and leadership. Is there any reasonable hope that contemporary political science is capable of rising to this challenge—of becoming the mainstay of an education that aspires to dialectical liberation? What place is there for Socrates or the Socratic spirit in contemporary political science departments?

Within the discipline of political science, the teaching of the great books has a uniquely paradoxical, and therefore uniquely thought-provoking, status. Political science is by far the oldest of the social sciences and boasts a star-studded history, beginning with Socrates, Thucydides, Plato, and Aristotle and extending to such giants as Hegel, Tocqueville, and Marx. As a result, it was taken for granted until a couple of generations ago that the study of this illustrious history ought to be a central and required part of the discipline. But this very fact—that the study of the great books was taken for granted—meant that such study had gradually become more and more antiquarian and pedantic. Fewer and fewer political scientists—including, unfortunately, those who were scholars of the history of political thought—possessed or even thought much about a compelling *justification* for the required study of the history of political thought and its great books. Such justifications as were perfunctorily offered in introductions to required courses and textbooks were either formulaic and platitudinous or else raised more doubts than they answered (see Sabine 1961, esp. v–vi). The study of the great books in political science departments was ripe for devastating (and not altogether unjustified) criticism.

That criticism emerged in the 1930s and 1940s under the twin banners of Science and Progress. The argument goes as follows. Political science ought, like the other social sciences (and maybe even the humanities, if they wish to be up-to-date and respectable), to strive to be a genuine science: a science modeled (in a properly adapted form, to be sure) on the natural sciences. But, it is argued, the history of science is not a central or required part of genuine science, of the natural sciences. The study of the history of science, of mathematics, and of medicine is at most a mere adornment for, or curious ancillary to, the education of a competent physicist or mathematician or doctor. Science, in general, is a progressive and cumulative enterprise, in which the earlier stages may be envisaged as the lisping babyhood or awkward adolescence that at best prefigure the later stages of an ever-ascending process of discovery and consolidation of knowledge. The continued insistence that political scientists be compelled to acquire competence in the history, and especially the ancient history, of the discipline is thus perceived as a relic of a prescientific, unprogressive mentality that ought to be left behind.

For a time this new outlook drove the old history of political thought and its somewhat befuddled or embarrassed scholarly custodians to the wall, placing them on the verge of extinction. But in the late 1940s and 1950s an intrepid, erudite, and philosophically very powerful counterattack was suddenly launched across the broadest possible front. The new scholars and teachers who spearheaded this counterattack did not leave it at defending the study of the history of political thought; they claimed, on the basis of the insights afforded by the great books in that history, to demonstrate that the scientistic conception of political, or, indeed, of social science in general, represents a narrow, inhuman, morally irresponsible, and philosophically indefensible notion of political and social science. The battle continues to this day. The counterattack did not win, or come close to victory; but it established a beachhead, within which rage more or less friendly dialectic debates, and from whose perimeter renewed assaults are continually being launched and repelled. Now this means to say that within political science the study and teaching of the great old books is, and has for some time been, obviously and unmistakably controversial; and for that very reason, teachers of the great books who are political scientists are compelled to justify, therefore to question, and therefore to think in a sustained way about, the meaning or purpose of the study of the great books.

The counterattack on behavioral political science in the name of the history of political philosophy, and of the study of the great books that are the core of that history, raised fundamental questions: What is political science? What ought it to be? What are or should be its goals and aims? Nor did the counterattack stop here. It went on to ask: What is education? What are or should be its goals? What is or ought to be the place of political science, properly understood, within education, properly understood?

More pointedly, the counterattack insisted on asking: Why, or for what, is political and social science ultimately good? Now scientistic political and social science cannot answer—strictly speaking, it cannot even address or deal with—this question. Modern science in general tends to conceive of itself as grounded in a conception of reason or objectivity that contends that reason or objectivity is possible only in the realm of facts, or at best of intermediate, but not of ultimate, values. Given an end, science can tell us the most efficient way to promote that end; in some cases, it may be able to tell us something about which ends conflict with one another. But positivistic science or reason (which is, of course, not embraced by every good scientist or social scientist) cannot objectively arbitrate among ultimate ends. Scientific thinking so understood cannot, therefore, provide the ultimate ground for ranking ends or goods. Such science cannot even provide the ground for our choosing efficiency or reasonableness over "creative chaos"; placid harmony over exhilarating conflict; a will to construct over a will to destroy. Value-neutral science in general, and scientistic political science in particular, is constitutionally incapable of explaining why it itself is good.

But the question of the good, and in particular the good or worth of political science, is fundamental to politics. Politics, and the political authorities, must explicitly or implicitly raise and answer the questions of whether or not free scientific inquiry is to be cultivated or restricted within the political community; of the rank or place in the scale of priorities of every controversial element in human existence; and ultimately of good and evil. Politics is the realm in which human beings, through coercive laws and rulers and civic action (including bloody warfare and revolution) determine collectively the ultimate ordering of a society's priorities—what is honored and promoted, what is tolerated, what is dishonored or forbidden. Politics at its fullest is the attempt to understand and to foster the common good: justice. A "science" of politics that cannot raise and pursue the questions of the ultimate good and the ranking of human endeavors is not a true science of politics. The supposedly "progressive" turn to the model of contemporary science, a turn that had come to dominate the social sciences and that was increasingly dominant even in the humanities, stood revealed, not as progress toward enlightenment, but as a decay into obfuscation and forgetting of the most important political questions.

This does not mean to say that the scientific analysis of political and social data, with a view to identifying explanatory variables and correlations, and arriving at some degree of predictive power, is to be relegated to the sidelines; but that study must understand itself as subordinate to or under the guidance of and in service to a higher study, a civic art or true science of politics devoted to the pursuit of knowledge of justice or the common good, of virtuous citizenship and far-sighted statesmanship. This higher and more fundamental reach of politics *is* the central and abiding preoccupation of the great books in the history of political philosophy. It is in those great books that we find unraveled or unpacked the whole vast complexity of, the ceaseless debates or arguments over, the meaning of justice and the common good. The entire galaxy of thinkers who make up the illustrious history of political thought, however much they disagree, all agree on this most fundamental meaning of political science education; and it is this high conception of the profession that, I contend, must be brought back to life. The turn away from the great books, however much it may be excused by the boring and antiquarian way in which those books might once have come to be taught, is the starkest symptom of a fundamental crisis in political science, a crisis that consists in political science's having lost sight of its highest legitimate goal and responsibility.

To be sure, most courses in political science will quite properly preoccupy themselves with recent history and with the nature of presently existing political systems. But these studies and courses could and should be cognizant of a core of great books to which sustained and provocative reference is regularly and systematically made. There is no reason why many courses should not contain some readings from the greats, whose unorthodox questions and synoptic perspective would cast an unexpected, not to say startling, light on the contemporary political scene. A similar observation holds for courses in the other social sciences. Students and faculty alike might find new worlds of surprising questions, and an enlarged, more critical self-consciousness, opening up before them if history classes took their bearings in part from the political and philosophic histories of Tacitus, Philippe de Comines, and Hume; if they tested with sympathetic scrutiny the great nineteenth-century philosophers of history; if sociologists put Tocqueville's and Montesquieu's enormously broad comparative studies of forms of society at the center of their teaching; if anthropologists followed Lévi-Strauss's lead and reflected on the source of their discipline's dominant issues in the questions of Rousseau and his critique of both the biblical and classical conceptions of the origins of society.

Yet we must try to prevent the reading of the few old books that truly matter from becoming routine or rote. When students walk into the first lecture in an introductory course, or when they sit down to the first meeting of a graduate or undergraduate seminar, I would expect them to react to the presence on the syllabus of antiquated texts with doubts and questions. And to make sure all the students share those doubts and questions, I advocate making these issues a theme, not only of the opening class, but in some sense of every class. How can one devote any important part of a course, which is meant to be the introduction to, or continuation of, some branch of political

science, to the study of old, even very old, books? How can one justify a syllabus, whether for a beginning or for an advanced course in political theory, on
which there appears hardly any required reading less than a century old, a
syllabus most of whose texts were written by authors who lived in remote and
long-dead political cultures? Does not the study of politics mean, naturally
and necessarily, the study of the urgent and overwhelming issues of our day?

My initial response would be simple, though necessarily provisional, for
"the proof of the pudding is in the eating": the issues with which we are
going to deal by way of the great books are more important, more fundamental, than the burning issues of the day. The latter will certainly not be forgotten. They will rather be given new weight and significance, by being comprehended as instantiations of deeper, more permanent or abiding issues, which
current issues presuppose and emerge out of, but which the noise of the
current controversies can also cover over.

What are these more profound and abiding issues that ought, in a truly
liberal education, to take precedence—if only by remaining, looming, in the
background? A beginning or provisional list, culled from the most obvious
surface of the great books, would include: What are, or should be, the goals
of a healthy and decent society? What is freedom? What is excellence or
virtue? What constitutes human dignity—is it freedom, or virtue, or the
capacity to love? To what extent, and how, should government foster freedom, virtue, love, and dignity? What is love? Who or what is worthy of
love? What is friendship, and what is a good friend? What are the relations
of love and friendship to civic duty? Do God and divine law exist? If so, or
if not, what is implied for the life of the citizen and the human being? What
is the relationship between the obligations, the virtues, and the fulfillment
of the citizen or statesman, and the obligations, virtues, and fulfillment of
the human being simply? What is the moral responsibility or civic obligation
of the artist? What is a philosopher, and what is the moral responsibility or
civic obligation of the philosopher? And, speaking comprehensively, what
are the deepest alternative answers to these questions; how is the debate
among these alternatives articulated?

Even from this incomplete list, it is obvious that a study of great books
cannot be confined to the texts traditionally labeled "works of political
theory." The poets, the dramatists, the theologians, the scientists (especially
insofar as they have transcended the narrow and artificial limits of so much
contemporary science) must also be attended to with painstaking care. The
study of great books is necessarily, then, in tension—I would say, in a fruitful
and invigorating tension—with the artificially exaggerated boundaries of

specialization that so unfortunately sunder the contemporary "university" into a kind of congeries of intellectual ghettos. Among other things, the inclusion of great books in the reading lists of courses compels colorless or self-satisfied technicians and specialists to come into an arena where they must justify—and therefore transcend—their "specialties" in the light of questions that ought to provide the framework and structure for all specialization, within the manifold and dynamic dialectical *unity* that ought to constitute the "*uni*versity."

Yet, to repeat, I do not mean for one moment to suggest that the pressing concrete issues of contemporary life are to be left behind. Indeed, one of the major purposes of studying politics and society, love and death, religion and science, in the light shed by the classic works is to escape the fashionable academic abstractions of excessively scientist or "theoretical" social science and literary theory. Truly great books are never abstract, in the sense of abstracting from the gripping questions of human fate and existence. Truly great books vindicate, while enlarging and deepening, the good citizen's perspective on the issues that really count.

The model of what it means to treat politics in a manner at once philosophic and truly empirical is Aristotle's *Politics*. Aristotle's method is truly "empirical": it is *the* model of the empirical, because his study is derived directly from the lived *experiences*, the passionate concerns, of citizens and statesmen. Aristotle begins not from scientific "models" and a constructed jargon, but from the shrewd, articulate prescientific self-justifications of intelligent participants in grave civic controversies. Through critical dialogue with the warring participants, Aristotle attempts to ascend to a more comprehensive and richer awareness of the given alternatives, and of the place of these alternatives within the whole range of possible human alternatives. To find a modern complement to the Aristotelian model, we need look no further than Tocqueville's *Democracy in America*. Tocqueville there insists on the need to analyze the possibilities of American democracy within the comparative perspective afforded, not just by other contemporary regimes, but by an all-embracing consideration of the greatness and decadence, the strengths and weaknesses, of the previously dominant, undemocratic forms of society. But Tocqueville always begins with, and repeatedly returns to, the opinions, self-justifications, and self-explanations of the great participants in the drama of American politics.

For American students of politics, the models of Aristotle and Tocqueville suggest that the study of the great books requires a concomitant immersion in the history and evolution of the great issues that have from the start divided and animated the United States. An American student's study of the great books will be solidly founded only if the student responds honestly to his or her undeniable primary concern as a human being—the concern with one's own people. For only then will the discussion of human problems become real, and only then will the self-criticism that is the heart of dialectic be frank and direct in its target. The issues dividing the American political tradition should be viewed in the light of the overarching quarrels that have historically moved political thought. Merely American disputes become universal when we understand how they exemplify the conundrums characterizing the political nature of human beings in all times and places.

A study of American politics and political history guided by the spirit of Socratic dialectic would seek to bring to light the agonizing complexity, the moral costs and benefits on both sides, of the great divides in our historical development. It would dictate, for example, a reading of the Founders, not as icons, but in the light of the fascinating debate or dialogue between the Federalists and the Anti-Federalists. It would seek to reenact the Lincoln-Douglas debates in order to retrieve the depth of their analysis of the competing moral claims of popular sovereignty on the one hand and the insistence on limiting popular sovereignty by the idea of natural rights on the other. It would attempt to follow the unfolding arguments among black leaders—from Martin Delaney to Malcolm X—over the specific contributions, obligations, and legitimate demands of blacks within American political culture. As regards this last, we may note that a Socratic approach to the implications of the black experience within America resonates especially with the early W. E. B. Du Bois's attempt to delineate the potential contribution of blacks to America. Du Bois saw "no truer exponents of the pure human spirit of the Declaration of Independence than the American Negroes." But at the same time, he saw African-Americans as the bringers of talents and virtues that are otherwise insufficiently stressed in the liberal democratic ethos: piety and reverence; light-hearted but determined humility; loving and jovial, as opposed to cruel and cranky, wit; and, Du Bois insisted, a taste for the depths of musical sorrow that breeds contempt for the vulgar music typical of the United States.

All in all, we black men seem the sole oasis of simple faith and reverence in a dusty desert of dollars and smartness. Will America be poorer if she replace her brutal dyspeptic blundering with light-hearted but determined Negro humility? or her coarse and cruel wit with loving jovial good-humor? or her vulgar music with the soul of the Sorrow Songs?[3]

3. "Of Our Spiritual Strivings," in *The Souls of Black Folk* (1903), in Du Bois 1988, 370; see also "The Sorrow Songs," in Du Bois 1988, 536ff.

By the same token, and in conformity with the early Du Bois's deliberate, while unsentimental, searching out of the excellences rather than the deficiencies of black Americans, and of the Founders to whose principles black Americans had remained so loyal, a Socratic approach to the study of the American tradition would discourage both irresponsible debunking of and thoughtless applause for our heritage. The Socratic spirit counsels us to strive harder to disinter and bring to light those all-too-rare, but still decisive, moments, controversies, movements, and figures who exhibit the best qualities of the American political tradition. It advises us to resist the sophisticated tendency to reduce the deeds and words and thoughts of all citizens and statesmen to mere class or selfish interest. It makes us hesitate to bandy about charges of racism, sexism, or capitalist oppression in characterizing the shining exemplars of our political tradition. None of this requires mythologizing our past. What is called for, rather, is a sympathetically critical study that passes judgment while recognizing the responsibility involved in passing judgment: a study that tries to make more intelligible the successes, as well as the more routine inadequacies or failures, in our political, legal, and constitutional development. In the words again of Du Bois: "Above our modern socialism, and out of the worship of the mass, must persist and evolve that higher individualism which the centres of culture protect; there must come a loftier respect for the sovereign human soul that seeks to know itself and the world about it" (1988, p. 437).

The Relation between Civic and Dialectical Education in the Postmodern Age

Yet has my advocacy of dialectical liberation not led me to overlook the danger such liberation may pose for civic health and education in civic virtue? Socrates himself was severely doubtful of the possibility of any easy or simple harmonization of the two goals, or indeed kinds, of liberal education. His last and most emphatic word on dialectic in the *Republic* is, I have noted, a word of warning. Socrates drives home his point by means of another striking metaphor (537e–538e). The danger that accrues to a young person from the premature or improperly directed study of dialectic is like the case, Socrates says, of a

changeling child reared in much wealth in a large and great family amidst many flatterers, who on becoming a man perceived that he did not belong to those who claimed to be his parents, and was unable to find those who really gave him birth. . . . during the time when he did not know the truth, he would honor his father and mother and his other apparent kin rather than the flatterers, and would be less likely to overlook any need they might have, and less likely to do or say anything to them against the law, and would be less likely to disobey them in important matters than the flatterers . . . but when he perceived the way things are, he would slacken in his honors and his serious attention to them, and intensify the same in regard to the flatterers, be persuaded by the latter more than before, and start living in accordance with [the ways of] the latter, having unconcealed relations with them, and, unless he were a decent person by nature, he would care nothing for that father and the other artificial kin.

Similarly, Socrates says:

We have convictions from our childhood about just things and noble things, convictions under which we are brought up as if under parents, obeying them as rulers and honoring them. . . . and then there are other practices opposed to these convictions, practices that bring pleasure, and that flatter one's soul and draw it to them. They do not persuade those who are at all men of measure, who honor rather the ancestral ways, and obey them as rulers. . . . but when to someone so disposed, the question is put: "What is the noble?"—and, when he answers what he heard from the lawgiver, the rational argument refutes him, and this refutation is repeated often and in many ways, he falls into the opinion that nothing is any more noble than base; and the same happens regarding the just and the good and the matters he especially held in honor. What, then, do you think he will do as regards honoring and obeying as rulers these things?

This Socratic admonition is an important key to the nature of the writings published by Plato and Aristotle. Both make clear the superiority of the philosophic life and its culmination in dialectics; but the actual practice of dialectics is something their writings lead up to, or adumbrate, or introduce, rather than fully unfold. Plato's dialogues are dramatic works in which, as we have seen very strikingly in the case of the *Republic*, the dialectic is celebrated and even introduced, but, in its strictest or highest sense, sharply curtailed, at least on the surface. All of the dialogues would seem to be written in response to Plato's criticism of philosophic writing, a criticism Plato presents through the mouth of his Socrates in the *Phaedrus* and in his own name in the *Seventh Letter* (341c–d, 344c):

There is not nor will there ever be a writing of mine about these matters. For it is not to be put in words like other studies; but from long intercourse concerning the matter, and from living together, suddenly, like a spark jumping out from a blazing fire, it comes into being in the soul and now feeds itself. . . . But if it appeared to me possible to write or speak adequately to the many, what nobler thing might we accomplish in life than to write down for humanity the great benefit, and bring to light nature for everyone? But I do not consider the attempt to talk about these things to human beings to be a good thing, except to a few who are capable of finding out by themselves with just a small indication. . . . Therefore a serious man will avoid writing about serious matters, which would only cast humanity into envy and perplexity.

And if we inspect the writings of Aristotle that have come down to us, we see that not one of them is, on its surface at any rate, dialectical in the strict sense. Indeed, Aristotle explicitly avoids—even while drawing attention to the need for—a dialectical inquiry into politics and morals:

It must not escape our notice that there is a difference between reasonings from first principles and reasonings to first principles. For it was well of Plato to puzzle over this, and he used to inquire whether the path being followed was from the first principles or to the first principles, just as in the stadium it can be from the judges to the end or the other way around. Now we ought to begin from what is known. But these things are such in two senses: known to us and known simply. Probably now we ought to begin from what is known to us. Therefore he who is attending in an adequate way to discussion of the noble and just things, and the political things in general, must be nobly trained through habituation. For the first principle is that something is so; and if this is sufficiently apparent, there will be no need to ask for the reason. (*Nicomachean Ethics* 1095a31–b8)

Plato and Aristotle were convinced that all societies—even, or especially, healthy republics—are necessarily closed. Every society will have certain fundamental sanctities or moral absolutes whose doubt is truly upsetting to that society, and that a responsible philosopher will in public treat with the greatest caution. The Socratics held that for the good of both civic virtue and philosophic intransigence, it was advantageous, as well as necessary, to accept the natural limits on the openness of society: to live, free from false hopes, in the awareness of an inevitable and insuperable, if varying, degree of alienation between authentic philosophers and the rest of society.

Truly to understand this feature of the relation between free thinking and civil society is to understand the relation between the virtues of wisdom and moderation; it is, in the words of the modern Platonist Leo Strauss, to accept and to understand "the sacrifices which we must make so that our minds may be free" (Strauss 1963, xvi). But today, of course, we live in a society—indeed, in a civilization—that is founded on philosophic arguments for "enlightenment": for a permissive, tolerant, commercial, and technological world in which a "free commonwealth," in Spinoza's immortal words, is one where "every man may think as he pleases, and say what he thinks" (*Theologico-Political Treatise*, ch. 20, title). Is this ideal truly achievable by human beings? The arguments on both sides of this fundamental issue will comprise one of the preeminent and abiding themes of any education in the great books worthy of the name. But a further question comes plainly into view for anyone who begins to take seriously the possible truth of the Socratic conception of politics and philosophy: how do the Socratic principles apply, how ought they to be applied, to this new, unclassical, and un-Socratic form of society, which Socrates, after all, never envisaged?

To begin with, we should not lose sight of the fact that—as Strauss's use of the term *sacrifices* reminds us—Plato does not regard the closed character of society simply as a good thing. He sees it rather as a fact of life: at best, as a necessary accompaniment of law and order, virtue, and civic as well as philosophic liberty. Plato is certainly not interested in intensifying the closedness of society. On the contrary, all his dialogues delicately explore, in one way or another, the limits to that closedness, or the possible ways in which individuals and groups within various regimes might be opened up, however slightly, to some experience of the dialectic that is the heart of the philosophic life. Let us never forget that Plato has Socrates proclaim in his most public and well-known utterance that "the unexamined life is not worth living for a human being." Yet at the same time, Plato is deeply wary of false or deluded liberation, of a supposition of openness that turns out to be a closed-mindedness all the more severe because deluded into supposing itself open. Socrates' face-to-face critique of the sophists in the Platonic dialogues reveals over and over again the manifold serpentine charms of this sophisticated trap of self-deluded, closed-minded "openness." Plato or a Platonic perspective surely does not presume that what declares itself to be openness necessarily *is* openness: true openness reveals itself only by its manner of reacting to the discomfiting pressure of philosophic questioning. The most urgent practical question from a truly Platonic perspective then becomes: how, in each given political situation, can the maximum possible openness that is *genuine* be achieved?

The answer to this question will not be discovered by seeking recipes of some sort in the Platonic dialogues. What is required is original reflection, rooted in the dialogues: a reflection that takes into account, above all, the *specific* dangers or threats to both civic and philosophic virtue that are found in each new political circumstance.

In our democracy, while the threats to civic virtue may seem pretty palpable, the threats to philosophic inquiry or virtue may well appear far fewer than in any closed society, and certainly fewer than in the democracy that executed Socrates. From this observation one might well draw the conclusion that our major concern ought to be with civic rather than with philosophic education. Should we not perhaps be even more worried than Socrates was about the possibility of the sort of corrosive impact of dialectic that he warns against? Our society is already so permissive: should we not throw our weight on the side of discipline, austerity, and restraint—including restraint on intellectual skepticism? This extremely conservative application of classical republican thought, while not altogether unpersuasive or mistaken, appears to me to be based on too narrow or superficial a diagnosis of our spiritual situation.

There is obvious truth to the proposition that philosophic inquiry is far less likely to lead to physical persecution in liberal democracy than in most previous sorts of republican and nonrepublican society. Yet this obvious truth tends to veil the deeper and more complicated truth that our open society purchases its freedom of expression at enormous risk to real intellectual independence, intrepidity, and diversity. In addition, there is a discernible link between the weakened condition of our intellectual integrity and the relative laxness of our civic spirit: the two have an important source in common. Some widespread, if vague, awareness of this deeper truth has emerged from our discovery of the link between intellectual and civic virtue in Eastern Europe. Western intellectuals and artists have registered astonished recognition that intellectual life, though perhaps restricted to fewer persons, seems to have a greater moral force, and that the arts seem to have a more serious sense of moral vocation, and a more devoted if narrower audience, under communist tyranny than under liberal democracy. As Italo Calvino has observed, comparing the situation of the writer in Eastern Europe with the situation of the writer in the West, "this is the paradox of the power of literature: it seems that only when it is persecuted does it show its true powers, challenging authority, whereas in our permissive society it feels that it is being used merely to create the pleasing contrast to the general ballooning of verbiage."[4] Similarly, when Philip Roth returned from Eastern Europe in the early 1980s, he described the difference in the situations of artists in the East and in the West as follows:

The difference was in freedom, and the differences from my point of view were almost comically vivid: in my situation, everything goes and nothing matters; in their situation, nothing goes and everything matters. Every word they write has endless implications, whereas in the States, one often doesn't have the sense of making an impact at all.[5]

As Isaiah Berlin wrote in *Two Concepts of Liberty* (one of the most broadminded and thoughtful defenses of liberalism written in this century), "integ-

4. *New York Times*, February 8, 1990, p. B1.
5. Ibid.

rity, love of truth, and fiery individualism grow at least as often in severely disciplined communities or under military discipline, as in more tolerant or indifferent societies" (Berlin 1958, 13–15, 48). I am inclined to believe Calvino goes too far in suggesting that tyranny or persecution are *required* for the full revelation of the powers of literature, but the contrast between East and West to which he is reacting does testify to the fact that our contemporary "tolerant or indifferent" societies face a peculiarly complex and grave spiritual problem.

What most threatens us, I would suggest, is not un˜ ˜˜˜ng skepticism, or revolutionary discord, or the excesses of passionate diversity, but rather the deadening conformism to a bloodless and philistine relativism that saps the will and the capacity to defend or define any principled basis of life. This threat endangers civic and philosophic life equally. The causes of this peculiar syndrome are no doubt many, and I do not pretend to understand or even to recognize them all. But an especially troubling one—especially troubling because rooted in the very nature of our society as a mass democratic order—is the theme of Tocqueville's inquiry into the spiritual strengths and weaknesses of modern mass democracy. Tocqueville begins from the classical observation that a strictly open society is a myth: every society is in some sense closed, because

without ideas in common, there is no common action, and, without common action, there may still exist human beings, but not a social entity. In order for society to exist, and, even more, to prosper, it is then necessary that the spirits of all the citizens be assembled and held together by certain leading ideas; and that cannot happen unless each of them comes from time to time to draw his opinions from the same source, and unless each consents to receive a certain number of ready-made beliefs.
(*Democracy in America* 2.1.2)

"The question," then, as Tocqueville says, "is not to ascertain whether there exists an intellectual authority in the democratic centuries, but only where it is lodged and what its limits are" (ibid.). Tocqueville answers the question through a characteristic comparison between the complementary strengths and weaknesses of modern democracy and traditional aristocracy. Whereas aristocracy tended to breed the authoritarianism of individuals and classes, democracy subjects individuals to the herding pressure of public opinion, armed by the almost irresistible, and potentially enslaving, psychological logic of extreme egalitarianism:

When conditions are unequal and men dissimilar, there are a few individuals who are very enlightened, very wise, with great strength of intelligence—and a multitude who are very ignorant and severely limited. Those who live in aristocratic ages are then naturally inclined to take as the guide for their opinions the superior reason of a man or a class, while they are very little disposed to recognize any infallibility in the mass of men.

The contrary holds in centuries of equality.

To the extent that citizens become more equal and more similar, the inclination of each to believe blindly a certain man or a certain class diminishes. The disposition to believe in the mass of men augments, and it is more and more public opinion that rules the world.

When the person who inhabits democratic countries compares himself to all those who surround him, he feels with pride that he is equal to each of them; but when he comes to contemplate the collectivity of his fellows, and to place himself alongside this great body, he is overwhelmed by his own insignificance and his weakness.

This same equality that renders him independent of each of his fellow citizens taken one by one leaves him isolated and defenseless before the action of the great number.

The public therefore has among democratic peoples a singular power of which the aristocratic nations could not conceive an idea. It does not persuade; it imposes its beliefs, and makes them penetrate into the souls by a sort of immense pressure of the spirit of all on the intelligence of each. . . .

Thus intellectual authority will be different, but it will not be less; and, far from believing that it is likely to disappear, I prophesy that it will easily become too great and that it is capable finally of confining the action of the individual's reason within limits more narrow than is proper for the grandeur and the happiness of the human species. (Ibid.)

This inner dwarfing of the human mind, this sapping of each individual's civic self-confidence and critical spirit, is strengthened in its demeaning effects by a second powerful and characteristic democratic bad tendency. The moral momentum of the doctrine of equality can easily push inhabitants of mass democracy to believe that individuals and small groups never count for much in civic or historical terms; that the human will and the human capacity for thought effect little in history, but are themselves the effects or by-products of deeper and broader material, psychological, and social factors. It is not "methodology," it is a perverted egalitarian moralism, made possible in part by the absence of any countervailing alternatives, that prompts even, or especially, the most "progressive" inhabitants of modern democracy to assume this cynical view of the drastic limits on human *praxis* and intellectual independence. Viewed through this prism, history and current events are seen as governed or determined, not by great exceptions, not by heroic or wise leaders and staunchly fraternal solidarities, but instead by unseen, systemic, or subconscious mass phenomena that no one can manage or influence, and before which the only reasonable posture is pathetic submission or inner withdrawal. To continue with Tocqueville:

In centuries of equality, all men are independent, isolated, and weak in relation to one another; there is little sign that anyone's will directs, in a permanent fashion, the movements of the crowd; in these ages, humanity seems always to go forward of its own accord. To explain what happens in the world, we are therefore reduced to looking for certain great causes that, acting in the same manner on every one of our peers, carry them all to follow voluntarily the same route.   (Ibid. 2.1.3)

As one major, specific educational antidote to these dangerous penchants of the modern democratic mentality, Tocqueville repeatedly recommends that the young be taught to study and enjoy the classics. The merely traditional, ornamental, or snobbish role of the classics is of little interest to Tocqueville. But he argues that certain specific strengths (and not only strengths, but even some failings or blindnesses) of the classical writers are the needed corrective counterweights to the specific blindnesses to which democratic readers and scholars are prone. The classical texts, especially the classical texts of political history and theory, recall us vividly to the capacities individuals do have to act, and to write or think, with a deliberateness and care that is indelibly effective.

It suffices, in fact, to cast a glance on the writings antiquity has left us to discover that, if those writers sometimes lack variety and fecundity in their subjects, and boldness, movement, and generalization in their thought, they always show the signs of an admirable artfulness and a care in details; nothing in their works seems done with haste or by chance; everything is written for those who understand, and the search for ideal beauty constantly shows itself. There exists no literature that puts into sharper relief than does the ancient the qualities that naturally tend to be missing in democratic writers. There is therefore no literature that ought more to be studied in democratic ages.   (Ibid. 2.1.15)

It seems, in reading the historians of aristocratic ages, and especially those of antiquity, that, in order to become master of his fate and govern his fellows, man has only to know how to master himself. In reading the histories written in our times, one would say that man had no power, either over himself or over his circumstances. The historians of antiquity taught how to command. Those of our days teach scarcely anything but how to submit: in their writings the author often appears great, but humanity is always petty. . . . such a doctrine is particularly dangerous in the epoch in which we now live; our contemporaries are only too inclined to doubt free will, because each of them feels himself limited on all sides by his weakness. But they do recognize the strength and independence of men united in social groups. We must not let this idea become obscure, because our task is to elevate souls and not to complete their debasement.   (Ibid. 2.1.20)

To attain their full validity, these Tocquevillian reflections need only to be updated and extended. For do we not see all around us the postmodern manifestations of the syndromes Tocqueville first described? In society at large, the ever-more-overwhelming presence of media that give voice to a seemingly omnipotent "public opinion"; in literature, the criticism and teaching that boast of their historicist reduction of all writers to the status of creatures of their class, gender, culture, subconscious, and so on; among historians, the scornful dismissal of political and constitutional history in the name of economic, social, and demographic history; and, worst of all, a moralistic, leveling relativism that now increasingly pervades even grade schools? Democratic tolerance and equality at their truest and most sublime promise to every human being the opportunity to ascend to a just rank in the natural hierarchy of talents and attainments, of virtue and wisdom. But democratic tolerance and equality in our day are haunted by the dangerous tendency to degenerate from the ideal of fertile controversy between competing moral and religious ways of life into the easygoing belief that all ways of life and all points of view are equal; thence to the notion that none are really worthy or in need of profound examination and passionate defense; and finally into the stridently moralistic belief that those who do insist on arguing for the superiority of their way of life or beliefs are "elitist," "anti-democratic," and hence immoral. In this last stage, the germ of intolerance and repression lurking in the bloodstream of the open society threatens to run amok. For it begins to lead people to charge that even those who argue for the superiority of liberal principles—for the principles of right imbedded in the Constitution as conceived by the Founders and grounded in the political philosophies of the Enlightenment, for the civil duties and rights required in a healthy democratic republic—somehow violate the new moral code of relativistic equality. And at this point toleration and democracy have reached a fever pitch where they have begun to self-destruct.

An education that provides a taste of genuinely Socratic skepticism is not the cure for all these ills. But it could make a contribution to their amelioration. The introduction of college students to the perennial issues at once dividing and animating our Great Tradition is not likely, I would argue, to intensify the specific sources of moral decay in our time. On the contrary: *serious* questioning of, *serious* arguing over, our most fundamental sources of political and moral principle may issue, at its best, in a rekindling of the embers of the controversies that attended the birth of the modern liberal democratic ethos. From these embers there may well spring up a renewed, thoughtful, and therefore undogmatic or reasonably qualified appreciation for the strength and validity of the principles underlying our Constitution. The "common sense" of our society, the soil from which our elemental and ordinary moral judgments spring, is in a crucial respect unlike the moral soil

Aristotle and the Greek thinkers stood upon. Ours is a political and moral culture derived from modern philosophy: from a specific philosophic transformation of prephilosophic thinking. For better or for worse, the vitality of our liberal democratic political culture depends on the vitality, or the revitalization, of the political philosophy that is its matrix. But political philosophy is not ideology; if or when it begins to degenerate into ideology, political philosophy atrophies; to prevent or stave off this slow spiritual death, the primordial wonder or doubt out of which philosophy grows must constantly be renewed in the forge of dialectic argument.

Yet this proposition will have practical effect only if it is admitted, and acted upon in a Socratic spirit, by those to whom the profession of higher education is entrusted. The future of our educational institutions in the postmodern age depends decisively on a vastly heightened sense of responsibility among university teachers. For it would be foolish to deny that the liberation through dialectical examination of which I have been speaking is attended with real risks and dangers. Education of the sort I have been attempting to describe is not a game, and the great books, once taken seriously in the way I am advocating, lead into deep waters. Those who embark on the enterprise may not return home the same men and women who set out. They may find themselves compelled to declare an inner independence from some or all of the fundamental presuppositions of our modern civilization—in the name, perhaps, of Moses, or of Plato, or of Dante. Plato and Xenophon make it clear that while the charges on which Socrates was convicted—impiety and corrupting the young—were false, it is nonetheless true that the misguided citizens who voted to convict Socrates were dimly and crudely aware of genuine potential dangers in the misuse or abuse of Socratic questioning. The mighty shield against this danger is what Socrates called *eros*, love, of the truth. In the final analysis, Socrates suggested, all human love seeks and needs a glimpse of truth as its foundation. The quest for the truth, in the humbling awareness of how far short we will inevitably fall in our erotic or needy pursuit of it, can be the foundation for the firmest attachments and for a truly common humanity—for a sense of the humane, and an immunity to the inhumane—that emerges as the natural expression of the common love of the truth. The great books may be said to be the products of such love: they may be understood as the gifts—handed down to us—from such lovers. As a result, they are, with a very few exceptions, immune to corrupting abuse. It is no accident that the three most obvious exceptions—I have in mind the works of Marx, Nietzsche, and Heidegger—raise unprecedented doubts about the existence or the strength of this *eros* for the truth. They thus usher in radical modernity, with its subjectivity of "values" and its "progressive," "historicist" forgetfulness of the great books, as well as of the common humanity of erotic reason aspiring to the thinking kept alive in the great books. We cannot, of course, turn our backs on the challenges of these most recent, and most sinister, great books; given the overwhelming predominance of "postmodernism" among contemporary academics, we are not likely to be able to do so. But we can and must struggle to keep alive the great debates that preceded and still preoccupied Marx and Nietzsche and Heidegger, the debates that are the ever-renewed proof of the permanence of Socratic *eros*.

Select List of Works Cited

Bataille, Georges
  1955 "Hegel, la mort et le sacrifice" (Hegel, Death and Sacrifice). *Deucalion*
        5:21–44.
  1961 *Le Coupable* (The Guilty One). 2d ed. Paris: Gallimard.

Berlin, Isaiah
  1958 *Two Concepts of Liberty.* Oxford: Oxford University Press.

Churchill, Winston
  1941 *Blood, Sweat, and Tears.* New York: G. P. Putnam's Sons.

Crespi, Franco
  1988 "Assenza di fondamento e progetto sociale" (Absence of Foundation, and
        Social Project). In *Il pensiero debole* (Weak Thinking), edited by Gianni
        Vattimo and Pier Aldo Rovatti, 6th ed., 243–59. Milan: Feltrinelli.

Dal Lago, Alessandro
  1985 "La Pensée comme oscillation" (Thought as Oscillation). *Critique*
        41:82–89.

De Man, Paul
  1953 "Montaigne et la transcendance" (Montaigne and Transcendence). *Critique* 9:1011–22.
  1988 *Wartime Journalism, 1939–1943.* Edited by Werner Hamacher, Neil
        Hertz, and Thomas Keenan. Lincoln: University of Nebraska Press.

Derrida, Jacques
  1967 *L'Écriture et la différence* (Writing and the Difference). Paris: Editions du
        Seuil.

Dewey, John
  1935 *Liberalism and Social Action.* New York: G. P. Putnam's Sons.

1939 *Freedom and Culture.* New York: G. P. Putnam's Sons.
1942 *German Philosophy and Politics.* Rev. ed. New York: G. P. Putnam's Sons.
1946 *The Public and Its Problems.* Rev. ed. Chicago: Gateway Books.
1948 *Reconstruction in Philosophy.* Boston: Beacon Press.

Du Bois, W. E. B.
1988 *Writings.* New York: Library of America, 1988.

Glendon, Mary Ann
1987 *Abortion and Divorce in Western Law: American Failures, European Challenges.* Cambridge, Mass.: Harvard University Press.

Hartman, Geoffrey
1988 "Blindness and Insight." *New Republic,* 7 March, 28–31.

Heidegger, Martin
1953 *Einführung in die Metaphysik* (Introduction to Metaphysics). Tübingen: Max Niemeyer.
1961 *Nietzsche.* 2 vols. Pfüllingen: Günther Neske.
1975 *Die Grundprobleme der Phänomenologie* (The Fundamental Problems of Phenomenology). Frankfurt am Main: Vittorio Klostermann.

Hess, Walter
1956 *Dokumente zum Verständnis der modernen Malerei* (Documents for the Understanding of Modern Painting). Hamburg: Rowohlt.

Kandinsky, Vasily
1985 *Oeuvres de Vasily Kandinsky.* Edited by Christian Derouet and Jessica Boissel. Paris: Centre Georges Pompidou, Musée d'Art Moderne.

Kojève, Alexandre
1962 *Introduction à la lecture de Hegel: Leçons sur la "Phénoménologie de l'esprit"* (Introduction to the Reading of Hegel: Lectures on the Phenomenology of the Spirit/Mind). 2d ed. Edited by Raymond Queneau. Paris: Gallimard.
1970a "Pourquoi concrete" (Why Concrete). In Vasily Kandinsky, *Ecrits complets* (Complete Writings), 2:395–400. Paris: Denoël-Gauthier.
1970b "Lettres à Georges Bataille" (Letters to Georges Bataille). *Textures,* June, 61–71.

Krüger, Gerhard
1931 *Philosophie und Moral in der Kantischen Kritik* (Philosophy and Morality in the Kantian Critique). Tübingen: J. C. B. Mohr.

Kundera, Milan
1980 "Afterword: A Talk with the Author, by Philip Roth." Translated by Peter Kussi. In *The Book of Laughter and Forgetting.* Translated by Michael Heim. Harmondsworth, England: Penguin Books.

Levinson, Sanford
1988 *Constitutional Faith.* Princeton: Princeton University Press.

Long, Rose-Carol Washton
1980 *Kandinsky.* Oxford: Clarendon Press.

Lyotard, Jean-François
  1977a *Instructions paiennes* (Pagan Lessons). Paris: Editions Galilée.
  1977b *Rudiments paiens* (Pagan Beginnings). Paris: Union générale d'éditions.
  1979 *La Condition postmoderne: Rapport sur le savoir* (The Postmodern Condition: Report on Scholarship). Paris: Editions de Minuit.
  1983 *Le Différend* (The Different). Paris: Editions de Minuit.
  1984 *Tombeau de l'intellectual et autres papiers* (Tomb of the Intellectual and Other Papers). Paris: Editions Galilée.
  1985 "Histoire universelle et differences culturelles" (Universal History and Cultural Differences). *Critique* 41:559–68.
  1986 *Le Postmoderne expliqué aux enfants* (The Postmodern Explained to Children). Paris: Editions Galilée.
  1989a "Figure Foreclosed." In *The Lyotard Reader*, edited by Andrew Benjamin, 69–110. Oxford: Basil Blackwell.
  1989b "Philosophy and Painting in the Age of Their Experimentation: Contribution to an Idea of Postmodernity." Translated by M. Brewer and D. Brewer. 1872In *The Lyotard Reader*, edited by Andrew Benjamin, 181–95. Oxford: Basil Blackwell.
  1989c "The Sublime and the Avant-Garde." Translated by Lisa Liebmann. 1984. Rev. ed. In *The Lyotard Reader*, edited by Andrew Benjamin, 196–211. Oxford: Basil Blackwell.

Lyotard, Jean-François, and Richard Rorty
  1985 "Discussion entre Jean-François Lyotard et Richard Rorty" (Discussion between Jean-François Lyotard and Richard Rorty). *Critique* 41:581–84.

Lyotard, Jean-François, and Jean-Loup Thébaud
  1985 *Just Gaming (Au juste)*. Translated by Wlad Godzich. Minneapolis: University of Minnesota Press.

Mahdi, Muhsin, and Ralph Lerner, eds.
  1972 *Medieval Political Philosophy: A Sourcebook*. Ithaca, N.Y.: Cornell University Press.

Mansfield, Harvey C., Jr.
  1988 "Democracy and the Great Books." *New Republic*, 4 April, 33–37.

Michnik, Adam
  1979 *L'Eglise et la gauche* (The Church and the Left). Paris: Editions du Seuil.

Milosz, Czeslaw
  1989 "The Telltale Scar." *New Republic*, 7 & 14 August, 27–29.

Newmann, Barnett
  1948 "The Sublime Is Now." *Tiger's Eye*, 15 December.

Nichols, James H., Jr.
  1990 "Pragmatism and the U.S. Constitution." In *Confronting the Constitution*, edited by Allan Bloom, 369–88, 529–32. Washington, D.C.: AEI Press.

Orwin, Clifford, and Thomas Pangle
  1984 "The Philosophical Foundation of Human Rights." In *Human Rights in*

Our Time: Essays in Memory of Victor Baras, edited by Marc Plattner, 1–22. Boulder, Colo.: Westview Press.

Pangle, Thomas L.
1973 *Montesquieu's Philosophy of Liberalism: A Commentary on the Spirit of the Laws*. Chicago: University of Chicago Press.
1988 *The Spirit of Modern Republicanism: The Moral Vision of the American Founders and the Philosophy of Locke*. Chicago: University of Chicago Press.
1989 *The Rebirth of Classical Political Rationalism: An Introduction to the Thought of Leo Strauss*. Chicago: University of Chicago Press.

Queneau, Raymond
1947 *Le Dimanche de la vie* (The Sunday of Life). Paris: Gallimard.
1961 *Cent mille milliards de poèmes* (One Hundred Thousand Billion Poems). Paris: Gallimard.

Rorty, Richard
1979 *Philosophy and the Mirror of Nature*. Princeton: Princeton University Press.
1982 *The Consequences of Pragmatism*. Minneapolis: University of Minnesota Press.
1985a "Le Cosmopolitisme sans émancipation: En réponse à Jean-François Lyotard" (Cosmopolitanism without Emancipation: In Response to Jean-François Lyotard). *Critique* 41:569–80.
1985b "Habermas and Lyotard on Postmodernity." In *Habermas and Modernity*, edited by Richard J. Bernstein, 161–75. Cambridge, Mass.: MIT Press.
1988 "That Old-Time Philosophy." *New Republic*, 4 April, 28–33.
1989 *Contingency, Irony, and Solidarity*. Cambridge: Cambridge University Press.

Rudolph, Frederick, ed.
1965 *Essays on Education in the Early Republic*. Cambridge, Mass.: Harvard University Press.

Sabine, George H.
1961 *A History of Political Theory*. 3d ed. New York: Holt, Rinehart & Winston. Originally published in 1937.

Searle, John
1990 "The Storm over the University." *New York Review of Books*, 6 December, 33–42.

Shaftesbury, Anthony Ashley Cooper, 3d earl of
1964 *Characteristics of Men, Manners, Opinions, Times*. 1711. 2 vols. Edited by John M. Robertson. Indianapolis: Bobbs-Merrill.

Shell, Susan
1989 "Preserving the Humanities." Address to the Madison Center Conference on the Humanities, Washington, D.C., October 10.

Stern, Fritz
1975 *The Failure of Illiberalism: Essays on the Political Culture of Modern Germany*. Chicago: University of Chicago Press.
Stewart, Dugald
1854 *Dissertation Exhibiting the Progress of Metaphysical, Ethical, and Political Philosophy, since the Revival of Letters in Europe*. Vol. 1 of *The Collected Works of Dugald Stewart*. 10 vols. plus a supplementary vol. Edited by Sir William Hamilton. Edinburgh: Thomas Constable. Originally published in two parts, 1815 and 1821.
Storing, Herbert J.
1970 *What Country Have I? Political Writings by Black Americans*. New York: St. Martin's Press.
Strauss, Leo
1959 *What Is Political Philosophy? And Other Studies*. Glencoe, Ill.: Free Press.
1963 *The Political Philosophy of Hobbes: Its Basis and Its Genesis*. Translated by Elsa M. Sinclair. Chicago: University of Chicago Press.
1977 "Farabi's Plato." In *Essays in Medieval Jewish and Islamic Philosophy*, edited by Arthur Hyman, 391–427. New York: KTAV Publishing.
1983 *Studies in Platonic Political Philosophy*. Chicago: University of Chicago Press.
Thompson, Wayne C.
1975 *In the Eye of the Storm: Kurt Riezler and Crises of Modern Germany*. Iowa City: University of Iowa Press.
Troeltsch, Ernst
1976 *The Social Teaching of the Christian Churches*. 2 vols. Translated by Olive Wyon. Chicago: University of Chicago Press.
Vattimo, Gianni
1980 *Le avventure della differenza* (The Adventures of the Difference). Milan: Garzanti.
1987 *La fine della modernità: Nichilismo ed ermeneutica nella cultura post-moderna*. (The End of Modernity: Nihilism and Hermeneutics in Postmodern Culture). 2d ed. Milan: Garzanti.
Weiss, Peg
1979 *Kandinsky in Munich: The Formative Jugendstil Years*. Princeton: Princeton University Press.

Index of Names

Adams, John, 100, 107–8, 113, 132, 149,
   150–51, 176–77
Adorno, Theodor, 51
Alfarabi, 6
Algazel, 77
Anaxagoras, 121
Antiphon, 194
Appius Claudius, 135
Aristides, 130
Aristotle, 6, 8–9, 25, 58, 94, 101, 105–13,
   120–24, 127–30, 140–41, 164, 181,
   185–86, 197, 200–201, 206, 209–10, 217
Augustine, St., 13, 118
Avicenna, 116

Bacon, Francis, 62, 132, 196–97
Bataille, Georges, 22
Beckett, Samuel, 51
Bentham, Jeremy, 75
Berlin, Isaiah, 58, 212–13
Bethmann-Holweg, Theobold von, 71
Bismarck, Otto von, 82
Blackstone, William, 149
Braque, Georges, 25
Burke, Edmund, 4, 25
Bush, George, 163, 165, 180

Cabell, Joseph, 172
Calvin, John, 58, 115, 117
Calvino, Italo, 212–13
Cassirer, Ernst, 39
Cézanne, Paul, 25
Churchill, Winston, 83–84, 90

Cicero, 115, 128
Clarke, John, 169
Comines, Phillip de, 204
Cotton, John, 97
Crespi, Franco, 54

Dal Lago, Alessandro, 54
Dante, 197, 217
Darwin, Charles, 53, 62
Defoe, Daniel, 196–97
De Gaulle, Charles, 86
Delaney, Martin, 207
De Man, Paul, 54, 56
Derrida, Jacques, 22, 52
Descartes, René, 132, 196
Dewey, John, 59–64
Diderot, Didier, 23
Douglas, Stephen, 207
Du Bois, W. E. B., 108, 207–8

Epaminondas, 176
Euclid, 137

Fanon, Franz, 79
Ferdinand I of Spain, 135
Fielding, Henry, 196
Franklin, Benjamin, 7, 126, 170–72, 180
Freud, Sigmund, 29–31, 77

Ghandi, Mohandas K., 57, 58
Goethe, Johann Wolfgang, 87
Gordon, Thomas, 132
Grotius, Hugo, 171

Habermas, Juergen, 53, 62, 128
Hamilton, Alexander, 8, 96
Hartman, Geoffrey, 56
Havel, Václav, 88–89
Hegel, Georg W. F., 3, 12–13, 20–23, 26,
    28–29, 51, 53, 62, 67, 73, 199, 201
Heidegger, Martin, 4, 5, 25, 33, 34–48,
    50–53, 58–60, 63, 74, 77, 199–200,
    217–18
Heine, Heinrich, 73
Henry, Patrick, 95
Heraclitus, 67
Herodotus, 106
Hesiod, 189–90
Hitler, Adolph, 26–27, 41, 67
Hobbes, Thomas, 10, 93–95, 97, 132,
    137–40, 145, 147, 181
Hooker, Richard, 117
Hume, David, 5, 95, 132, 147–49, 204
Hussein, Saddam, 73, 83
Husserl, Edmund, 186

Ibn Khaldun, 77
Ibn Tufayl, 197
Isaiah, 57
Isocrates, 106, 124, 128–29, 149, 170

Jefferson, Thomas, 63–64, 107–8, 151,
    172–74, 180
John Paul II, 84
Johnson, Philip, 20

Kandinsky, Vasily, 21–22
Kant, Immanuel, 3, 4, 10–13, 22–27, 39–40,
    50, 58, 59, 73
King, Martin Luther, Jr., 118–20, 123
Knox, Samuel, 174
Kojève, Alexandre, 20–23, 51
Krueger, Gerhard, 13
Kundera, Milan, 14, 89

Lacan, Jacques, 77
Lasch, Christopher, 80
Lauristan, Marju, 72
Lévinas, Emmanuel, 29–30, 32
Levinson, Sanford, 65–68
Lévi-Strauss, Claude, 204
Lincoln, Abraham, 74, 207
Locke, John, 3, 4, 5, 10, 73, 132, 134,
    136–38, 140, 142–47, 165–70, 174, 176,
    177, 180, 196–97
Long, Rose-Carol Washton, 21
Longinus, 28–29
Luxmoore, Jonathan, 84
Lycophron, 101

Lyotard, Jean-François, 14–15, 20–33,
    48–51, 55–56, 59, 62, 68

Machiavelli, Niccolò, 94–95, 101–2, 132,
    134–46, 140, 150
Madison, James, 93, 99–100, 149
Maimonides, Moses, 6, 116, 197
Malcolm X, 207
Manet, Edouard, 25
Mansfield, Harvey C., Jr., 61
Marx, Karl, 1, 2, 7, 26–28, 31, 53, 58, 71,
    73, 74, 77, 86, 88, 142, 201, 217–18
Melanchthon, Philip, 117
Mencius, 77
Mercer, John Francis, 95–96
Michnik, Adam, 88
Milosz, Czeslaw, 87, 89
Milton, John, 124–25, 149, 166–67, 170
Montaigne, 24
Montesquieu, 5, 8, 10, 53, 73, 85–86, 88,
    100–101, 132, 136, 140, 142–44, 147–49,
    174, 196, 204
More, St. Thomas, 154

Newmann, Barnett, 24–25
Newton, Isaac, 4
Nichols, James H., Jr., 61, 64
Nietzsche, Friedrich, 4, 19, 21, 32–33,
    34–46, 50, 52, 58–59, 60, 65, 73, 74,
    78–79, 81–82, 84, 87, 198–200, 217–18

Orwin, Clifford, 143

Paul, St., 141
Pericles, 111, 130, 165
Picasso, 25
Plato, 6, 9, 14, 29, 30–32, 43–44, 48–50,
    53, 58, 101, 108, 111–16, 120, 123–27,
    129–30, 141, 150, 164–65, 199–201,
    209–11, 217
Plutarch, 150, 151, 176, 196
Puffendorff, Samuel, 171

Queneau, Raymond, 22

Riezler, Kurt, 71–72
Rollin, Charles, 170
Rorty, Richard, 20, 54, 57–64
Roth, Phillip, 212
Rousseau, J.-J., 4, 58, 59, 204
Rush, Benjamin, 151, 171–72, 178–80

Sartre, Jean-Paul, 67
Schmitt, Carl, 53
Schumpeter, Joseph, 58
Searle, John, 76

Shaftesbury, Third Earl of, 29
Shell, Susan, 19–20, 57
Smith, Adam, 132
Smith, Samuel Harrison, 174–75
Socrates, 6, 7, 8, 13, 30–32, 48–50, 57, 115,
    119–24, 126–30, 164–65, 183–95,
    198–201, 207–11, 216–19
Spinoza, Benedict de, 3, 5, 132, 196–97, 210
Stalin, Joseph, 26
Stern, Fritz, 72
Stewart, Dugald, 146
Strauss, Leo, 6, 58, 85, 88, 140, 210–11
Sydney, Algernon, 149–50

Tacitus, 204
Thébaud, Jean-Loup, 32, 49–50
Themistocles, 130
Thomas Aquinas, St., 58, 116–18, 123,
    140–41, 197
Thompson, Wayne, 72
Thucydides, 111, 113, 130, 196–97, 201
Tocqueville, Alexis De, 80, 152–53, 181, 201,
    204, 206, 213–16

Tolstoy, Leo, 197
Troeltsch, Ernst, 117

Vattimo, Gianni, 33, 50–55
Vico, Giambattista, 4

Walesa, Lech, 89
Walker, Obadiah, 170
Washington, George, 151, 177
Watts, Isaac, 169
Weber, Max, 39
Webster, Noah, 151, 171–72, 175–80
Weiss, Peg, 21
Willard, Emma, 179–81
Wilson, James, 115, 117, 136–37, 146, 151
Wittgenstein, Ludwig von, 59, 68

Xenophon, 6, 7, 28–29, 111, 123, 126, 127,
    128, 164, 196, 217

Zarathustra, 57
Zeller, Edmund, 6
Zweig, Stefan, 72